"Amendments are hard, of course—there's a lot of corporate power to overcome—but given the stakes, this is surely an idea worth everyone taking very seriously!"

—**BILL McKIBBEN,** author of *Radio Free Vermont*

"A rallying cry not only for conservationists and wildlife biologists, but for pediatricians, teachers, psychologists, architects, city planners—everyone who is concerned about the welfare of all species, including human beings. Please read this important book."

—**RICHARD LOUV,** chairman emeritus of the Children & Nature Network and author of *Last Child in the Woods* and *Our Wild Calling*

"*The Green Amendment* asks us to imagine a world in which the right to pure water and healthy air exist on par with due process and free speech—and then shows us how to make it so."

—**SANDRA STEINGRABER,** PhD, author of *Living Downstream* and *Raising Elijah*, recipient of the Rachel Carson Leadership Award, and cofounder of New Yorkers Against Fracking

"Constitutional protection of natural and human communities may be our best hope for survival."

—**BRADLEY M. CAMPBELL,** President of the Conservation Law Foundation, former Commissioner of the New Jersey Department of Environmental Protection, and former Regional Administrator of the U.S. Environmental Protection Agency

"The beauty of her work and message is its clarity, simplicity, and the way in which it, in many ways, is dyed into the very fabric of the American Democracy and the American experience . . . . We have an American folk hero in our midst and her name is Maya van Rossum."

—**EMMY-NOMINATED JOURNALIST STEVE ROGERS,** producer of NJTV's *Here's the Story*

"Read this book and you will be infuriated and inspired. Infuriated because the book drags you through the environmental muck of fracking, pipelines, PFOA . . . But you will be inspired by the notion, transformed into a call for a constitutional amendment, that we, the people, have always had more power than we thought."

—**A. R. INGRAFFEA,** PhD, PE, Dwight C. Baum Professor of Engineering Emeritus and Weiss Presidential Teaching Fellow at Cornell University

"Maya's latest book . . . will help expand readers' knowledge and understanding of what it means to work to protect our fragile environment and the great efforts it takes to gain the political support that reflects the concerns of the majority of the world."

—**JOANNE FERRARY,** State Representative, D-New Mexico 37th District

"This book is an inspiration and a road map. It empowers individuals to take action to protect our precious air, land, and water. The stories of environmental heroism and the legal protections that all of us deserve make a huge contribution to the environmental movement. It is well-written, engaging, and informative."

—**ANTOINETTE SEDILLO LOPEZ,** State Senator, D-New Mexico

"This is activism 2.0. Important, timely, and passionate, *The Green Amendment* will revolutionize the way we approach our work to protect the environment."

—**GREG VITALI,** State Representative, D-Pennsylvania 166th District

THE
GREEN
AMENDMENT

THE
GREEN
AMENDMENT

THE PEOPLE'S FIGHT FOR A CLEAN, SAFE, AND HEALTHY ENVIRONMENT

SECOND EDITION

MAYA K. VAN ROSSUM

DISRUPTION
BOOKS
AUSTIN NEW YORK

Published by Disruption Books
New York, New York
www.disruptionbooks.com

Distributed by Disruption Books

For information about special discounts for bulk purchases, please contact Disruption Books at info@disruptionbooks.com.

Cover images © Shutterstock / Beskova Ekaterina; iStockphoto / Yevhenii Dubinko

Cover and book design by Sheila Parr

Library of Congress Cataloging-in-Publication Data available

Printed in the United States of America on 100% post-consumer waste paper.

Print ISBN: 978-1-63331-064-3
eBook ISBN: 978-1-63331-065-0

Second Edition

To the rivers, plants, and animals . . .
We must be their voice in our human world.
And to the future generations . . .
We must secure their future by fighting to protect our environment today.

CONTENTS

ACKNOWLEDGMENTS

I wish to express my immense gratitude to all the people and communities I have the honor of working with to fight for our rights to a clean, safe, and healthy environment. I want to thank my beautiful Delaware River, and all of the streams, plants, soils, critters, and natural communities that inspire me every day to rise up and advocate on their behalf.

Thank you to my family: my amazing husband, David Wood, for bringing unending love, joy, and support to my life, and my daughter, Anneke, and son, Wim, for being the budding advocates and special people that they are. Not only have they been amazing supporters of my work, but they have been proactive and engaged allies. Dave is the first to help me take on any needed task, from booking my flights to joining me at late night and early morning events so I have the support I need. Anneke has actively joined me in my environmental advocacy and advancing the Green Amendment message, using her dedicated talent for speaking up and speaking out in defense of our natural world; from the moment she was born, I knew she would be an amazing environmental ally, and every day she proves me right. Every day Wim is growing his voice for social and environmental justice, taking steps large and small to help others see the power and importance of treating all people and all of nature with respect, kindness, and gratitude. I want to give a special thank you to my four step-children—Steven, Jessica, Scott, and Tommy—for becoming such a wonderful part of my family and my world; they didn't know what they were getting into when their dad and

I got together, but they have blossomed into amazing people who every day show loving care for others.

Thank you to my mother, Marijke, and my father, George. I have no words to describe what spectacular people they were and how much I miss them. Each and every day, they inspire me to be a better person and to advocate more passionately for justice and the protection of communities and the Earth.

I want to give special thanks to Bridget Brady and Molly Atz, who joined me early in my Green Amendment journey. They have been with me every step of the way, and helped me face all of the immense challenges, from inspiring funders to support this work, to challenging the opposition, to keeping up the positive energy during the long workdays and workweeks we increasingly face. This movement would not be advancing so beautifully without their partnership and leadership.

I want to thank Suzanne Crilley, Bob Meek, and Kathleen Reidy for providing the financial support that allowed this second edition to happen. I knew more needed to be said and that updated information needed to get to the world. It is thanks to you that I was able to do so. Thank you for believing in me.

I want to thank Susan and Bruce Wallace for being there from day one and providing the financial support for the Act 13 legal action and the early years when we were launching this new national movement. The Green Amendment movement would not be where we are without your dedication to furthering environmental protection and making our world a safer and happier place for all.

I want to thank the whole Green Amendments For The Generations and Delaware Riverkeeper Network staff who support this work in a myriad of ways. There are many who have joined me in my journey over the years and every one has made a special and lasting contribution to our work together. Special thanks go out as well to the board of directors of both organizations for helping to energetically advance our work. Their dedication to helping save the planet is wonderfully uplifting.

I also wish to acknowledge the amazing grassroots and legislative champions in the Green Amendment movement. With your visionary activism on behalf of the environment, you help to make our world a better place each and every day.

Thank you to Franklin L. Kury who, as a Pennsylvania state legislator in the 1970s, had the courage and vision to propose an environmental rights amendment in Pennsylvania's constitution and ensured its ultimate passage. It is Franklin Kury's original leadership all those decades ago that inspired this movement.

Thank you to Chief Justice Ronald Castille for his insightful and powerful legal opinion that brought the Pennsylvania environmental rights amendment back to life.

Thank you to Jordan Yeager, Jonathan Smith, and John Dernbach for their amazing legal prowess that provided the legal foundation upon which Chief Justice Castille rendered his opinion.

FOREWORD

By Mark Ruffalo

In 1962, conservationist Rachel Carson published *Silent Spring*, a clarion warning to the world about the consequences of environmental degradation. Her book and her later efforts are often credited with sparking the birth of the modern environmental movement. It was a call to action to political leaders and regular citizens alike: to defend our natural resources with extraordinary urgency, on behalf of the planet and all of its species, and in the name of future generations. When Carson testified before Congress the following year, one senator described her work this way: "Every once in a while in the history of mankind, a book has appeared which has substantially altered the course of history." And indeed, in the more than fifty years since *Silent Spring*'s publication, we have won critically important battles, from the passage of the Clean Air and Clean Water Acts to the establishment of the Environmental Protection Agency. Yet any honest accounting of where we are as a country must acknowledge that what has been won is woefully insufficient, that in the broader war to prevent the poisoning of the world, we are losing badly.

The basic things we have come to expect can no longer be taken for granted. We cannot assume that it is safe to swim in our lakes and rivers. We cannot assume that the soil beneath our feet is safe for growing food. We can't even assume that the water coming out of our faucets is safe to drink.

We see this tragedy playing out across the country, in places like Flint, Michigan, where more than a hundred thousand people spent years drinking, cooking with, and bathing in lead-contaminated water. Residents had long reported brown, foul-smelling water and unexplained sickness, but state and local officials chose to do nothing—even after they were confronted with the reality of the danger. This incident is, perhaps, the most notorious, but it is far from unique. According to a 2016 analysis by *Reuters*, there are nearly three thousand areas in the country—with a population of more than ten million people—that have lead poisoning rates even higher than those in Flint.

Then there is hydrofracking and its deadly consequences—the poisoning of well water, of streams and rivers and lakes—as companies pump toxic chemicals into shale rock to release natural gas (none of which they are required to disclose). I live in the Catskills atop the Marcellus Shale, one of the country's largest fracking fields. I have seen firsthand the destruction this new technology has wrought—both the cost to human health and the cost to the pristine natural landscape. To corporations, and their political backers, these are simply the costs of doing business.

And this just scratches the surface. We see corporations build shoddy oil pipelines across critical water tables, downplaying inevitable oil spills. And yet it is the protestors who are demonized. I joined those at Standing Rock who were protesting the Dakota Access Pipeline, for example, and watched in disbelief as the air filled with tear gas. We see coal companies dumping ash and other poisons into waterways, poisoning wildlife and endangering communities downstream. We allow companies to build dangerous chemical plants in populated areas with lax regulations and insufficient safety protocols. In the aftermath of Hurricane Harvey, for example, one such plant exploded multiple times in the city of Houston, sending toxic benzene plumes over the city, along with other chemicals that the company still refuses to disclose. It seems that rarely a day goes by without another man-made environmental tragedy to mourn.

What is clear is that our leaders have let us down. At nearly every turn, the profits of big business are prioritized, consequences be damned. It amounts to a moral failing of the highest degree, one with horrifying and lasting consequences. It is stunning just how often, in the courts, in state legislatures, in Congress, the interests of corporations are deemed more important than the basic things we demand for survival. We are not the sum of dollars and cents; we are people of flesh and blood. And yet it is the dollars that do all the talking.

Existing laws have clearly failed us. They are neither strong enough nor serious enough to protect what matters most. This insufficiency has exacted a heavy price, one we expect to worsen over time. After all, the effects of climate change will surely exacerbate political and corporate negligence.

What we desperately need today is a new strategy, one that recognizes two things: that our efforts to protect the environment to date, however well meaning, are insufficient; and that we must mobilize the American people in common cause and common purpose. It is time to see a safe and clean environment not just as a preference or a privilege, but as a fundamental right, to treat it with the same sanctity as the right of free speech.

I believe the book you are holding in your hand has the power to spark a new movement, just as Rachel Carson's did so many years ago. It is written with sharpness and clarity as it puts forward a road map for a new environmental compact. The ideas within these pages are the very ones we must embrace if we are to shift the paradigm of environmental protection. As the Delaware Riverkeeper, Maya van Rossum has gotten her hands dirty—literally—in the work to battle pollution and its defenders. Her work here will move you—and empower you— to do the same. van Rossum has spoken fiercely and eloquently for the kind of change we all must seek, and has put admirable action behind her powerful words. I cannot imagine a timelier or more critically important piece of writing. It offers a fast and fascinating analysis of where we are as a country, and a bold and convincing strategy for where we must go. My sincere hope is that the words written here are read and repeated far and wide, and that its message becomes the basis of a new environmental era. In an age of environmental pessimism, van Rossum gives me hope.

Mark Ruffalo
Actor, clean water activist, founder of Water Defense,
and cofounder of The Solutions Project

FOREWORD

By Kerri Evelyn Harris

Every time something major happens—whether it brings us joy or sadness, excitement or pain—at some point we will inevitably step outside, take a deep breath, look off into the horizon, and find hope. We believe that everything will be okay if we look at something bigger than us; we can get perspective on our wins and losses through nature.

But sometimes that deep breath, that human reaction, is impeded by putrid smells, a taste of chemicals in our mouths, a horizon that is fuzzy, or a night sky that is absent of stars not because of cloud cover, but because of pollution. Perhaps we smell our shorelines, and it doesn't smell the way we remember as children. It smells dirty. We've gotten so accustomed to this that we just keep moving.

But, my friends, we can't keep turning away from the fact that we are destroying the very thing that brings us peace.

The Green Amendment aims to bring us to a place where the air we breathe is fresh and clean. Where we don't have to worry about becoming unhealthy when we swim in our natural bodies of water. Where we don't have to worry about chemicals or toxins in the soil when we plant fruit trees in our backyards or go to the grocery store and buy produce. Where we will know that our air, water, and soil are safe.

No longer will you have to worry that a business might pop up somewhere and leach waste into your land and your water supply.

No longer will our government agencies be able to turn the other cheek, because they will be required to do the work that they were appointed to do: protect you, your families, and your communities.

As a veteran, activist, community advocate, and organizer in Delaware, I have taken a stand for the people of my state so that we can all demand something better. I want us to look forward and imagine new possibilities. Time and time again, I hear a rallying cry of "people over profits." Well, people are at the very foundation of the Green Amendment's call for clean air, clean water, and healthy soil. The Green Amendment requires our government to actually consider the health and well-being of all of us.

Some people will say that there are already regulations in place that are supposed to protect us. But if that is the case, why are we still fighting the same fights? Why in 2021 did we see the ocean literally on fire?

We're seeing the effects of climate change on a regular basis in ways that we never expected, and we think, *Oh wow, it's nice to have snow when we don't usually get any here.* But there's something wrong with that.

What about when there's flooding that destroys your home and kills your friends and family? When there are tornadoes and hurricanes at record numbers? When we cannot keep rebuilding because we don't have the fighting spirit we used to?

Maya van Rossum is now called the Mother of the Green Amendment movement—what a fitting term. She has made it her life's mission to make sure we are all healthier and happier, and that we have clean air, clean water, and healthy soil as a constitutional right.

I have seen Maya in rooms with people who are labeled as far right, and I've seen her in rooms with people labeled as far left. I've seen her in rooms with people of every political identity, every affiliation, every racial group—moderate, independent, urban, suburban, rural—to deliver a message of a better tomorrow to each and every one of them. She is consistent regardless of whom she's speaking to because she understands that without clean air, clean water, and healthy soil, none of us can thrive. Maya comes with an explanation. She's not just describing a problem but getting us to the next step: how do we fix it?

We all talk about how our elected officials should do better; Maya has helped deliver a way to hold them accountable and to make sure they put us first. We talk about our life and our liberty and our pursuit of happiness—things given to us by our makers, but also enshrined in the Declaration of Independence—and the Green Amendment addresses exactly that.

For me, the Green Amendment means making sure that my state of Delaware, the lowest lying state in the Union, doesn't end up completely underwater. It means knowing that my children can swim on our shores without concern for catching a flesh-eating bacteria from a small scratch. For me, it means my children not suffering from asthma at the rate that they do. For me, it means my state not having so many cancer clusters. For me, it means building a stronger economy: good jobs in industries that don't kill us in the name of being job creators.

For me, it means no other person losing their mother to cancer, as I did, and wondering if it was caused by environmental factors because she seemed to do everything right to take care of her health.

This book will share with you where Maya has gone since the first edition, the stories—sad and joyful, painful and exciting—that are happening in different parts of the country. Hopefully it will inspire you to push for a Green Amendment in your state and join the national movement to make this a federal calling.

As you're reading this book, I hope that you think to yourself: What would the Green Amendment mean for me? What would it mean for my family? Allow that to be your charge forward. Allow the answers to those questions to be the reasons why you take action, even through something as simple as writing a letter to your elected officials at the state or federal level and letting them know that you want more for yourself and your family.

And please, choose to do the work necessary to create the change you want to see in the world; join the Green Amendment movement to help create a healthier America.

Kerri Evelyn Harris

CHAPTER ONE

MY GREEN AMENDMENT EPIPHANY

Early in 2008, my family drove up to my late mother's beautiful sixty-eight-acre patch of forest in Columbia County, central Pennsylvania. For over twenty-five years, this rustic valley had served as my mother's oasis.

She'd bought the land years earlier with an inheritance from her parents. Her father had died suddenly when my mother was a teenager, and the grief would shadow her for the rest of her life. She wanted to do something special and enduring in his memory. My opa (the Dutch word for "grandfather") loved nature and believed in social justice. And so it was no surprise when my mother decided she would purchase a piece of forest she could both protect and enjoy, as a way to honor him.

The journey to find her special sixty-eight-acre forest all those years ago became a driving joy. We visited many parcels together, crisscrossing Pennsylvania to find just the right spot. And when she found Iola—the name of the little village down the road, which we adopted to refer to her special forest—it was love at first sight.

We'd camp together in Iola over countless weekends and on mini-vacations. The little stream running through was so clean, we would use the water for our morning coffee. My daughter was introduced to Iola when she was just a few months old, and she and my mother would go on their own camping adventures now and again. But usually it was the three of us. We hiked every inch of that beautiful forest time and again, always making a stop at the spot with the native lady's slipper orchids my mother loved so much—a personal sanctuary that became all the more exceptional when my mother learned that these lady's slippers were a threatened species in Pennsylvania. She had always loved orchids, and so to learn that she was protecting a little fragile patch threatened by human incursion brought her a profound thrill and sense of responsibility.

When she told me she'd be entrusting her precious forest to me after she was gone, I was overwhelmed by my own grief over the impending loss of my mother, in parallel with the awe and honor of knowing she trusted me with her forest legacy. She shared her plan with me not long after we learned that she had pancreatic cancer, when she was thinking seriously about every aspect of her life. After my mother passed, and once her estate was settled, I set about securing the loans necessary to build the dream cabin she had designed—and joyfully talked about during our Iola hikes—but never had the chance to build. By 2008, the cabin was complete, and my husband, Dave, and I, along with our new blended family, were taking our first trip up to enjoy it. This trip to Iola was filled with both memories of joy and tears of loss.

While there, Dave and I decided to drop in on our neighbor Mason. As we sat in Mason's lumberyard office, he filled us in on some recent happenings in the area. He mentioned that representatives of gas drilling companies had approached several neighbors, describing a new technology that could extract gas from deep inside the Earth without harming the surrounding environment. "They're offering us lots of money for access to our land," Mason said. "They say there's absolutely no adverse environmental impacts, and that the drilling will help revitalize our economy and community."

Absolutely no adverse environmental impacts. That's what they said back then about the process of extracting natural gas from shale rock formations using horizontal directional drilling and hydraulic fracturing (commonly known as "fracking").

"Did you sign on?" I asked.

He shook his head. "A lot of the neighbors are just signing leases with the drilling companies, but I'm taking the time to look into it first. There's a lot of pressure from the drilling reps for folks to sign. But it sounds too good to be true. I'm going to wait awhile."

Reviving a Forgotten Right

I'm the Delaware Riverkeeper, and my job is to protect the Delaware River and its watershed, 13,539 square miles of land spanning the states of Pennsylvania, New Jersey, Delaware, and New York. Much of the watershed lands in New York and Pennsylvania rest atop the Marcellus Shale deposit, a massive stretch of gas-rich shale running from New York State down to West Virginia. Around the same time we spoke with Mason, we learned that the drilling companies were also aggressively targeting properties and landholdings for development in portions of the Delaware River watershed. As 2008 wore on, my organization, the Delaware Riverkeeper Network, received more and more calls from residents in our watershed with similar stories of industry representatives knocking on doors and soliciting easements to drill for gas. My conversation with Mason had alerted me to the impact these sudden offers were having on landowners and communities. The excitement, confusion, and fear were palpable. For the good of my watershed, we would need to determine the truth about fracking, carefully comparing the industry's claims with the experiences of communities and the findings of scientific experts.

My colleague, Delaware Riverkeeper Network's Deputy Director Tracy Carluccio, and I acted quickly, learning about fracking and its potential impacts. The more we investigated, the more apparent it became that drilling and fracking are hardly innocuous. Although scientific evidence linking fracking with water pollution, the contamination of drinking water, methane gas emissions, increased seismic activity, extreme weather events, and human health hazards was still emerging for our region and the Marcellus Shale, we discovered that the extraction process had already devastated environments and communities in Texas, Michigan, and other states early to the shale gas boom. We were also hearing horrific stories from communities in central and western Pennsylvania where fracking had already taken place.

We paid a visit to see for ourselves what was happening in these Pennsylvania communities outside of our watershed. As we discovered, fracking operations were emitting noxious gases into residential communities and towns. They were disturbing humans and animals with 24/7 light and noise pollution. They were destroying vast swaths of forest, as shale gas extraction requires massive land clearing to accommodate drilling pads, roads, wastewater impoundments, compressor stations, pipelines, and natural gas processing facilities. Their heavy truck traffic was overwhelming commuters and local roads not designed to carry an immense load, increasing accidents, including fatal ones, and inflicting costly road wear and tear that stressed local government budgets.[1] And they were sucking up vast quantities of water while simultaneously polluting groundwater supplies and streams.

Despite this environmental devastation, the fracking shale gas industry had continued to expand throughout Pennsylvania, West Virginia, and Ohio, primary states sitting atop the coveted Marcellus Shale deposits. Within our watershed and across the region, companies were approaching more property owners to secure drilling leases. Everywhere the gas companies went, they touted the same argument: We have a way to extract natural gas from the ground. Natural gas is an environmentally friendly, largely nonpolluting energy source that's good for addressing climate change—and we have a way to extract it from the ground without posing harm to the environment, your property, or your family. We will pay you a bonus up front when you sign a lease that allows us to drill on your property. Once we start getting gas, you will get royalties. You will make a good, healthy income for years to come. You can pay off your debts and start to enjoy your life. You can even start to think about retirement.

People began signing leases. Unfortunately, many who signed soon came to regret their choices. As early as 2009, residents of Clearville and Avella, Pennsylvania, reported sick and dying livestock—as well as dangerous levels of contamination in the soil around drill sites.[2] In Dimock, Pennsylvania, water began turning brown and making people sick, animals began mysteriously shedding their hair, and a water well spontaneously combusted. Dimock residents watched in horror when, in September of that year, a series of spills from a Cabot Oil and Gas well sent acid- and detergent-laced fracking water surging into surrounding wetlands and nearby Stevens Creek. Other communities reeled as their homes and schools, long ensconced in beautiful forests and gently flowing streams, now gazed out onto noisy, smelly, and hazardous industrial operations. As the months ticked along, more families started suffering all sorts of harms: nosebleeds, headaches, loss of memory, dizziness, agitation, and the sickening of farm animals or domestic pets. Families were terrified. People no longer felt safe in their homes, they weren't able to enjoy their properties for family get-togethers or fun in the yard, and they lived with the ever-present fear of getting sick.

Alarmed, Tracy and I voiced our concerns before the Delaware River Basin Commission (DRBC), a regulatory agency with authority over the Delaware River watershed. After collaborating with other community leaders, mobilizing residents, lobbying politicians, submitting written comments, testifying at hearings, and representing the concerns of the seventeen million people who rely upon the Delaware for drinking water, we managed in May 2010 to convince the DRBC to enact a moratorium on shale gas extraction, drilling, and fracking within our watershed. This moratorium would remain in force until the DRBC's five commissioners passed regulations that would allow drilling and fracking while at the same time protecting the river's water quality—a hurdle that by this time we knew they could never overcome (and a fact that we eventually proved through our extensive research and advocacy).

The drilling industry assured the DRBC that fracking benefited communities, the environment, and business, and that the industry could frack in a way that would not harm the river. Industry officials, lawyers, and landowners also threatened legal action if the DRBC did not open the watershed to shale gas extraction. By 2020, the industry raved, America would achieve energy independence—relying on its own natural resources instead of foreign sources of fossil fuels—and put Americans to work in the process. At most, they said, fracking was a temporary nuisance. It posed less of a threat than coal, its dirty, carbon-dioxide-emitting energy competitor. Despite these industry lies, or perhaps in response to them, a growing number of individuals and organizations joined us in our opposition.

As more accounts documenting fracking's destructiveness accumulated, and as scientific studies documenting near- and long-term ecological impacts mounted, it became obvious that we needed to do more to stop the industry. Our moratorium on shale gas extraction in the Delaware River watershed represented the cutting edge of protection, but it was fragile—it could be lifted with a vote of five people (the DRBC commissioners) and just a few weeks' notice. In fact, for a few weeks during the fall of 2011, the lifting of the moratorium seemed imminent. In the end, our hard-fought defense held because we lobbied hard behind the scenes and there was a massive public outcry that prevented the vote.

After this close call, we at the Delaware Riverkeeper Network and our partner organizations resolved to work for a comprehensive and permanent ban on fracking in the watershed. At the same time, we wanted to put in place layers of protection so that we'd be safe if the DRBC ever tried to lift its moratorium. The more layers that existed, the more communities we would help, bringing us closer to the day when we would stop all shale gas extraction everywhere, for everyone.

In New York, communities had invoked their municipal authority to ban fracking town by town, and the courts had upheld their right to institute these local protections. Could fracking opponents accomplish similar town-by-town bans in Pennsylvania? That was unclear. Pennsylvania communities could certainly make various legal arguments in support of a ban, but to date no court decision had actually upheld such a local ban.[3] So most Pennsylvania communities wishing to institute protections resorted to using zoning laws to place constraints on drilling and fracking, ensuring that these operations could take place only in industrial zones and not in agricultural districts, residential areas, or critical environmental or historic preservation zones.

In response, the fracking industry got busy in the halls of the state capitol in Harrisburg. Pitching drilling and fracking as a job-creating engine for the state, they covered up the environmental, public safety, and community devastation that was already resulting. They liberally spread around lobbying dollars to help solidify needed legislator support.

Enticed by the industry's promise of quick wealth, or perhaps just by the big contributions they would receive in their election campaign coffers, Pennsylvania's politicians reaffirmed their support of drilling, fracking, and shale gas, passing a sinister piece of legislation in 2012 that came to be known as Act 13. The law granted the shale gas industry a bag of goodies from its regulatory wish list. This came as no surprise, as we later learned that industry proponents themselves had written the law and delivered it to legislators, many of whom didn't even bother to read it.

Act 13 required that every municipality, and every zoning district within every municipality, permit access to the drilling and fracking industry. Schools, residences, protected waterways, wildlife sanctuaries, public parks—all were now open to intrusion by the shale gas fracking industry. Not only was every community obliged to allow drilling and fracking operations in every part of their community, but the drilling industry was also given the power to seize land through eminent domain for purposes of storing its gas underground. While the law mandated that the industry notify public water authorities in the case of accidental spills threatening water supplies, the industry didn't have to notify people who obtained their water from private wells.

To make the bill more palatable, the fracking industry had included several carrots, such as an "impact fee" that would channel industry money into the state's general budget and also disseminate it to local communities to remediate fracking-related damages, fund schools, or support other local priorities. We at the Delaware Riverkeeper Network knew, however, that the environmental impacts inflicted by fracking and shale gas extraction would be far more devastating than any impact fee could cover. We suspect that may be in part why Act 13 included a medical gag rule. Doctors who treated patients suffering from exposure to the industry's chemicals could obtain information about potential exposures needed to help their patients only if they signed nondisclosure agreements. The information secured couldn't be shared with anyone, including other doctors who might help them properly diagnose and treat their patients. By any measure, Act 13 was a travesty—a bald-faced capitulation to the industry. An enormous grassroots effort to stop the bill emerged, waged by the Delaware Riverkeeper Network, municipalities, and environmental organizations from across Pennsylvania. In February 2012, however, the legislature approved the bill, and shortly thereafter, Governor Tom Corbett signed Act 13 into law.

Alarmed and outraged, my Delaware Riverkeeper Network brought legal action, joining forces with seven vulnerable towns and a concerned physician. Three attorneys would lead our legal team—Jordan Yeager, John Smith, and Jonathan Kamin. While plotting our strategy for the litigation, Jordan and I agreed that although the Delaware Riverkeeper Network would present a number of rationales for striking down the law from the environmental perspective, chief among them would be a long-ignored provision of the Pennsylvania Constitution, the environmental rights amendment.

In 1971, driven by the vision of a junior state legislator, Franklin Kury, who sought stronger state environmental protections that could not be easily undone, Pennsylvania had passed an amendment to its constitution's Declaration of Rights—article 1, section 27—that explicitly protected the right of people to a healthy environment, and that established the government's obligation to protect the state's natural resources. The provision stated:

*The people have a right to clean air, pure water, and to the pres-
ervation of the natural, scenic, historic and esthetic values of the
environment. Pennsylvania's public natural resources are the
common property of all the people, including generations yet to
come. As trustee of these resources, the Commonwealth shall conserve and maintain them for the benefit of all the people.*

With the inclusion of article 1, section 27, Pennsylvania's constitution elevated environmental rights to the status of other fundamental
rights and freedoms, such as free speech, freedom of religion, due process, and the right to bear arms. The constitution's power transcended
that of any piece of legislation. It proclaimed the supreme law of the
state, enshrining our most deeply held values. And yet, when presented
with early opportunities to interpret and apply the constitutional language, Pennsylvania's courts had treated article 1, section 27 as a statement of policy rather than as a binding statement of law.

Still, we believed that Act 13 violated both the spirit and the letter
of the state's environmental rights amendment—and that the amendment was not a mere policy statement. We were determined to test this
conviction in court. By including the constitutional argument as a cen-
terpiece of our legal efforts, we hoped to obtain a decision that would set
a powerful new precedent regarding the environmental rights of Pennsylvanians. It was a risky bet, but the stakes couldn't have been higher:
pure water, clean air, and a healthy environment.

In a protracted series of actions and appeals, our legal team presented the case for why Pennsylvania courts should find Act 13 unconstitutional. Attorney Jordan Yeager took the lead in crafting our part of
the case and in arguing that Act 13 violated our environmental rights
as guaranteed in article 1, section 27. In December 2013, in a landmark
decision, the Pennsylvania Supreme Court declared fundamental provisions of Act 13 unconstitutional, reinstating property and municipal
zoning rights. Article 1, section 27 was a linchpin of the plurality opinion
authored by Chief Justice Ronald D. Castille. In rendering its decision,

the court vindicated the environmental rights amendment's importance and power, promising all generations of Pennsylvanians that they would benefit from pure water, clean air, and a healthy environment, and giving them the ability to defend that right in court if it were violated. The court, through Chief Justice Castille's carefully crafted plurality opinion, also made clear that our environmental rights are not granted by the Pennsylvania Constitution or any legal document created by people. Rather, they are inherent and indefeasible rights given to us by nature, by virtue of our birth, and thus inalienable. The plurality of the court also emphasized that these environmental rights do not just belong to present generations living on the Earth today, but extend to the future generations yet to come, thus ensuring a higher obligation of protection.

Industry lawyers, lobbyists, and even their friends in state government quickly tried to discount our environmental rights victory and claim it did not set a precedent that could, would, or should control future cases. The suggestion that our win based on environmental rights did not set legal precedent was quickly stomped out when, in June 2017, a majority of the Pennsylvania Supreme Court explicitly adopted Chief Justice Castille's analysis.[4] The strength of article 1, section 27 for protecting environmental rights and natural resources for the benefit of present and future generations of Pennsylvanians is now beyond dispute.

As the Delaware Riverkeeper, I felt deeply moved and inspired by our triumph. We had thwarted the gas companies' arrogant efforts to take over the state and ruin its environment. The fracking industry was still inflicting harm, but we had prevented the industry's exponential expansion and sent a message to their cronies in the legislature that "fractivists"—as we are now often called—are a force to be reckoned with. But the victory was even bigger than that. We had established that harmed Pennsylvanians, impacted community leaders, and good government officials could use constitutional provisions to affect transformational change when it came to environmental protection.

Over time, this led me to an epiphany that would plant the seed of a national movement. Environmental rights are worthy of constitutional recognition and protection. But not just any language anywhere will do. The right words and constitutional placement are key. Green Amendments are what we need.

A National Movement Begins and Grows

Across the country, concerned individuals fighting a range of environmental battles are at the mercy of powerful business interests and the lawmakers they influence. Environmentalists have sought protections via legislative remedies—laws like the Clean Water Act, the Clean Air Act, the Safe Drinking Water Act, the Endangered Species Act, and others, along with a wealth of state counterparts. Yet this legislative approach has largely failed us. Our precious natural resources have continued to degrade, and we are facing a growing climate crisis. Business interests enjoy a powerful advantage in how the laws are written, whether they pass or fail, how they are implemented, and how rigorously they are enforced (or not enforced). These corporate and industry proponents enjoy access to politicians that regular people simply do not have. They have bought the science needed to make their case, and they've leveraged economic arguments to cloud the facts both in the courtroom and in public debate.

But more than that, when government officials or advocates have dared to oppose their plans, companies and industry groups have gone to courts of law and mobilized property rights and other widely recognized constitutional liberties and legal claims to justify environmental degradation. Lacking recourse to the constitution, people harmed by environmental degradation have been at the mercy of elected officials and powerful business interests. When legislators have passed laws that encourage dramatic ecological harm, when government officials haven't properly enforced existing environmental protections, or when laws that are supposed to protect our environment have been used to disproportionately impact people of color, Indigenous people, and/or low-income communities, environmental protectors and community groups have too often—for lack of a sufficiently strong legal rationale—lost our battles. In Pennsylvania, thanks to our 2013 case, this situation is starting to change. We faced down a powerful, well-funded industry group with a stranglehold over legislators and regulators, and we triumphed—because we had the state constitution on our side.

This fight led me to wonder: Was Pennsylvania's environmental rights amendment unique among the fifty states? I hadn't learned about environmental rights in school, and as an attorney it was definitely not part of day-to-day parlance. But if Pennsylvania was different, how was it different?

I began to investigate.

First, I needed to be clear about what made Pennsylvania's environmental rights amendment special—what made it a "Green Amendment" (as I was starting to call it). Jordan Yeager, lead attorney on the Act 13 case, and his colleague Lauren Williams, who had also been an essential member of the Act 13 team, joined me in preparing a checklist of what makes article 1, section 27 special. For one thing, it is located in the Bill of Rights, placing environmental rights on par with other fundamental rights. For another, it is self-executing, meaning its own terms afford it legal strength and enforceability. It makes clear, in plain language, that it protects life-sustaining elements of the environment, provides generational protections, and establishes that *all* government officials in the state are obliged to safeguard Pennsylvania's natural resources and the environmental rights of all people. Somewhat hidden, but no less powerful or enforceable, are its environmental justice protections as well as the climate protections it can provide.

With my Green Amendment checklist in hand, I polled every state constitution across our nation—and what I found was quite astonishing. Almost every state constitution mentions aspects of the environment; some even employ eloquent references that sound as though they bestow environmental rights. But only Montana had a constitutional amendment that raised environmental rights to the same high standing as Pennsylvania. A close look at all the other states revealed that they don't recognize environmental rights as being on par with other political rights deserving of the highest legal recognition and protection. Many provisions merely refer to environmental protection or rights as good public policy or make these rights dependent on additional state action to realize the actual protection they seem to promise. As a result, these provisions are largely ineffectual. A handful of states have no provisions whatsoever protecting or even discussing the environment. And of course, I didn't need to bother with the US Constitution: I already knew that clear recognition and protection of environmental rights is glaringly absent at the federal level.

Imagine what would happen if strong constitutional provisions similar to Pennsylvania's existed across our nation. Imagine if each state passed a constitutional environmental rights amendment—a Green Amendment—that equals or exceeds Pennsylvania's. Imagine if we passed a federal constitutional provision guaranteeing that the government has no more ability to harm your environmental rights than it does to deny you due process or overturn your right to free speech. In courts of law, constitutional protection would change wishful thinking about the environment into a clear and well-deserved entitlement. Instead of hoping and pleading with lawmakers to do the right thing, constitutional amendments would elevate environmental rights to the status of our most cherished liberties. Life, liberty, the pursuit of happiness, *and* a healthy environment would now be recognized by all as inherent and indefeasible rights that all government officials must protect for the benefit of all generations, even those yet to come.

Beyond leveling the playing field in contests between environmentalists and industry, constitutional amendments at the state and federal levels promise to effect a broader cultural and intellectual transformation. Explicitly recognizing a right to a clean and healthy environment would alter how people think about the environment and our relationship to it. My Green Amendment mantra—pure water, clean air, a stable climate, and a healthy environment—would take on the stature of an entitlement in people's minds, becoming far more than what it is now:

an aspirational, but unenforceable, goal. We would all take it personally when companies destroy the forests and wetlands around us, or when they pollute our air or water. We'd feel outraged, perceiving that industry wrongfully took something of ours to which they had no right. We'd feel more of an obligation to protect the Earth for others.

After all, we're not the only ones who possess a right to a clean and healthy environment—there is the next generation, and the generations after that. There are also the plants, animals, trees, and rivers with whom we share this Earth. With constitutional recognition, we would feel more empowered because we would *be* more empowered. In addition to fighting for the very environment that sustains us all, we would be fighting for a constitutional right that belongs to us—and that government officials would not be legally empowered or entitled to take from us. Constitutional amendments protecting the right to a clean and healthy environment have the power to change everything about how people interact with one another, with the world, with our decision makers, and with future generations.

Enshrining environmental rights within a constitution's declaration of rights—and holding lawmakers accountable on the basis of those rights—was a breakthrough for me in our fight against the fracking industry. I'm writing this book to share this breakthrough with anyone who cares about human welfare and our natural world.

My message is simple: *you can do this*. You might feel beaten down by the seemingly impossible battles you're waging, but take heart. You have a new strategy now to draw on—environmental constitutionalism and the power of a Green Amendment. It is a winning strategy that will forever change the foundation upon which you pursue your advocacy.

Amazingly, my vision for nationwide change is starting to take hold. On November 2, 2021, with a decisive 70 percent of the vote, the people of New York determined to add a Green Amendment to their state constitution. And from coast to coast we are starting to see Green Amendment proposals put forth in other states. Even if the politics seem daunting in your state or in our nation as a whole, there is something so profoundly and morally sound about all of us having a right to clean water and air and healthy environments, that it resonates across the political spectrum. I've seen it, and you will too. By working together efficiently, effectively, and in close collaboration from the get-go, we are best positioned to get the most meaningful constitutional language, avoid the pitfalls, and take on the industry opposition we know will build quickly against us. I formed my organization Green Amendments For The Generations so we can do just that: work together to secure this most powerful change state by state, and then as a nation.

No matter where you happen to live, I'm here to say that you should dramatically raise your expectations when it comes to the environment. You have a *right* to pure water, clean air, a stable climate, and healthy environments. This right is inherent and indefeasible. It *belongs* to you. Many politicians rail against entitlements and dismiss millennials as an "entitled generation," but they've got it wrong. Entitlement is not a dirty word. It is a recognition of rights. And make no mistake: when it comes to the environment, you *are* entitled. When your right to a healthy environment is challenged, you should rise up as firmly and passionately in defense of that entitlement as you would rise up to defend your right to free speech, freedom of religion, trial by jury, and private property. Standing up for your environment doesn't hurt jobs or industry, as those profiting from environmental devastation often contend. As I'll show later in this book, your right to pure water, clean air, a stable climate, and healthy environments actually *underlies* many other social goods, including a strong economy.

This book offers a brief but comprehensive look at the power of environmental constitutionalism to effect change from the point of view of an activist. Throughout the chapters to come, we will explore a range of critical environmental issues, along with the health, environmental justice, and generational impacts of pollution and degradation. I will relate how grievous the harms have been despite the existence of environmental laws and regulations, and explain the difference a meaningful constitutional amendment—a Green Amendment—in our state and federal constitutions could make. We'll take on some of the key arguments that environmental defenders face, so we can all be well prepared to confront those false arguments head-on. I close the book hoping to inspire you to join me in a national Green Amendment movement—one focused on securing constitutional Green Amendments state by state and at the federal level—so that as a nation we can meaningfully secure our environmental rights; ensure environmental justice for all people regardless of race, ethnicity, or socioeconomic status; more powerfully address the climate crisis; and more broadly embrace the mindset of environmental constitutionalism to improve our lives, empower our communities, and save our Earth.

Following my mother's death, my family continued to venture to Iola to enjoy the forest. But over a period of years, nearby shale gas extraction ruined my mother's natural haven. Pollution, noise, and the ever-present fear of increased drilling intruded on our oasis. Eventually, this all became too much. We returned the land to its original owner, entrusting him to protect it as best he could.

Sadly, my family's story has been replicated throughout the region, the state, and the country. The culprit has not just been fracking, but has included a variety of damaging industries, technologies, and forms of development.

Let's stand up for our right to a clean and healthy environment. Let's take our country back from the industrial interests that seek to exploit our natural world for their own profit. Let's rise up together and demand our environmental rights. Let's change our constitutions to recognize that our right to life, liberty, happiness, and a clean and healthy environment far overshadows the rights of others to pollute for profit.

A Green Amendment in every state constitution and in the US Constitution: It can happen. It starts with you. Right now.

CHAPTER TWO

LIVING IN THE
SACRIFICE ZONE

Would you send your kids to school near a working oil refinery? Would you let them play tag or hopscotch amid giant smokestacks spewing out a witches' brew of chemicals? Of course not. That's crazy. Unthinkable. Yet that's exactly what Rosaria Marquina of Manchester, Texas, did each day. Her seven-year-old boy Valentín attended JR Harris Elementary School, which *USA Today* ranked as one of the nation's most polluted. When kids at JR Harris Elementary play outside during recess, their developing bodies ingest toxic levels of benzene and 1,3-butadiene issuing from the community's numerous oil refineries and petrochemical plants, as well as from the ships and barges that navigate the nearby Houston Ship Channel.[1] Valentín breathed that foul air every day—until doctors diagnosed him with leukemia.[2]

Rosaria pulled Valentín out of the school. But Valentín had a little sister, six-year-old Mónica. She still attended JR Harris Elementary. Financially strapped, Rosaria had no choice but to live in this toxic neighborhood and enroll her children in its public schools. Imagine how hard it must have been for her to say goodbye to her daughter each morning when she dropped her off. "I don't know whether I am giving her an education or a death sentence," Rosaria said to a reporter.[3] Public officials reassured her that her kids were safe at school, that the community's pollution problems didn't pose health risks to her children. With constant exposure, they develop natural defenses within their bodies, she was told. "If that's true," she wondered, "what happened to Valentín?"[4]

In 2016, Manchester ranked among the country's most environmentally degraded places.[5] Children growing up there were over 50 percent more likely than other American kids to develop acute leukemia.[6] The pollution was obvious, unmistakable. Because of Houston's famous lack of zoning, children played on jungle gyms and ran miles on the school track with industrial compounds spewing pollution in the near background. The community's César E. Chavez High School is located within a mere *quarter mile* of three major oil refineries.[7] Small homes with tricycles and monkey bars bordered chemical storage facilities. Residents nursed lifelong coughs and endured unremitting noxious odors. They washed the accumulated soot off their cars each morning and were told that the fruit they grew in their yards was too toxic to eat.[8] This was simply part of the fabric of everyday life in Manchester, Texas.

But the story of Manchester's pollution didn't end there. In this city, industry didn't just engulf schools and houses. It penetrated *beneath* the community as well. Pipelines crisscrossed one another beneath the ground, transporting natural gas and oil to refineries. Jay Olaguer, director of the Houston Advanced Research Center's air-quality science program, found the cancer-causing contaminant benzene leaching from these underground pipelines. Using cutting-edge tracking equipment, as well as CT scans and tests of human lung tissue, his study revealed dangerously high levels of benzene emissions within Manchester. Human lung cells begin to exhibit signs of asthmatic irritation and inflammation after just four hours of exposure to Manchester's oil facilities.[9] Imagine the fate of Manchester's residents, whose exposure to such contaminants is constant.

Residents of Manchester believe the pollution from nearby industry—pollution they can smell—is compromising their health, and they want out. But the cost of moving can prove prohibitive. "I want to get out of here and go to the country and find some cleaner air. It would be better for me and the kids," Eugene Barragan, a fifty-six-year-old resident who has multiple growths in his lungs, told a reporter. "When I work hard, I start coughing and coughing, and can't stop." While the Texas Commission on Environmental Quality rated the environmental compliance of refineries and chemical plants as satisfactory, a University of Texas study found that children who live within two miles of the Houston Ship Channel have a 56 percent higher risk of acute lymphocytic leukemia compared with children living ten miles away.[10] Regardless of what Texas regulators say, something is devastatingly amiss in Manchester—and rather than providing the needed protection for the people, environmental laws seem to be giving industry cover to keep operating without addressing these grievous harms.

The New Sacrifice Zones

During the Cold War, experts coined a powerful euphemism to describe areas damaged irreparably by nuclear radiation. They called them "sacrifice zones."[11] These places were so devastated by the manufacture of nuclear weapons that they became inhospitable to life—humans, animals, plants. They were areas that the US government had literally sacrificed for the sake of the nuclear arms race. Since the Cold War, many communities have been knowingly sacrificed, this time in service not to national security, but to industry. Toxicity is so pervasive in Manchester, Texas, that it has become a permanent health hazard. And so the people of the city are being sacrificed—knowingly, intentionally, and with the full blessing of the law—ostensibly for the sake of local and national economies.

Perhaps you don't live in a clearly identified sacrifice zone. Does that mean your area is safe? The available scientific data demonstrates that widespread environmental catastrophe is underway throughout the country and the world. As former NASA researcher and professor of mathematics Dave Pruett observes, environmental degradation is so widespread that "we're all in the sacrifice zone now."[12] Indigenous communities, communities of color, and low-income communities already suffer disproportionate environmental pollution and degradation—too often imposed by the intentional acts of government officials, or as the result of the knowing design and/or implementation of our system of laws and government. So at the same time that mounting environmental degradation and a spiraling climate crisis are expanding the scope of environmental harm, this damage also perpetuates, and grows, the footprint of environmental racism.

Most people believe that the United States of America is a nation of laws, and that these laws are adequate to protect us from environmental harm. We have the Clean Water Act, the Clean Air Act, the Safe Drinking Water Act, and the National Environmental Policy Act, to name a few. These federal statutes are complemented by an array of state laws also focused on issues of air, water, species protection, habitat preservation, toxic contamination, and more. In fact, we have so many environmental laws that developers, industry representatives, and conservative politicians complain loudly about them. They take to the airwaves, contending that environmental laws are unnecessary and interfere with their ability to carry out their operations, manufacture their products, extract targeted resources, turn a profit, and create jobs.

This could not be further from the truth. Corporations are fully pursuing their operations and creating jobs, but our environment and health are not being fully, fairly, properly, or equitably protected. Environmental degradation of all forms is underway in every part of every community in the United States of America. We're loading our water, air, and soils with pollution. We're allowing construction to take place in wetlands, old-growth forests, streams, and rivers. We're shattering the Earth's geology and turning formerly bucolic areas into pollution-spewing industrial sites so as to extract every last drop of fossil fuel. We're changing our climate in deadly ways. All of this is occurring despite the system of federal, state, and local environmental laws we have in place. It's occurring despite the existence of environmental protection agencies at the local, state, and federal levels.

More Dangerous Than War

The general public tends to focus on environmental degradation at times of great emergency, largely forgetting about it once the emergency has passed. Many people thought a lot about petrochemical pollution in 2010, when the BP Deepwater Horizon spilled over four million barrels of oil into the Gulf of Mexico.[13] Heart-wrenching photos of brown pelicans coated in globs of oil flashed across television screens. Journalists conducted interviews with members of fishing communities devastated by the impact on their livelihoods. Witnesses saw swirling rainbows of deadly oil spreading endlessly across the water. While chemical contamination from that devastating spill continues to impact communities, sea life, and environments, how much attention do the news media and the general public pay today?[14] How often do most of us think about the impacts of that spill?

Let's consider a few facts that get lost when sensational spills and other environmental calamities aren't claiming the headlines. We learned as schoolchildren that water is essential to life and that our bodies are composed of over 60 percent water. Despite this reality, we allow sewage, industrial runoff, and unregulated pharmaceuticals to contaminate our limited freshwater supplies. In fact, we don't just allow this pollution to happen—we invite it. We *intentionally inject* contamination into our waterways, either as a way to dispose of contaminated waste or because adding toxic chemicals to fresh water allows us to carry out industrial operations like fracking to extract gas or oil from shale.

Surface water pollution adversely affects more than half of the world's population, causing millions of deaths every year. At least half the world's groundwater is so polluted that it is unsafe to consume.[15] America's pollution levels track this global trend, with approximately half of our streams, lakes, and bays suffering significant pollution—and far too many of our drinking water supplies laden with harmful, cancer-causing chemicals. [16] Though Erin Brockovich brought the dangers of one such chemical, chromium-6, to the national spotlight in 1993, the United States Environmental Protection Agency (EPA) has still failed to take the steps required to remove it from our drinking water.[17] Chromium-6 now infects the tap water of over 200 million Americans and will cause approximately twelve thousand cancer deaths by century's end.[18] As environmentalists, scholars, and economists have predicted, clean and healthy fresh water is becoming so scarce that it will soon be the "new oil."

The state of our air is no better. According to the American Lung Association's *State of the Air 2021* report, more than 40 percent of our country's population lives where there are unhealthy levels of ozone or particle pollution.[19] This equates to 135 million people who are breathing unhealthy air. Scientists have linked air pollution to major killers like heart disease, asthma, and cancer, including bladder and lung cancers.[20] In fact, an astonishing 10.2 million people die annually from air pollution.[21]

Contrary to what the authorities in Manchester, Texas, may argue, our bodies don't develop "defenses" against air and water pollution. Instead, our bodies fall victim to it. They sicken. They die. And think about this: every year, more people die from water pollutants than from all episodes of war and global violence combined.[22] That's right, pollution kills more people than *war*.

Air pollution might also be the key to unlocking the mysteries of neurodegeneration. Concerning data from around the world are linking air pollution to dementia and Alzheimer's disease, two of the most devastating medical enigmas of our time and illnesses that afflicted my father and my grandfather. A 2017 University of Toronto study found that people living within fifty meters of a busy freeway or thoroughfare had a 12 percent greater likelihood of developing dementia than those living more than two hundred meters away.[23] Assistant professor Hong Chen, the paper's lead author, said, "Little is known in current research about how to reduce the risk of dementia. Our findings show the closer you live to roads with heavy day-to-day traffic, the greater the risk of developing dementia."[24] Seventeen additional studies published in 2016 also linked air pollution with dementia. It's frightening to think that living near a busy road could make us literally lose our minds, but it's looking more and more like that might be the case for many of us.

Children are not spared the mind-altering and body-damaging ravages of pollution exposure. Too often, they are even more vulnerable. Over the course of the twenty-first century, the prevalence of childhood developmental disorders has significantly increased.[25] Autism rates have continued to climb since 2000 (when specialists began tracking such figures).[26] The rate of attention deficit hyperactivity disorder (ADHD) has increased by between 33 and 52 percent, depending on the age and gender of the child.[27] And asthma afflicts 8.5 percent of children across the United States—with higher rates still, ranging from 10 to 15 percent, among children of color and those living below the poverty level.[28] Such disorders stem from many different causes, with exposure to pollution inarguably playing a role. Scientists at Harvard and the Massachusetts College of Pharmacy and Health Sciences found that exposure to fine particulate air pollution in utero or early childhood increases the risk of autism in children.[29] And according to the National Resource Center on ADHD, exposure to lead or pesticides is a potential cause of ADHD in children.[30] In addition, a well-documented association exists between asthma (as well as asthma-related deaths) and air pollution.[31]

For some children, the damage from pollution exposure begins in the womb. Studies are demonstrating that air pollution can affect a developing fetus, causing a lowered IQ and potentially behavioral syndromes.[32] In utero exposure to air pollution is also being linked to low birth weight, which in turn can cause respiratory distress in infants, put them at greater risk of infections, and cause or contribute to neurological or gastrointestinal problems.[33] It may be hard to accept, but our pollution is harming children in devastating ways before they are even born.

Cancer, autism, asthma, ADHD, Alzheimer's, dementia—these are but a few of many harmful effects that pollution has on our bodies. But we humans are not the only ones who have suffered thanks to the largely silent scourge of environmental degradation. When formerly pristine areas are transformed into sacrifice zones, our animal friends suffer, too. Over the long term, their suffering only intensifies and broadens our own.

Victims of the Anthropocene

By any standard, sturgeon are remarkable creatures. They've swum the world's oceans since the age of the dinosaurs, making them some of the most ancient fish in existence today.[34] Some species of sturgeon can live between 50 and 150 years and grow in excess of a thousand pounds.[35] A quick look at these animals can convince you of their uniqueness. With bony plates accompanying their standard fish gills, they look prehistoric. As Dr. Dewayne Fox, a longtime researcher of the Delaware River population and professor at Delaware State University, relates, "Sturgeon in their present form look like they did seventy-three million years ago."[36]

The Delaware River is home to a genetically unique line of Atlantic sturgeon, one that is found nowhere else on Earth. Despite their longevity as a species, however, in 2012 Atlantic sturgeon (including our Delaware River population) joined shortnose sturgeon on the federal Endangered Species List.[37] Around the world, sturgeon are among the most imperiled of all species, according to the International Union for Conservation of Nature.[38] How did they become critically endangered after freely roaming the seas for 200 million years?

Historically, the culprit was humans' taste for caviar. During the nineteenth century, the world transformed fish eggs, cured with salt, into a delicacy. The global caviar industry transported wild sturgeon eggs (roe), harvested from the Black and Caspian seas, throughout Europe. After years of overfishing, however, European sturgeon populations dwindled, and the industry moved west. The nineteenth-century Delaware River was so populated with sturgeon that it became known as the caviar capital of North America. The sturgeon of the Delaware River fueled a massive caviar industry, creating jobs and generating wealth for the region.[39]

By 1900, however, sturgeon populations dwindled, and they have flirted with extinction ever since.[40] Scientists estimate there are currently fewer than three hundred spawning adults left of the Delaware River's genetically unique line of Atlantic sturgeon. According to Dr. Erik Silldorff, an aquatic ecologist who specializes in the species, there are so few Atlantic sturgeon left in the Delaware River population that some years there may be no females entering the river to spawn.[41]

Sturgeon haven't mounted a comeback over the past century, despite multiple regulatory and grassroots efforts. As Dewayne explains, sturgeon species "have suffered population declines because of pollution, dams that block access to spawning areas, dredging, unintended bycatch during fishing operations, and vessel strikes."[42]

In the Delaware River, dredging and deepening of the river's main navigation channel to accommodate larger ships have taken a significant toll on the species. Adult sturgeon swim up the river's navigation channel, where they fall victim to large ships, says Dewayne. "Some ships bump on [the] bottom; you can see the scour marks," he explains. "When you have two ships with twenty-foot-diameter propellers passing in opposite directions, that takes twenty-five percent of the channel. We get a lot of animals cut in half."[43] Deepening also increases the inflow of water from the ocean, diminishing freshwater habitat essential for sturgeon spawning. Water diversions upstream, including for power generation and industry, and periods of drought also reduce freshwater flows into the river, allowing the salt line to further advance. Other industrial activity, like nuclear power plants, which suck up river water for cooling purposes, also make the Delaware River hazardous for sturgeon.[44]

Layered on top, making the river even more inhospitable for sturgeon and other fish, is a lack of oxygen in key reaches of the river. A fifty-year-old regulatory standard requires agencies to manage pollution discharges only at a level that will assure an average 3.5 mg/l of dissolved oxygen in certain segments of the river. The Delaware River Basin

Commission—the very same DRBC that set this standard in 1967—then released a 2018 expert report identifying 6.3 mg/l or higher as the necessary level to support the spawning and rearing of Atlantic sturgeon. The 2018 report observes that most key species of fish in the Delaware suffer lethal and sublethal effects when dissolved oxygen is below 5 mg/l.[45] In response to the research, the DRBC has received multiple petitions from fish and environmental organizations, in no small part led by my Delaware Riverkeeper Network, urging the commission to follow the science and upgrade the standards. But the DRBC has refused to do so.

Without a higher standard, not only are the oxygen levels suboptimal on a regular basis, but there is no buffer when things go wrong in the system. In the summers of 2019, 2020, and 2021, the river's dissolved oxygen fell below 3.5 mg/l multiple times, at one point getting as low as 2.8 mg/l in a critical segment essential for Atlantic sturgeon procreation. Despite the alarm bells of concern this raised for the public, the DRBC continued to defend its lack of action—an abdication of responsibility that industry has lobbied for and applauds. The DRBC instead takes the position that the issue is complicated, so it needs to keep studying it before it can act. But it's not complicated; on the contrary, it could hardly be clearer.[46] The sturgeon need 6.3 mg/l or more of oxygen in their water—almost double the DRBC's 3.5 mg/l standard, and more than double the recent low of 2.8 mg/l. Can people thrive on half the oxygen their bodies need? No, they can't! When human beings lose access to optimal levels of oxygen, their brains and bodies suffer.[47] The same is true for sturgeon.

Because the DRBC and other regulatory agencies responsible for protecting the quality of the Delaware River refuse to follow the known science, the Atlantic sturgeon's already perilous future is even more dire. As Erik laments, "Even when all the signs show that we were continuing to inflict irreversible harm on a species well recognized as having suffered population collapse, rather than take meaningful and needed action, our government agencies are turning a blind eye. And as a result, we may lose the Delaware River's Atlantic sturgeon."[48]

Despite the dire circumstances of Atlantic sturgeon all along the East Coast—and despite legal obligations to protect them—government agencies continue to overlook the devastating consequences of their actions. For example, the US Department of Transportation Maritime Administration (MARAD) has been using its regulatory authority and budget to secure expansion of shipping traffic on waterways it has designated as Marine Highway Routes. The problem is many of these designated waterways are known to have a critical role in the life cycle of sturgeon and other endangered and threatened species, such as North Atlantic right whales, loggerhead sea turtles, freshwater mussels, chinook salmon, bull trout, humpback whales, blue whales, sea lions, and others.[49]

"The Endangered Species Act is clear: MARAD must work with expert wildlife agencies to ensure its projects, grants and programs are not jeopardizing the continuing existence of species on the brink of extinction," says Jared Margolis, senior attorney for the Center for Biological Diversity. "But they are choosing not to—and in so doing, are forcing the environmental community to step in with legal action."[50] As an environmental activist and attorney myself, I find it incomprehensible that community organizations like my Delaware Riverkeeper Network or the Center for Biological Diversity should have to invest our precious donation and grant dollars in legal actions to force government agencies to comply with the law. But sadly, that is often the case. Worst of all, too often our legal actions lose—because the laws as written allow these government failures to go unaddressed and unchanged.

Loss of species—thanks to development, pollution, and other forms of environmental degradation—is hardly limited to sturgeon. Approximately 80 percent of the world's flora and fauna inhabit forests.[51] Without forests, these plants and animals perish, while climate change and greenhouse gas emissions increase, disrupting global water cycles and degrading our air quality.[52] Between 2001 and 2011, the United States destroyed nearly seventeen million acres of forested land in the contiguous forty-eight states.[53] Though forests still account for approximately one-third of the world's surface area, every year we are losing forest cover for a landmass half the size of England.[54] The World Wildlife Fund calculates the loss as forty-eight football fields of forest every sixty seconds![55]

Wetland ecosystems are so diverse and valuable that they've been nicknamed "biological supermarkets," because they provide food to different plants, animals, and microorganisms while helping address climate change by storing significant levels of carbon in their plant and soil communities.[56] Yet since the first Industrial Revolution, more than 85 percent of the world's wetlands have been lost because of human activity.[57] Between 2008 and 2011 alone, we destroyed nearly twenty-four million acres of grassland, shrubland, and wetland—a surface area larger than Indiana.[58] Priceless ecosystems are disappearing before our eyes.

As a result of habitat destruction and pollution, most wildlife inhabiting the world today are under siege. According to a World Wildlife Fund 2020 study, populations of wildlife around the globe—including birds, mammals, reptiles, amphibians, and fish—have decreased by an average of 68 percent within just forty-six years (1970–2016).[59] Freshwater species have been the hardest hit, declining 84 percent on average.[60] An estimated one million animal, plant, and insect species are at risk of extinction, predicts the World Wildlife Fund, if things don't change.[61] And Stanford biologist Paul Ehrlich has demonstrated that extinction rates are the highest they have been since the disappearance of dinosaurs sixty-six million years ago.[62]

Indeed, the "species holocaust" we're experiencing is so extreme that some specialists see it as marking a change in geologic time. The Holocene era, which encompasses the entirety of human civilization, has given way to the human-centered Anthropocene era.[63] One of Ehrlich's collaborators, Gerardo Ceballos of the Universidad Nacional Autónoma de México, offered a terrifying assessment of the fate of life on Earth: "If [the rate of species loss] is allowed to continue, life would take many millions of years to recover, and our species itself would likely disappear early on."[64]

For now, of course, we humans are still here—and so are the last of the sturgeon. We still have an opportunity to reverse course and alter the devastating impacts we are inflicting.

We need nature for more than just food, air, water, and space to live. We also need to bask in nature's majesty; for the sake of our psychological and emotional health, we need respite from our bustling lives. For many of us, we need the spiritual peace of knowing we honored nature's rights to be and thrive. Unfortunately, our ability to enjoy the bounty of nature has also become a casualty of environmental degradation. We're paving over nature, with little thought as to how it coarsens our own lives.

They Paved Paradise and Put up a Route Extension

The city of Trenton, New Jersey, has seen more glamorous days. Since manufacturing left the area, jobs are few, and crime and poverty rates are high. But this city once possessed riches you couldn't measure in dollars. It had free and easy access to the Delaware River. From anywhere in the city, you could navigate your way to a cluster of trees that marked the edge of an embankment. From there, you could descend to the cool, refreshing water below. Kids played in this area, swinging from tree branches into the water and frolicking along the shore's edges, while adults fished on the upriver portion. The local folks called this reach of my Delaware River "South Trenton's Jersey Shore." Many inhabitants didn't have the time or the financial means to visit the beaches of Cape May or other resort areas along the New Jersey Shore's Atlantic Ocean. But they had the Delaware River.

Then the New Jersey Department of Transportation (NJDOT) stepped in, deciding it needed to convert a two-lane scenic road into a four-lane highway. This would make it quicker, easier, and cheaper for large, heavy trucks to motor through the region rather than having to navigate the streets and bridges of South Trenton. To build this new highway expansion, NJDOT decided to tear down the stately corridor of sycamore trees along the river's embankment and fill in part of the Delaware River. Trucking in tons of fill for the river and its bank, the agency planned to perch the highway alongside the river, cutting the community off from its once free and easy access to the water's edge.

The state's plan was foolhardy to begin with. With this priceless community treasure in peril, my Delaware Riverkeeper Network voiced strong opposition. The Tri-State Transportation Campaign, headed by the venerable attorney Janine Bauer, identified a network of pre-existing highways with sufficient capacity to accommodate the truck traffic and orient it around the city.[65] The highway extension was not needed. NJDOT nonetheless insisted on walling off the city from its remaining waterfront.

Janine and I organized against this new section of highway, the Route 29 Extension, as strongly as we could. Ed Lloyd, one of the state's most highly regarded environmental attorneys, joined the fight, bringing with him the legal resources of the Rutgers Environmental Law Clinic. Protecting this reach of river and its plants and animals was one of our major objectives, but we also argued against the expansion because this river belonged to the community, especially its youth. It was their oasis, something they deserved, a special place they were entitled to enjoy.

Sometimes, as with the overturning of Act 13, you score a major victory. As most environmental advocates and activists will attest, however, such victories are uncomfortably few. Even though we had all the ingredients necessary to achieve success—a solid transportation solution; important public interests that needed protection; environmental laws; and large-scale community, legal, and professional opposition—the state still decided to build that Route 29 Extension.

Shortly after the final decision was made, I received a call from Ed saying, "Maya, you won!"

I detected sarcasm, but over the phone I couldn't be sure. "What do you mean, 'we won'?" I asked.

"Well, the state just called and told me so." Yes, Ed was definitely being sarcastic.

The state had designated funds for a walkway running parallel to the river and adjacent to the highway. As the state attorney explained it to Ed, locals would supposedly be able to use this walkway, which would sit at least ten feet above the waterline, to view the river and cast lines for fish. There was also talk of a stairwell from the walkway that would take folks down to touch the water.

"The state tells us it is a perfect compromise," Ed added. Of course, it wasn't perfect as planned, nor is it perfect as it currently exists.

Inexplicably, and contrary to their arguments for why the Route 29 Extension was needed, shortly before the expanded highway opened to traffic, the state banned large, heavy trucks from using it and rerouted them along the more rational route Janine and the Tri-State Transportation Campaign had identified.[66] Now the Route 29 Extension serves Trenton's workforce, who can flee the city and its problems a little faster once the workday ends. Homes that once enjoyed a view of nature now face a highway wall. Visitors to this once peaceful part of the Delaware River are now plagued by high-speed traffic zipping past and battering their ears. Breathing in exhaust and struggling to hear the sounds of nature, local residents can't begin to touch, feel, and enjoy the river water.

South Trenton's Jersey Shore is dead. And guess what! For no good reason. Once there was a river here, and now there is a highway. Needed by nobody. To the detriment of an entire community.

What happened to South Trenton is happening, in one form or another, around the country and globally. Extensive habitat destruction is dramatically curtailing humanity's access to nature. More than 50 percent of the world's inhabitants live in either suburban or urban contexts, and the United Nations Population Fund estimates that this number will skyrocket, with five billion of the estimated 8.5 billion total population living in developed areas by 2030.[67] Never in human history has our species been so urbanized, so removed from wilderness, nature, and natural spaces.

Human beings evolved in nature. Today, however, the artificial light and noise we confront thanks to anti-green development corrode our happiness and health. Noise pollution causes increased stress, hypertension, heart disease, and stroke.[68] In 2011, the World Health Organization determined that in Western Europe every year, noise pollution results in the loss of one million healthy life years,[69] and a 2010 study determined that those living near noisy airports are at much greater risk of heart attack.[70]

As with so many aspects of environmental degradation, children are at risk of even greater harms from noise pollution. Studies show that learning, reading, and memory in children are all affected by excessive nonnatural noise.[71] This means noise pollution is not only undermining quality of life for our children when they are young, but having a harmful effect throughout their entire lives.

Personally, I'm not sure whether it is a relief to know that the increased stress I feel from too much noise pollution is not just in my imagination. When my husband and I bought our current house, we went to great pains to ensure that our days working in the garden, evenings in the backyard, and nights sleeping with the windows open (year-round, regardless of the weather) would not be assaulted by the rumble of traffic. Sadly, over the years, nearby trees were cut down and houses were built at key "pinch points" for such noise. Now, far too often I find myself lying awake at night, or turning up the volume on my music during the day, to combat the ugly auditory invasion.

By allowing ourselves to become distanced from nature, we risk more than disease and a lack of well-being. We risk dehumanization. Take our connection with the human senses. While we're taught as children that human beings have five senses, scientists believe we actually have as many as ten to thirty.[72] Personally, I believe people are born with a deep connection to the Earth, including an ability to perceive its joys and its pains. By spending so much time glued to our screens, however, we're blocking out this connection and not allowing ourselves to fully develop these senses. When we don't experience the sensory cornucopia that nature provides, we're not fully alive. What kinds of artistic, cultural, and scientific innovations might we achieve if we venture into nature more, activating and tapping into these super-senses? If we don't stop degrading the environment, we'll never know.

As the author Richard Louv observes, unchecked urbanization might eventually sever our links with nature—or it could lead us to reshape our relationship with the environment in positive ways. With the help of nature-conscious "biophilic designers," we could create nature-rich workplaces, schools, homes, and cities, which are proven to be more productive and happy places.[73] If we increase the biodiversity in our urban parks, we become psychologically healthier, experience less stress, have lower body mass indexes (BMI), and enjoy enhanced creativity. Louv's research demonstrates that even providing people with access to places like South Trenton's Jersey Shore can enhance human longevity and energize the human spirit.

Locked In

Every year is getting hotter. First, 2014 was declared the hottest year ever recorded; then came 2015 and 2016, each hotter than the year before.[74] The year 2019 rivaled the all-time-high temperatures of 2016, closing out the hottest decade in recorded history.[75] Shortly thereafter, 2021 crushed temperature records over a four-day period in the US Pacific Northwest and Western Canada as the mercury climbed to 110 degrees Fahrenheit, according to the National Oceanic and Atmospheric Administration. Roads buckled from the heat. People suffered. And temperatures soared even higher in parts of British Columbia, reaching 116 degrees Fahrenheit.[76]

What does it all add up to? Climate-change deniers argue that just because the surface temperature of the Earth increased exponentially in a single year or two or seven, this doesn't prove that climate warming is accelerating. Temperatures fluctuate year to year as a result of normal weather patterns, they say.

I'm not here to argue whether human-caused climate change is real. I don't need to. The climate science is clear: Humans have released an unprecedented amount of carbon dioxide, methane, and other greenhouse gases into our atmosphere. Those emissions are producing widespread, irreparable changes here on Earth.[77] Once levels surpass a certain threshold, a cascade of uncontrollable changes will occur. The Earth's climate and the fate of its inhabitants will become, in the words of climate scientists, "locked in."

Other forms of environmental degradation are locking in as well. I have had the thrill of seeing one of the Delaware River's Atlantic sturgeon, but at the rate we are impacting this species, my son, Wim, may never experience this thrill for himself. I wonder similarly about other iconic species of the Delaware River system.

For over forty years, scientists have been annually counting how many red knot rufa, a migratory shorebird, stop at the beaches of the Delaware Bay to gorge themselves on the eggs of horseshoe crabs in order to fuel their spring migration to breeding grounds in the arctic. Over these four decades, red knot numbers have plummeted along with those of the horseshoe crabs and their energy-rich eggs.[78] During this time, I have worked together with my daughter, Anneke, and with internationally recognized experts Dr. Larry Niles and Dr. Amanda Dey, helping to affix scientific tracking bands to help measure population health (or lack thereof). On these days, Anneke and I have enjoyed the camaraderie of volunteerism, and the thrilling moment the birds are set back into flight once their statistics and tracking bands have been secured.

But the red knot count data in 2021 brought a devastating blow—the lowest numbers recorded to date. "I think it's reasonable to wait and see what the rest of the data says. But the fact remains that we've been doing a count since the 1980s, when it was up around 90,000, and now it's down to 6,800," Larry told reporters. While he is careful not to draw conclusions about the ultimate fate of the birds based on one year's count, his concern is clear.[79]

For my part, I also worry. And I wonder: will Anneke's children have the same opportunity to witness the beauty and majesty of the red knot rufa and their annual visit to the Delaware Bay?

It's undeniable that by irreparably altering our environment, we're preventing future generations from enjoying and benefitting from nature. When we poison a stream, the damage might last for hundreds of years. Likewise, when we invest in fossil-fuel infrastructure such as pipelines, power plants, and compressor stations, we create a disturbing degree of permanency. We commit ourselves to decades of using the infrastructure and the dirty fossil fuels it carries. While industry will reap economic benefits from that infrastructure in the short term, as a community and a nation we are subjecting our children, for generations, to its manifold costs. We are also preventing ourselves from embracing a path fueled by clean, renewable energy.

By the time he was eleven, Wim was already confused about why I had to fight gas drilling wells and pipeline projects, and why we had to lose our special forest in Columbia County. Upon learning that our own home is fueled by solar panels, he asked, "Why aren't we just putting solar panels on everybody's roofs?" Today, at age sixteen, his confusion is even greater—and it's complemented by anger. Wim is not alone in experiencing this mix of emotions. Many of the young people I meet and work with can't believe that so many of today's adults and decision makers are so cavalier about our choices and what it means for their future.

Through other choices we make—such as our tendency to treat rainfall as wastewater rather than a resource—we are depleting water resources for future generations. Felling forests, filling wetlands, flattening our landscapes, and packing down soils for development prevent rain from soaking into the soil. So instead of recharging the groundwater, providing needed baseflows for streams and replenishing drinking-water aquifers and wells, that rain rushes off the land in a torrent, through human-made systems of curbing and piping. From there, it is dumped directly and unceremoniously into rivers and streams, causing flooding in communities downstream. The rush of rainfall also delivers to those communities all the pollution that exists in its path, from oil and trash to winter salts and excess fertilizers. While other development methods and stormwater strategies exist that can alleviate or avoid most of these harms, outdated management techniques are the ones most often embraced by our laws and most used by developers. With each new development project that fails to protect our vital natural systems, we lock our children into worsening droughts, floods, and pollution.

In destroying the natural world, we're preventing our children from benefiting from nature, we're impoverishing their awareness and experience of it; we're even impacting our children's capacity to learn and grow.

In *Last Child in the Woods* (a must-read for all parents and educators), Richard Louv explores the rich body of research demonstrating that children learn better when they enjoy access to nature and the great outdoors.[80] Kids residing in the inner city or dense metropolitan areas, surrounded by cement, can't focus or learn as efficiently. Their creativity and imagination can falter, and with it their self-confidence. Even the ability to peer out of a classroom window and spot a tree enhances a child's capacity to learn.

When kids aren't running around climbing trees and crawling through creeks, when they're confined to their backyards or playing mostly organized sports, when they spend too much time on their phones or tablets, they're unable to develop in a holistic, well-rounded way. As environmentalist George Monbiot suggests, "Natural spaces encourage fantasy and role play, reasoning and observation. The social standing of children there depends less on physical dominance, more on inventiveness and language skills."[81] Our polluting habits and the continuing destruction of naturally healthy spaces rob our children of the carefree joy, the wonderful sense of discovery, and the important skills-development associated with unstructured play in nature.

George Monbiot considers children's seclusion from the joys of nature "a second environmental crisis" facing the world.[82] In addition to diminishing creativity and cardiovascular health, and accelerating developmental disorders and obesity, this crisis will produce a generation of children who won't love nature, and who won't fight for it. As Monbiot observes, "Without a feel for the texture and function of the natural world, without an intensity of engagement almost impossible in the absence of early experience, people will not devote their lives to its protection."[83]

But sometimes, in our dark moments of deepest worry, there comes a silver lining. While the Covid-19 pandemic thoroughly disrupted our lives starting in the early months of 2020—in some ways making us even more dependent on technology for interaction and engagement—at the same time it reconnected many of us, particularly our children, with the beauty and value of time in nature. Being forced to quarantine in and around our homes for months on end took many people back to the simple pleasures, and the many benefits, that nature provides. Walks in the woods, time in the backyard garden, canoeing or kayaking on a local river—these experiences not only brought the joy of nature back into people's lives, but also reduced stress, anxiety, and depression.

The added time in nature helped children with emotional and behavioral issues. And nature benefited, too. As one study noted, the "empty roads, improved air quality and the sudden drop in noise and light pollution enabled birds, plants and animals to thrive in previously inhospitable environments, while also providing new opportunities for children to listen to birdsong or notice wildlife."[84]

Will this renewed appreciation last? Will it inspire us to use our system of government and laws to better protect the environment that is so essential for supporting and enriching all aspects of our lives? Rather than take a wait-and-see approach, I think we should build upon this renewed respect for what nature provides in all our lives.

The Old Weapons Aren't Working, but a New One Is On the Way

In 2007, fed up with the pollution that was degrading their health and communities, people in Houston, Texas, finally had enough. Concerned residents, environmental organizations, and honest municipal leaders demanded that the oil and gas industries be held accountable for pollution they had caused. Houston's city council got tough, devising a muscular set of environmental laws and enforcement mechanisms to halt pollution. Unconvinced by the industry's claim of healthy emissions levels, the city of Houston enacted a new regulatory regime, requiring emitters to purchase pollution permits, and criminally punishing industries that didn't comply with air quality and public health standards.[85] Fines levied against noncompliant plants and refineries ranged from several hundred to several thousand dollars per day.[86]

Unhappy with the new ordinances curtailing their power to pollute with impunity, the oil and gas industry took the city to court, appealing these ordinances to the state's highest tribunal.[87] In April 2016, the Texas Supreme Court faced a decision analogous to the Pennsylvania Supreme Court's when it debated Act 13. The Texas high court could choose either to rule in favor of community health or to bow to powerful corporate interests. Sadly, the court opted to side with industry over democracy—with the wealth of the few over the health of the many. On April 29, 2016, in an 8–1 majority ruling, the court delivered a landslide decision in favor of industry, overturning the city's health ordinances. Such a ruling was disappointing, but squarely in keeping with America's dismal history of legislative enforcement when it comes to the environment. In the United States, all the environmental degradation surveyed in this chapter has occurred *despite* an extensive regime of laws, regulations, and regulatory bodies ostensibly in place to protect the environment.

Our existing legislative-based environmental protections have failed us. And they have failed us for a variety of reasons. At times, as we'll see in later chapters, our elected officials have been in the pockets of industry. At other times, industry veterans have been appointed to lead regulatory bodies, or industry has exerted so much lobbying power that it has succeeded in changing the law to reduce environmental protections or do away with them altogether. Sometimes all of these factors have come into play at once, as was the case at the federal level following the 2016 presidential election, when Donald Trump began his unprecedented assault on the environment.

During his tenure as the forty-fifth US president, Donald Trump inflicted devastating harm on our already faltering legislative regime of environmental protection. He pulled the United States out of the Paris Climate Accords; rolled back or undermined more than 125 environmental protection rules and policies; seriously undermined government scientists entrusted with documenting the consequences of environmental and climate degradation; opened up to logging ancient forests such as the Tongass National Forest (with trees that are one thousand years old and soak up more climate-changing carbon than any other forest in the US); and installed yes-men with extensive anti-environmental records (and close personal and financial ties with heavy industry) in leadership roles of key agencies such as the Environmental Protection Agency and the Department of the Interior. Because Trump was working largely within the boundaries of our existing laws and political system, there were few checks to stop these abuses of leadership and power.

Most people are pretty shocked to learn that for the most part, existing laws *don't ban* pollution or environmentally devastating activities. Industries are perfectly able to pollute the air and water not in spite of, but *because of* the Clean Air Act and the Clean Water Act and their state counterparts—they simply need the right permits to do so. In the very act of purporting to restrict or regulate pollution, our laws legalize it. In fact, they create a presumption—even an expectation—that it is a right of business and government to pollute and degrade our environment. At the same time, industry has had an easy time manipulating existing laws in its favor. Industry representatives are adept at working the system.

The rest of us are paying the price. Sturgeon are dying. We're building highways over our riverfronts. Rates of cancer, asthma, autism, Alzheimer's, and other illnesses are rising. Our children are losing touch with nature. Kids are going to school next to oil refineries. Pollution is threatening the peace, sanctity, and safety of our homes. Jobs that depend upon healthy environments are being lost. Jobs that would advance environmentally beneficial economic growth are going uncreated. And we are facing a climate catastrophe that is putting our very existence in jeopardy.

Any way you look at it, we are losing. So too are the generations to come.

Unless we're prepared to live—and die—in the sacrifice zone, our country must radically rethink its approach to protecting the environment. And activists everywhere must lead the way. In Pennsylvania, we didn't rely on legislative protections. We tried a different strategy entirely. We overcame industry's control over the legislative process by passing and then claiming our constitutional rights. Article 1, section 27 of Pennsylvania's constitution safeguarded our rights to a healthy environment. While it took decades, Pennsylvania's constitutional provision is beginning to operate as it should have all along: as a constitutional check that protects people's rights to a clean, safe, and healthy environment.

I'm writing this book so that across our nation, we can seize the power of our constitutions to secure the environmental protections and justice we need. Working together to advance a national Green Amendment movement, we can avoid the pitfalls we encountered in Pennsylvania and benefit from the lessons we are learning as this movement grows.

In 2013, we took a massive step toward eradicating fracking from Pennsylvania. We continue to work toward that goal, but we already have fundamentally changed how decisions about our environment are made in Pennsylvania. As a result of our case, Jordan Yeager observes, Pennsylvania's decision-making must now be intentional and science-based; it must consider cumulative environmental impacts, and it must be tilted in favor of environmental protection. Our strategy itself was the true winner in court that day. By claiming a healthy environment as a fundamental liberty, and by ensuring that this right is recognized alongside other long-standing freedoms like free speech, freedom of religion, and the right to bear arms, people in states across America could better protect themselves, just as we have in Pennsylvania.

I believe that if we'd had a living and thriving constitutional right to a healthy environment when fracking came to Pennsylvania, we could have stopped the frackers in their tracks and kept them out. As it was, the frackers got there first. Now it will take time to use our Pennsylvania constitutional rights to get the protection from this industry we truly need—time that, in many ways, we don't really have. But in Pennsylvania, we do have the constitution, the strongest legal tool available under our US system of law, in order to make fundamental change. And now we have the thriving Green Amendment protections that we can use to prevent the next snake-oil solution industry presents—things like industrial carbon capture and sequestration, and blue hydrogen, which are being peddled falsely as solutions for the climate crisis but are themselves instigators and perpetrators of dramatic environmental harm.

Constitutional provisions to ensure a healthy environment comprise the linchpin of a new environmentalism. Unlike its alternatives, this brand of environmentalism draws on an authority more powerful than corporations, laws, and governments. This authority is the inalienable, indefeasible, inherent rights we all possess as residents of this Earth. Through passage of constitutional Green Amendments, "we the people" will be taking our power back when it comes to environmental decision-making. We'll be making clear to all government officials that the presumption now is in favor of protecting our water, air, climate, and environment first, before industry and profit.

Constitutional Green Amendments are our greatest hope for protecting the people of Manchester, the sturgeon, all of us here on Earth today, and our future descendants. As I've experienced firsthand, constitutional environmental rights and protections afford—to all of us who are concerned about our environment, our health, our safety, our children, our quality of life, our economy, and our quality jobs—newfound leverage against ineffectual or corrupt lawmakers and inadequate laws.

Let's turn our attention now to constitutional Green Amendments: what this new weapon is and how it has evolved over time.

CHAPTER THREE

THE RIGHT TO A HEALTHY ENVIRONMENT

Author and outdoorsman David James Duncan has had a tumultuous relationship with rivers. In 1983, Duncan published *The River Why,* a novel about fly-fishing, young brothers, and coming-of-age in the great outdoors. He then purchased a home on an unspoiled Oregonian waterway, seeking a peaceful place to raise his family and find further inspiration for his art.[1] At first his home was every bit the idyllic natural oasis he'd envisioned. But then the logging industry stepped in. Clear-cutters decimated the temperate forests surrounding his home. They polluted his river and degraded the delicate habitat of the owls, salmon, and marshlands that had helped inspire his life's work.

Determined to raise his young daughters in an intact ecosystem, Duncan moved his family to Missoula, Montana.[2] Another waterway beckoned him there: the mighty and historic Blackfoot River. The river's plunging depths, picturesque vistas, and trout-filled waters provided endless opportunities for fly-fishers, kayakers, and curious children. It also helped to sustain the region's thriving tourism and agriculture sectors.

But the Blackfoot watershed was also under assault. In 1989, voracious metal prospectors—Arizona-based Phelps Dodge and Colorado's

Canyon Resources—began scouring the watershed for gold. Estimating that eight million ounces of gold could be extracted from a mountain in the Blackfoot headwaters, the companies formed a venture known as Seven-Up Pete. Its purpose: to construct one of the North American continent's largest open-pit gold mines. Eager for new revenues and swayed by Seven-Up Pete's promises to protect Montana's pristine environment, state regulators approved the company's development plans and delivered the necessary permits.

Duncan's investigations into the venture, along with graduate student Gus Gardner, told a different story.[3] Seven-Up Pete planned to employ a controversial and sinister technique called "cyanide heap-leach mining." Along the butte of the upper Blackfoot, where elk calve and sandhill cranes nest their eggs amid soaring pine trees, Seven-Up Pete would continuously detonate ammonium nitrate bombs until it removed the entire mountain, inserting in its place a gash in the earth more than one thousand feet deep.[4] It would deploy millions of gallons of cyanide-laced water to separate gold from rock, yielding a mere one ounce of product for every 245 tons of rock it processed![5] This was the lowest-grade ore that anyone had ever attempted to mine on such a monumental scale.

As Duncan details in *My Story as Told by Water*, "The estimated 570 million tons of 'waste rock' excavated to create the pit will be sculpted into a coffin-shaped riverside mountain—larger than New York's Central Park, taller than the Washington Monument—from which heavy metals, sulfuric acid, and nitrates will leach into the Blackfoot watershed forever."[6] For the following twelve to fifteen years—the mine's estimated life span—Seven-Up Pete would "dewater" from the pit ten thousand to fifteen thousand gallons every single minute, depressing the Blackfoot Valley's water table by more than one thousand feet, evacuating the surrounding wetlands, springs, and ponds of water, imperiling one of the few remaining US habitats of the river-dwelling bull trout, and returning billions of gallons of poisonous water into the Blackfoot.[7]

The community met such extreme exploitation with incredulity and defiance. A tremendous public battle ensued, pitting corporate mining against courageous residents. Realtors, religious leaders, vegans, taxidermists, nature lovers, regional artists, and celebrities like Robert Redford banded together to save the river. Emblazoning their cars with bumper stickers that read "The Blackfoot is more precious than gold," these residents did everything they could to protect the environment, their livelihoods, and their health against the proposed environmental assault.[8]

This advocacy was complemented by litigation. The Montana Environmental Information Center (MEIC) and Women's Voices for the Earth (WVE)—two environmental nonprofits like the Delaware Riverkeeper Network—filed an appeal, contesting the corporate mining venture's rights to send polluted water surging into the Blackfoot and neighboring watersheds.[9] They pursued a novel legal strategy: instead of fighting the mining venture by appealing to state legislation or regulation, they sought recourse through Montana's constitution. After all, the state's constitution should reign supreme, superseding any state policy, regulation, or legislation.

In addition to article 2, section 3 of the Montana constitution's Declaration of Rights, which affirms the "right to a clean and healthful environment" as inalienable among all persons, article 9 further safeguards inhabitants' rights to a protected and improved environment. "The state and each person," article 9, section 1 reads, "shall maintain and improve a clean and healthful environment in Montana for present and future generations." In the breakthrough *MEIC v. Montana DEQ* (1999) decision, the state supreme court ruled unanimously in favor of Montana's environmental health, rescinding the rights of mining companies to irrevocably degrade the watershed.

As with our Act 13 victory in Pennsylvania, the MEIC case produced an inspiring piece of jurisprudence that would continue to shape the state's environmental agenda for decades. Justice Terry Trieweiler, who wrote the court's opinion, stated the case for the environment in stirring terms: "Our constitution does not require that dead fish float on the surface of our state's rivers and streams before its farsighted environmental protections can be invoked."[10] The environmental rights conferred by Montana's constitution, stipulated Justice Trieweiler, were "both anticipatory and preventative." Nonprofits and other concerned individuals didn't have to wait until degradation was underway to take legal action. The court empowered them to prevent environmental despoliation before it occurred.

As our Act 13 victory and the MEIC decision demonstrate, constitutional provisions present an exciting opportunity for communities seeking to preserve nature's bounty. Activists have long relied on legislation to save our planet—all too often without success. Following the Act 13 and MEIC cases, Pennsylvanians and Montanans interested in protecting the environment have resurrected a powerful tool. In Pennsylvania, we used the constitution to prevent legislation that forced the approval of fracking within every part of every community. Since that victory, we have deployed our state's robust constitutional provision to wage other important environmental battles. Our colleagues in Montana have done similarly.

What would happen if activists deployed this strategy in all fifty states, and ultimately at the federal level? What would happen if people everywhere began asserting their inalienable right to a clean and healthy environment, rising up when industry and its political allies trample on that right?

A Brief History of Environmental Constitutionalism

Let's review the origins of this potentially fearsome weapon in the environmentalist's arsenal. As a strategy, environmental constitutionalism first emerged out of the political and social ferment of the 1960s. Rachel Carson's seminal book *Silent Spring* (1962) had raised public awareness about the perils of pollution and helped galvanize the modern environmental movement. Afterward, a series of media spectacles heightened fears among everyday Americans that industrial fecklessness, carelessness, and greed were ruining the country's natural resources. In 1969, for instance, a pile of trash and oil-laden debris caught fire off Cleveland's Cuyahoga River, leaving the impression that the river itself was on fire. *Time* magazine detailed the story to a horrified nation, describing the river as a waterway that "oozes rather than flows," because of rampant industrial pollution.[11]

To blunt outrage over environmental degradation, the Nixon administration accelerated its planned establishment of the Environmental Protection Agency and began drafting the Clean Air Act. But by the 1970s, Americans were fighting back in other ways. They flocked to join environmental groups. And they sought to claim their right to a healthy environment. Individual states began enshrining environmental protections in their constitutions. Over the next few decades, approximately one-third of America's states drafted or amended their constitutions to address environmental protection in some fashion.[12] Senator Gaylord Nelson of Wisconsin even proposed an environmental amendment to America's federal constitution, but his proposal was quickly shot down (as were subsequent efforts to pass such an amendment).[13]

Despite their proponents' laudable intentions, most state-level constitutional amendments in the United States have had little impact. Although sometimes rhetorically beautiful, these amendments have been largely ornamental—and certainly not strong enough to overcome the many inadequacies in our environmental laws. Virginia, for example, in article 11, section 1, employs lovely language about the value of people having "clean air, pure water, and the use and enjoyment for recreation of adequate public lands, waters and other natural resources," but then undermines that language by declaring environmental protection a mere prerogative of the state, a policy to be aspired to rather than a right of the people.

Michigan's provision is somewhat better, mandating that the state legislature protect natural resources, but still stopping short of defining an individual right: "The conservation and development of the natural resources of the state," reads article 4, section 52 of Michigan's constitution, "are hereby declared to be of paramount public concern. The legislature shall provide for the protection of the air, water and other natural resources of the state from pollution, impairment and destruction."

While article 20, section 21 of New Mexico's constitution proudly declares "protection of the state's beautiful and healthful environment . . . to be of fundamental importance," it relegates the environment to the "Miscellaneous" section of the constitution. Furthermore, the constitution entrusts the boundaries of constitutional environmental protection to the political agenda of the legislature, but with a focus on "control of pollution and control of despoilment of the air, water and other natural resources" rather than recognizing a right of the people to a clean, healthy, and safe environment. When legally tested, the New Mexico Court of Appeals confirmed the legislative limitations of the language and made clear that New Mexicans unhappy with environmental protection in the state could take it up at the "ballot box during each election cycle."[14]

Other states that stopped short of affirming a general enforceable right included provisions in their constitutions that allowed for protection of natural resources but for economic and recreational purposes. States like Idaho, Kentucky, Minnesota, and Vermont focused on preserving the right to fish, hunt, and trap as part of their communities' historic heritage, but their constitutions don't discuss rights to clean and healthy water, air, or environments. Notably, their provisions also don't recognize how environmental degradation impacts these enumerated rights. As any fisher will tell you, it is one thing to be able to catch a fish, but quite another to know that you can safely eat it.

Illinois, Hawaii, and Massachusetts were among just a handful of states that seemingly granted people the explicit right to a healthy environment, but then embedded within the language limitations on its use and enforcement—including vesting authority in the legislature, which rendered the constitutional promise of an environmental right illusory. In these states, as with others, the failure to recognize these protections in the constitution's declaration of rights assured they would be denied the same deference given to other fundamental rights such as speech, property, and gun rights. Court decisions assessing and applying state environmental provisions nationwide are confirming their vulnerabilities and lack of strength.

The assessment of State Senator Antoinette Sedillo Lopez of New Mexico, with regard to her state's constitutional language, carries a sentiment that resonates across many states with similarly feeble provisions. "In 1972 the people of New Mexico voted for Article 20 Section 21 intending to protect their rights as people to healthy water, air, soils and environments," she said in a press release. "But the people, unfortunately, did not accomplish that goal; instead, they gave all of the power to their legislators, who have passed laws more focused on permitting pollution rather than preventing it. While those who advanced Article 20 Section 21 meant for us to secure a higher level of environmental protection in the State, they didn't get the language or placement correct."[15]

During the 1970s, only two states, Montana and Pennsylvania, passed the strongest form of constitutional protection able to produce real environmental change. Both states located these environmental provisions within their constitution's declaration of rights, thus placing them on par with other cherished freedoms. Instead of simply using inspiring language that proclaims the right to a healthy environment, Montana and Pennsylvania employed muscular constitutional provisions that ensure this right for all state residents. Montana and Pennsylvania defined the right to a healthy environment as an inherent, indefeasible, and inalienable personal liberty.

Senator Franklin Kury, the architect of Pennsylvania's amendment, first ran for state office in 1966 on a platform promising clean water, largely in response to the devastating environmental impacts of the state's coal industry. Senator Kury's election, in which he defeated the senior Republican incumbent in the state legislature, was the upset of that year's election cycle. "The environmental revolution was just hitting Pennsylvania at that time," the former state senator recalls, describing "a very big upswell to pass" environmental legislation that would protect the water, air, and land. "We passed all this environmental legislation that people were talking about . . . . Then it occurred to me we needed to have something stronger than a statute. Because while statutes were very popular, and relatively easy to pass, they could be just as easily unpassed or amended."[16] With the goal and vision of a constitutional amendment that would provide meaningful, permanent protections for environmental rights, Senator Kury crafted language to be added to the state's Bill of Rights.

In a striking sign of the times, the Pennsylvania legislature voted unanimously in support of the proposed language that would read:

> *The people have a right to clean air, pure water, and to the preservation of the natural, scenic, historic and esthetic values of the environment. Pennsylvania's public natural resources are the common property of all the people, including generations yet to come. As trustee of these resources, the Commonwealth shall conserve and maintain them for the benefit of all the people.*

Next, it was up to the people to decide. On May 18, 1971, by a supermajority vote tally of four to one (approximately one million versus 250,000), Senator Kury's amendment was adopted by the Pennsylvania electorate. With that vote, the people of Pennsylvania secured article 1, section 27 of their constitution, giving themselves an enforceable right to a clean and healthy environment—and obligating the state to protect their rights and natural resources for present and future generations. The state senator recalls, "The public was so upset with the way that the coal companies and the railroad companies and the steel companies had raped and exploited this state for a century. They were saying, 'Enough is enough.'"[17]

Of course, bold declarations of rights, such as Pennsylvania had now achieved, mean nothing if plaintiffs don't ask courts to apply them in meaningful ways. In Pennsylvania, decades passed before constitutional environmentalism yielded tangible benefits, largely because early plaintiffs brought ill-considered test cases for the newly minted provision.

In the early 1970s, a company contracted with America's National

Park Service to construct a 307-foot observation tower overlooking the sprawling Gettysburg Battlefield in Pennsylvania. The Commonwealth of Pennsylvania challenged the permit based on article 1, section 27 of the constitution. The tower, the state alleged, would detract from the battleground's natural beauty and historic setting. The court found against the state, suggesting it hadn't provided sufficient evidence that the observation deck compromised "the natural, scenic, historic or aesthetic values of the Gettysburg environment."[18] But the court went further than simply denying the state the outcome it desired. It also took the opportunity to undermine the constitutional power of the environmental rights amendment so recently passed, declaring it to be more a statement of policy than a pronouncement of an enforceable constitutional environmental right. As Chief Justice C. J. Jones pronounced in his dissent, "In one swift stroke, the court has disemboweled a constitutional provision."

In the Gettysburg case, the lack of compelling facts inspired an outcome that undermined the state's recently passed constitutional provision for over forty years. It is embarrassing that Pennsylvania's inaugural environmental lawsuit, fought on constitutional grounds, sought to prevent a relatively insignificant harm instead of protecting the state's priceless waterways, wilderness, or endangered species. The observation tower, the state alleged, represented "a [despoliation] of the natural and historical environment" that would "disrupt the skyline, dominate the [battlefield] setting from many angles, and . . . further erode the natural beauty and setting" that marked the place of an awful "brothers' war."[19] To cite the construction of the tower (which by some accounts was well designed to be unobtrusive, aesthetically pleasing, and of "great educational value") as a violation of a constitutional right seems extreme by almost any measure.[20]

As lawyers like to say, bad facts make for bad law. Because of lawsuits like *Commonwealth v. National Gettysburg Battlefield Tower*, which championed aesthetic concerns instead of environmental stewardship and protection, it took over four decades for Pennsylvania's environmental rights amendment to achieve a profound environmental victory in the court system.

The Gettysburg case carries a great lesson: to overcome the present environmental crisis, we must remain laser-focused on protecting water, air, soils, plants, animals, wilderness, climate, and equitable environmental justice for all. If we interpret environmental provisions too broadly and use them where other legal means are clearly more appropriate, we're only handing our opponents ammunition to dismiss our cases in court. And in the process, we're damaging the legitimacy and effectiveness of constitutional environmental rights protections.

Preventing Government Overreach

Given the limited impact of constitutional protections to date, why should we think that they hold such promise? Well, just look at those few jurisdictions where we *do* have strong constitutional provisions. In addition to our transformational Act 13 victory and the defeat of Seven-Up Pete's industrial gold mining plans, an emerging body of case law continues to define what it means to have an enforceable right to a healthy environment, transforming it from merely another good idea into a law of the land that provides genuine and meaningful protection.

In 2001, just two years after Montana's supreme court rescinded its mining permits to Seven-Up Pete, the court reviewed the district court decision of *Cape-France Enterprises v. Estate of Peed*. In this case, two family members, Lola Peed and Martha Moore, partnered to buy a piece of property upon which to build a hotel. Cape-France Enterprises planned to subdivide its property in Bozeman, Montana, selling a five-acre parcel to Peed and Moore. To secure approval for the subdivision, Cape-France needed to drill a well so as to confirm a viable water supply for the property. Preliminary investigations revealed that a neighboring dry-cleaning business might have contaminated the groundwater with perchloroethylene (PERC), a toxin that causes cancer and organ failure in humans and is poisonous to aquatic life. Drilling a well at the site would confirm the presence of needed water; but if the toxin was also present, drilling could flush it into the local groundwater system.

Concerned about the environmental impacts and its potential legal liability, Cape-France Enterprises refused to drill the well. Peed and Moore sued. Recognizing that drilling the well could expose people and the environment to dangerous toxins, and citing the state's environmental rights provision, the Montana Supreme Court found the threat of harm too high and determined that no compelling state interest existed that would warrant enforcing the well-drilling obligation. The court determined the contract was thereafter null and void.[21]

With each new environmental rights case, we are laying the foundation upon which the law is building. Of notable significance, the Montana Supreme Court recognized environmental rights as fundamental and determined that they "may be infringed only by demonstrating a compelling state interest." A "compelling state interest" now represents a significant legal threshold and qualifying metric. It affords us a clear test for evaluating whether the state might legally infringe on environmental rights while carrying out other duties. The state is, after all, fundamentally interested in enforcing contracts, like the one the Peed estate made with Cape-France. Contracts represent the backbone of private property rights and other fundamental liberties. When balancing the fundamental liberty of a healthy environment and contracts in this dispute, the court sided with the environment, because it had no "compelling state interest" to act otherwise.[22]

Informed decision-making—and a meaningful remedy—is emerging as another entitlement of a constitutional environmental right. In the winter of 2020, the Montana Supreme Court returned to the state's Green Amendment for essential environmental and community protections. Once again, industrial gold mining operations were threatening serious harm, and once again state environmental regulators were siding with the industry over the environment and the people.

A company called Lucky Minerals Inc. had secured a permit for mining investigations and future operations in Emigrant Gulch, just fifteen miles north of Yellowstone National Park. Over two years, the company would develop dozens of well pads and drill deep into the earth. Nighttime drilling, requiring massive lighting rigs, would light up the night sky. Development of construction roads would open up as-yet inaccessible natural areas. Construction, drilling, and habitat fragmentation would inflict grievous and irreparable harm by disturbing and displacing grizzly bears; potentially causing female wolverines to abandon their dens; threatening acid mine pollution to the Yellowstone River (a prized trout stream); and permanently damaging ecosystems important to lynx, bears, elk, moose, deer, and wolverines. The areas to be harmed were also essential for supporting ecotourism in the region—an important economic driver and job creator.

Alleging that the state had failed to undertake a fully robust consideration of the environmental implications of the project before giving approval, the Park County Environmental Council and the Greater Yellowstone Coalition challenged the drilling license and the underlying law that supported its approval. While the drilling would inflict unacceptable harm, the law, they claimed, prevented protection of their constitutional environmental rights by allowing construction to proceed while additional court-ordered environmental reviews were underway.

On December 8, 2020, the state supreme court sided with the challengers, declaring the legal provision unconstitutional and Lucky's license invalid. Among the constitutional guarantees, the court explained, is that there will be remedies "adequate to prevent unreasonable degradation of natural resources," and this assurance includes that "the government will not take actions jeopardizing such unique and treasured facets of Montana's natural environment without first thoroughly understanding the risks involved." The court recognized that if Lucky Mining were allowed to undertake its industrial drilling exploration before the state had finalized its review, that review would only have served to inform the people of Montana—"perhaps tragically"—about the consequences of the state's actions when it was too late to prevent, mitigate, or remedy the harm. "A remedy implemented only after a violation is a hollow vindication of constitutional right if a potentially irreversible harm has already occurred," the court quoted from the historic constitutional record.[23]

Pennsylvania's Green Amendment jurisprudence is also building—even more quickly and robustly than Montana's. Since our 2013 defeat of the pro-fracking Act 13, the Pennsylvania Green Amendment has provided essential protections that otherwise would not have succeeded. In 2017, the Pennsylvania Supreme Court once again took a comprehensive look at the state's constitutional environmental rights, solidifying their standing as legally on par with other bill of rights protections. The Pennsylvania Environmental Defense Foundation had challenged the diversion of funds paid to the state from the leasing of state forest lands for fracking operations.[24] Because the state lands and natural resources involved were part of the environmental trust that the state was constitutionally obliged to "conserve and maintain" for both present and future generations, article 1, section 27 of the Pennsylvania Bill of Rights prevented the blanket misappropriation of the funds for the state's general operating budget. Instead, the constitution required that trust income be used to prevent and remedy the degradation, diminution, and depletion of the public natural resources. As the court further explained, the proceeds must "remain in the trust and must be devoted to the conservation and maintenance of our public natural resources." The court also affirmed the self-executing nature of the Pennsylvania Green Amendment and therefore the ability of people to turn directly to the constitution to protect their environmental rights even in the absence of legislation. Referring back to Chief Justice Castille's decision in our Act 13 victory, the court reaffirmed that the state's trustee obligations enumerated in the constitution "create a right in the people to seek to enforce the obligations."

In 2021, when helping to further parse out which income streams were subject to this constitutional obligation, the state supreme court turned to the generational protections promised by Pennsylvania's amendment. The court reinforced the "cross-generational dimension" of the constitutional right, making clear that government decision-making "cannot prioritize the needs of the living over those yet to be born."[25] Providing generational justice regarding environmental rights could prove to be a linchpin for securing meaningful government action in time to avert climate catastrophe. In addition, as we can see in Pennsylvania, while Green Amendments are proving an essential tool for protecting environmental rights from government overreach, they also embolden better decisions to avoid harm.

For decades, the crowded communities of Delaware County, Pennsylvania, had enjoyed the forest and hiking trails that pass through the Don Guanella site in Marple Township. Spanning 213 acres and owned by the Archdiocese of Philadelphia, this land is home to a unique old-growth beech forest and the Whetstone Run, a stream with high water quality and health. Inexplicably, the archdiocese had been planning to sell off the forest for development. How could a religious order charged with protecting God's creation so callously seek its destruction for money? Community and watershed groups, among them my own Delaware Riverkeeper Network, joined forces as the Whetstone Coalition. We used every path of advocacy and science we could. We hired experts and lawyers to challenge the plans to cut down the forest for development. We urged the Marple Township Board of Commissioners to use their authority to just say "no."

The battle to save the Don Guanella woods spanned years. Every drive by this oasis of green in a quickly urbanizing area struck at the heart—mine included. When the night finally arrived for a crucial township vote, Mike Molinaro of the Marple Township Board of Commissioners took center stage:

> I've listened to people, and I've heard what they said, and I'm not going to say anything different because we have a duty, I believe, under article 1, section 27 of the Pennsylvania constitution, to protect and preserve the Commonwealth's natural resources . . . . I personally believe this trumps everything else, any code you may have, any "by right" you say you may have, anything else. The role of us as municipal government is to protect our natural resources as best we can, especially when there's not that many left. I mean,

if you look at Delaware County, and you look at this area—this is it. This is the last little piece that we have, and we're not, and I'm not, going to let houses be built on it. So, I believe this is our duty to protect these woodlands for not only us, not only Delaware County, PA, but also for future generations, so they can look back and say, "You know, this board stood up to this builder, and they did what was right."[26]

That night, December 14, 2020, the Board of Commissioners voted unanimously (7–0) to reject the proposed residential development plan. Later the county would purchase the site, ensuring its permanent protection.[27]

More cases are emerging in Pennsylvania to help build the copious body of jurisprudence that is allowing us all to recognize what it truly means to have an enforceable right to a clean, safe, and healthy environment. As you'll discover in future chapters, the Pennsylvania amendment is also being used to secure cleanup of a long-ignored toxic site and to advance much-needed drinking water protections, among other important advancements.

Environmental Rights Are Human Rights

Just as there is a new awakening for environmental rights here in the United States, the right to a clean and healthy environment is also gaining attention internationally. In 2021, the Human Rights Council officially recognized that having a clean, healthy, and sustainable environment is indeed a human right. But as Jim May, a leading authority on international environmental rights, founder of the Global Environmental Rights Institute, and cofounder of the Dignity Rights Project and the Environmental Rights Institute at Widener University Delaware Law School, explains, "There's a bit of a mismatch between actual outcomes legally . . . and the narrative internationally about the role that environmental rights can play legally. Because it's been fairly inconsequential so far internationally."[28]

Globally, as is the case in the United States, constitutional measures protecting the environment vary in scope, power, and breadth. In Gambia, environmental stewardship is conceived as a matter of national policy alone—Gambian people have no recourse to the courts should their environmental constitutional rights be infringed.[29] In Portugal, the constitution treats a clean and healthy environment as a fundamental constitutional right, on par with other fundamental liberties. Portugal even allows victims of pollution or environmental degradation the right to seek compensation in court.[30] In 2008, Ecuador went even further, becoming the first country to grant protections to nature itself.[31] Instead of granting nature the status of property and endowing people with the right to a healthy environment, Ecuador's constitution vests nature (often referred to as Pachamama, an ancient Incan Earth deity) with the right to exist and flourish.

According to Jim May, "Lots of countries have environmental rights provisions. By my count, eighty-four expressly incorporate a right to a healthy environment. About less than one-third of those are found in fundamental rights provisions, so-called bill of rights provisions, or are otherwise actionable. That takes us down into the late twenties. And of those twenty or something, less than half of those provisions have been subject to judicial review." By contrast, in Pennsylvania since our 2013 legal victory, we're seeing how environmental rights provisions are making a difference. It is astounding to hear Jim say that our Act 13 case "signifies leading jurisprudence across the globe on implementing environmental rights amendments from the constitution. The Pennsylvania case is a leading light in environmental rights jurisprudence now, in 2021, and its progeny." Jim goes on to explain, "There are more cases with more remedies in Pennsylvania—in one state!—than in the rest of the world combined on environmental rights provisions."[32]

Wow! A "leading light" of environmental rights protection around the globe. That is truly an honor. But more important, it is confirmation that if we want environmental rights to receive the level of protection needed in the short term and the long term—to address our nation's and our world's most pressing environmental, human health, and human dignity issues, from clean water to the climate crisis—the Green Amendment movement is the right path.

A Personal Call to Action

In the United States, a constitutional approach seems especially promising and necessary when we consider how American jurisprudence has traditionally enabled environmental degradation. Supreme Court Justice Oliver Wendell Holmes is famous for prohibiting the false exclamation of "Fire!" in a crowded theater. But he also had something memorable to say about the environment. In the 1930s, New Jersey disagreed with neighboring states about water diversion policy, and appealed its dispute to the US Supreme Court. In deciding the case, Justice Holmes declared that "a river is more than an amenity, it is a treasure." When I first read this quote, I felt proud, because the litigants were vying over access to the Delaware River. Clearly, Justice Holmes took inspiration from our mighty Delaware River and crafted a stirring call to honor and protect our country's precious water systems.

But then I took a closer look at the entire quote. It read: "A river is more than an amenity, it is a treasure. It offers a necessity of life that must be rationed among those who have power over it." My heart sank. Instead of issuing a rousing call to cherish and safeguard nature, Justice Holmes promoted an irresponsible and domineering view toward rivers and the environment.

Indeed, *New Jersey v. New York* (1931) profoundly hurt the Delaware River and impacted everyone downstream. New Jersey petitioned the country's highest court to keep the Delaware River system intact, while neighboring states wanted to divert its water to quench the thirst of residents elsewhere, especially in the New York City metro area. In siding against New Jersey and in favor of diversion, the court inaugurated a sad chapter in the Delaware River's conservation history. The court's decision to ration the river represented another sad loss for the sturgeon, as well as for the watershed's other marine, plant, and human inhabitants. (The only saving grace, as you will read about in chapter 10, is that New York City recognized a responsibility of care in how it chose to exercise its option over the river.)

The more I thought about Justice Holmes's words, the more I realized that they spoke to the central environmental problem I first mentioned in chapter 2: Pollution and environmental destruction are not illegal in this country. People are free to pollute, damage, and devastate the environment so long as they obtain government permits or licenses to do so. The degrading ramifications of this legal construct are magnified by state and federal agencies that seem to embrace the pollution side of the regulatory language but not the environmental protection part.

John Dernbach, the Commonwealth Professor of Environmental Law and Sustainability at Widener University, is an attorney, advocate, and public servant who played a key role in securing our Act 13 constitutional victory—and whose scholarship has informed how the amendment has been interpreted since. As John puts it, our environmental agencies charged with implementing environmental laws essentially have two roles: "One is that they manage pollution at a politically acceptable level. That's really the truth of it. And the other, to a great extent, is that they slow down the rate at which things get worse. [Though of course] that's not always true."[33]

It is under the watchful eyes of these self-same agencies and laws that the DuPont corporation, over the decades, has secured numerous permits allowing it to discharge cancer-causing substances into the Delaware River. Blessed with governmental permits, PSEG Nuclear LLC operates the Salem Nuclear Power Plant, killing over fourteen billion eggs, larvae, and fish from the Delaware River every year—even though it could reduce those kills by over 95 percent with the installation of modern technology.[34] Sadly, government-issued licenses to pollute and degrade are rarely denied. The Delaware River lost at the hands of Justice Holmes's court, it lost to the South Trenton route extension, and it has lost to numerous dredging, nuclear, industrial, and development projects ever since.

But in 2013, the Delaware River and all of Pennsylvania's people and environments didn't lose. When we appealed to the Pennsylvania Constitution for protection, I (in my role as the Delaware Riverkeeper), the Delaware Riverkeeper Network, seven towns, and Dr. Mehernosh Khan were represented by three of the smartest attorneys I know. Together, we overturned a major pro-drilling and fracking law passed by Pennsylvania's governor and legislature. We scored a landmark, precedent-setting, environmental victory. "We had a legislature and a governor that passed a law . . . that would have ensured that fracking [would happen] in every zoning district, in every municipality where it could happen," remarks Jordan Yeager (one of the aforementioned smartest attorneys). "It would have led to the wholesale mass industrialization of huge swaths of the state. I don't think it's an understatement to say that [Pennsylvania's Green Amendment] saved a vast, vast amount of the community from being fracked."[35]

America desperately needs more of these kinds of victories. And it needs more states with stronger, more explicit constitutional provisions protecting the environment. Ideally, of course, we'd instantly amend our national Constitution with an environmental rights provision that meets my Green Amendment definition. But let's be realistic. Since the adoption of the US Bill of Rights two centuries ago, the American constitution has been amended a scant seventeen times. Many of these amendments reflected epochal transformations in American society and culture. The Thirteenth Amendment abolished slavery, the Sixteenth instituted the federal income tax, and the Nineteenth extended voting rights to women. While environmental protections merit a federal amendment, this will only become possible after a grassroots transformation has occurred across the nation and in the individual consciousness of our people.

The place to start is at the state level. State constitutions are more dynamic documents than the federal Constitution. (The state of Massachusetts, for example, has altered its state constitution 120 times.[36]) Furthermore, states have a tremendous amount of power when it comes to the environment—generally the federal government sets the floor, but the states are entitled, and I would suggest even obliged, to provide better protection. State constitutions provide individual states with the means to grant environmental health the highest possible protection, that of a recognized and enforceable right, within their jurisdictions. Even when we have a federal Green Amendment, we will still want state constitutional recognition. I'm of the mind that state constitutional action is not just logical but imperative.

I don't mean to suggest that securing constitutional change at any level is easy—in fact, that difficulty is one of its benefits. There is a higher bar to success than for typical legislation, but this heightened process also means constitutional protections are more enduring. In the United States, history has taught us that the government's commitment to the environment is subject to change. A visionary environmental policy agenda during one administration can easily turn into an "anti-environment" policy agenda the next. In contrast, once we secure constitutional environmental rights, we're unlikely to lose them due to this higher procedural bar. At the same time, armed with a Green Amendment, we have a powerful tool to keep in place other legacy environmental achievements. The rollback of a strong environmental agenda, program, or protection secured under a previous administration could raise constitutional objection by future elected officials or people—and thereby be upheld.

Pursuing a Green Amendment at the state level affords a unique opportunity to hold public conversations about a state's unique values, goals, and needs. Because these are local charters, each state's constitutional provision about the environment reflects local values. My home state of Pennsylvania adopted what I consider a minimum standard of environmental protection. Pennsylvania's provision succinctly and elegantly recognizes environmental rights as inherent, indefeasible, and generational. It ensures the right must be protected equitably for all people regardless of race, ethnicity, or socioeconomic status. The provision is self-executing, meaning no further state action is necessary to give it legal life. It provides individuals with the legal right to enforce it. And it places a clear obligation on all government officials to protect our environment and natural resources.

Montana's state constitution similarly recognizes environmental rights to be "inalienable" and protected in the state's bill of rights. The state requires the environment to be not only maintained but also improved for the benefit of present and future generations—and vests each Montanan with the duty to protect the environment. Montana's bifurcated path for securing environmental rights and duties—bill of rights language complemented by language elsewhere in the constitution, all of it supported by sound court interpretation—is yielding strong environmental rights recognition. (For the record, I believe including all of the protective environmental language in the Bill of Rights provides a greater assurance of proper legal interpretation, ensuring highest constitutional recognition for the rights and obligations included therein.) And so it is little surprise that this state joins Pennsylvania on the vanguard of contemporary constitutional environmentalism in America.

In 2021, New York state joined our Green Amendment family. Under the leadership of New York State Assembly Member Steve Englebright and Senator Robert Jackson—and supported by the environmental education, advocacy, and grassroots organizing of my Green Amendments For The Generations organization, the Delaware Riverkeeper Network, Environmental Advocates New York, and Adirondack Mountain Club, as well as the strong legal advocacy of prominent legal minds such as Elisabeth Haub School of Law professors Nicholas A. Robinson and Katrina Fischer Kuh—New York's Green Amendment proposal advanced through the legislative process and to a vote of the people. On November 2, 2021, supported by 70 percent of voters, the Bill of Rights of the New York Constitution was amended to ensure "each person shall have a right to clean air and water, and a healthful environment." This language meets the Green Amendment fundamentals of raising up environmental rights so they are on par with other fundamental rights. But my hope and goal is that other states follow the path of Pennsylvania, and other emerging Green Amendment leaders, in including essential elements such as generational language, specific mention of the climate, and the trustee language that have proven so beneficial in the interpretation and application of Pennsylvania's Green Amendment.

A growing number of states advancing Green Amendments are seizing on the opportunity to further strengthen environmental rights progress. While Hawaii's constitution meaningfully recognizes the state's obligation to act as a trustee of its natural resources for both present and future generations, it has yet to include enforceable environmental rights. Today, Hawaii's conversation about environmental rights for the people is being revisited under the leadership of state Senator Michael Gabbard and Representative Amy Perruso, who are advancing individual environmental rights that not only include water, air, environment, and climate, but also recognize the importance of beaches to that state.

New Mexico's Green Amendment champions, Senator Antoinette Sedillo Lopez and Representative Joanne Ferrary, are seeking to replace the current provision's weak language with explicit recognition of environmental rights, state trustee obligations, and generational protections. They also have gone to great lengths to consult with Indigenous leaders and environmental justice communities to secure their review and input. It was in New Mexico where language that embraces the cultural values of a clean and healthy environment important to Indigenous communities first emerged.

Informed by New Mexico's considerations, Maine, Arizona, Hawaii, and Washington are also considering the importance of the cultural values associated with the environment in their Green Amendment language proposals. Wanting to express more firmly the environmental justice values of a Green Amendment important to the state of Washington, Representative Debra Lekanoff appended additional explicit language in that state's Green Amendment proposal. Senator Juan Mendez of Arizona, along with leaders in New Jersey and Washington, is considering explicit inclusion of flora and fauna. Meanwhile, in Maine and Maryland, leaders want to ensure that the human health values of the environment are specifically recognized, so they included language promising the healthful qualities of the environment.

Delegate Evan Hansen of West Virginia liked the strength and elegance of Pennsylvania's language and recognized the political value of mirroring a successful amendment in a similar state—so his proposal borrowed Pennsylvania's phrasing verbatim. Likewise, Iowa is borrowing heavily from Pennsylvania's language, with State Representative Chuck Isenhart focusing much of his early work on getting the messaging just right—appealing to the down-to-earth values of everyday Americans and stressing that clean water and air are vital for us all.

Together we are demonstrating that although the Green Amendment fundamentals are nonnegotiable, there are many ways to express and embrace additional components that best reflect the personality of each state joining the movement. Whatever the emphasis or priorities, each state can arrive at its own vision and articulation of environmental rights protection. And every time a state adds a new provision, element, recognition, or style of presentation to their Green Amendment, it offers a new example and approach that will inspire and resonate with a new state joining our movement.

In addition to the legal benefits they provide, Green Amendments help reshape how people think about their rights to a clean and healthy environment—from something they hope for, to something they expect and feel empowered to fight for. Having an enforceable constitutional right promotes better public appreciation of environmental activism, with important consequences for activists themselves. Industry representatives and their political allies often try to shame activists with labels such as "radical," "extremist," or "ecoterrorist." They try to represent our perspectives as naive or anti-business. Over time, these attacks can take a psychological toll. With a constitutional amendment in hand, however, activists can more easily withstand such attacks and bolster their morale. By passing a progressive environmental rights amendment, the community publicly affirms its understanding of nature as worthy of safeguarding for ourselves and future generations. The playing field shifts; now it's industry that has become marginalized, and government that must explain its lassitude in protecting the environment. As Jordan Yeager so beautifully explains, "When we start getting people to think about their environmental rights, [. . .] there are ripple effects . . . . It shifts the burden onto government to establish that what [they're] allowing to happen isn't going to hurt us, before [they] allow it to happen."[37]

Student and concerned Delaware resident Afua Dapaah demonstrated well how quickly the sense of expectation can manifest. Within weeks of joining the campaign for a Delaware Green Amendment, she pointedly asked a legislative staffer during a meeting on the recently proposed Delaware language, "Why do we even have to have this conversation? Why do we have to ask for rights to clean water and air, for a safe environment and climate? We should have them already." The room of advocates who had joined the meeting nodded their agreement. The staffer quickly indicated he believed the state representative he worked for would be supportive of the proposal.[38]

In my own public conversations, I see firsthand the deep emotional impact that constitutional discussions can have. I meet with many communities up in arms about impending environmental desecration—an ill-conceived development project, a drilling operation, a scheme to fill a wetland and thus destroy a habitat. People too often feel frustrated at how little protection the law or their elected representatives provide. But when we talk about environmental rights, the room becomes electric. It dawns on people that they should have these rights and that government and industry should honor them. Audiences become incredulous upon realizing that these rights, in most instances, go unrecognized and unprotected.

After I gave a talk about Green Amendments in New Mexico before the members of an organization known as Indivisible Albuquerque, the whole room was energized. Person after person enthusiastically asked me questions.

"What next?"

"How can we make it happen here?"

"Do you have a legislative sponsor yet? Because I have a good one in mind!"

I had come that evening to share a good idea and hopefully garner some interest in learning more, yet I left the room knowing that New Mexico was going to be a leader in the movement. As I traveled with Molly Atz, a key member of my Green Amendment team, back to our Airbnb, we were bubbling over with excitement. This was my first talk on the subject in New Mexico. We hadn't known what to expect, but we couldn't have dreamed of a better reception. Given the stranglehold of the oil and gas industry, we knew that it would be an uphill battle—but that with this kind of passion, we would be victorious. And this public energy for Green Amendments is not unique to New Mexico. I have seen it nationwide.

As a country and world, we are facing many challenges. Pollution is harming our health, our children, and the quality of our lives, and it is creating cost burdens that are hard for government budgets to overcome. Those of us seeking environmental protection are struggling with the emotional turmoil we feel when we rise within our communities to seek redress for ongoing or threatened environmental harms—and all too often face disagreeable neighbors, or decision makers who exercise their position of power with inappropriate hostility to shut us down. And we are burdened by an antiquated legal system that has failed to give environmental protection the priority placement it needs in our modern world.

It's about time that we all stand up for the environmental health we truly deserve; that activists feel empowered to fight on the public's behalf; that industry no longer possesses unfettered access to the levers of power; and that government feels obliged to protect people.

It's about time we took back our power for environmental protection, providing nature the defense, protection, and restoration it—and we—so desperately need. No longer can government be simply trusted to do the right thing.

It's about time for public officials to know that we are laying the ground rules regarding environmental protection—and that now we're not only looking over their shoulders to watch what they're doing, but we're also ready to take action and secure our rights should they fail or betray us.

As Dr. Mohammad Akhter, former executive director of American Public Health Association and health commissioner in Washington, DC, observed when we gave a May 2022 presentation together before a Delaware audience, states without Green Amendments are starting from largely the same place. "The difference between a good state and a not good state is the size of the loophole the state has created for industry to climb through and contaminate our environment," he said. "A Green Amendment will guide us to a new way to do things and to protect people and our health."

To me it is very simple and clear. To rectify our present and future environmental crisis, we must elevate environmental rights above partisan politics, above misinformation campaigns, and above misplaced emphasis on property rights or industry economics. We can do this only if every state and the United States recognize a constitutional right ensuring every individual and every generation a clean, safe, and healthy environment. The first step toward achieving this noble goal is to generate state-level awareness and enthusiasm. And that's an accomplishment that all of us can help bring about.

CHAPTER FOUR

FRACKING AWAY OUR FUTURE

In 1988, Terry Greenwood gave up his career as a truck driver and mechanic and purchased a small twenty-acre farm in Daisytown, a sparsely populated borough in southwestern Pennsylvania's Washington County. It seemed like a great move, and for the next two decades, it was—Terry thrived as one of America's small independent farmers. Then, in 2007, the Dominion Energy company knocked on his door.[1] Engineers had advanced the hydraulic fracturing—fracking—technology necessary to access natural gas contained in underground shales. Terry's fields happened to reside over plenty of shale gas just waiting to be tapped. Dominion wanted to build wells on his land and exploit the gas resource.

Although Terry wasn't interested in having an energy company drill on his family farm, he had no choice. Dominion wasn't asking him to grant access to his land; the company simply brandished a lease it had on the property that dated from 1921, a lease Terry had no part in. As many residents of Washington County would soon discover, they owned their homes and properties, but not the "mineral rights" to their land.[2] Dominion informed Terry that it would site two industrial fracking wells on his farm. Construction would begin immediately, and there was nothing he could do about it. Terry begged the company to drill as far away from his cattle, hayfields, and home as possible, but the company refused. The gas wells, Dominion informed him, would operate a mere four hundred feet from his groundwater wells, and three hundred feet from his pond. To compensate Terry and his family for any inconvenience, the gas company provided a scant $400 a month in energy royalties.

Drilling on Terry's property began in December 2007. Week after week, Terry watched as the company transformed his peaceful, quiet, and bucolic oasis into an industrial site. The company paved over his six acres of hayfields, clearing land for industrial gas rigs to drill and construct gravel roads. Terry reported that the company treated him disrespect-fully, throwing garbage on his property and carelessly erecting an electric fence, which stunned one of his horses, removing the skin from its legs. In Terry's opinion, "The gas company doesn't care what they do, they don't have respect."[3]

By early 2008, a few months after fracking operations began, Terry noticed changes to the water on his property. The surface-water pond where his cattle drank turned a bright, brackish red. It was so obviously contaminated that Terry cordoned it off to protect his animals. He also appealed to the Pennsylvania Department of Environmental Protection (Pennsylvania DEP). Surely it would help. After all, reining in industrial contamination was its job, right?

To Terry's surprise, regulators claimed the water was "good" and then refused to conduct any soil testing. As they told Terry, the water on his property came from a pond and wasn't intended for human use.[4] Under these circumstances, there was nothing they could do. Terry countered that humans *would* be consuming the water. Cattle ingested it, which meant that anything present in the water would enter human bodies once people consumed the cattle. The Pennsylvania DEP declined to comment on this point.

In a sense, Terry was wrong. Humans wouldn't consume his cattle anytime soon. That's because his cattle started *dying* at unprecedented rates. In a typical year, Terry lost one or two animals to disease or accidents. In 2008, however, eleven of his animals perished. Four became blind, one developed a cleft palate, and some were stillborn. Photographs reveal that their eyes were bright blue and white, likely evidence of toxic chemical exposure. At least one stillborn calf was so mangled that its mother didn't bother to clean it off after birth, but instead discarded it like rubbish. Terry contacted the Pennsylvania DEP, but inspectors showed little sympathy. "That's a farmer's luck, losing cattle," an inspector told him.[5]

Terry knew that it wasn't farmer's luck. Dominion stored industrial wastewater in rickety pits on his property, and Terry had observed water gushing from these pits into his farmland, right where his animals roamed and drank.[6] He contacted the Pennsylvania DEP once more. Investigators conducted an inquiry and concluded that "there was no spill and no natural gas drilling contamination of Greenwood's pond water."[7] Dr. John Stolz, a professor of environmental microbiology at Duquesne University, who studied Greenwood's case, strongly disagreed with the Pennsylvania DEP's assessments.[8]

In addition to contamination of his pond, Terry also had to contend with poisoning of the water he and his family used for drinking, cooking, and washing. The well water on Terry's land became so contaminated that it resembled "iced tea," as he described it. The energy company told him and his family to stop drinking it immediately. A few months later, the well water disappeared altogether. Dominion initiated five attempts to access fresh water, puncturing holes in Terry's farm until the company finally struck liquid. While Pennsylvania's DEP insisted that this newly accessed well water was perfectly safe, it had a briny taste, and Terry suspected that it was laced with fracking chemicals.

With his water sources decimated and his animals sick and dying, Terry's property values and annual revenues plummeted. Terry dreamed of abandoning this nightmare and moving, but he couldn't afford to. Who would purchase a farmstead studded with gas wells and containing no reliable water? In the first four years of drilling on Terry's property, his son tabulated $50,000 in losses.[9] That didn't include his $125,000 farm, which had lost all its value.[10] As Terry gazed around his once idyllic rural community, he noted additional eerie catastrophes underway: "There's been dogs died, goats died, and people sick. You put the sick people and the animals together and you have a big problem. There's been more stillborn [human] babies around here too."[11]

Don't Be Fracking Crazy

Little did Terry Greenwood and his neighbors realize, but their county had been swept up in America's new energy boom. Beginning in the late 1990s, the oil and gas industry began eyeing Pennsylvania's Marcellus Shale.[12] Harvesting natural gas from America's vast shale deposits, such as the Marcellus, located below the Appalachian Basin, and the Bakken, resting below the northern United States and central Canada, had been a fossil fuel energy pipe dream for decades. The twenty-first century now marked a new energy era based on fracking.

Armed with innovative techniques and proprietary chemical concoctions, America's drilling and fracking industry promised to lead the country into a brighter, more independent, and profitable future. Beginning in the early 2000s, media headlines proclaimed the end of "dirty coal," which polluted the Earth, and the rise of natural gas, which was allegedly much cleaner. By the end of the 2000s, domestic fracked gas was also heralded as our ticket out of the global recession and our difficult relationships with volatile Middle Eastern states. According to news reports, natural gas promised to make the United States "energy independent" within decades.

The oil and gas industry allocated millions to lobbying efforts and slick marketing campaigns, funding studies about the merits of fracking and lining the pockets of local, state, and national politicians to ensure their support for fracking projects. They also began knocking on the doors of rural Americans, asking them to sign leases for gas exploration on their land. If local landowners agreed to the drilling, the energy companies promised, they'd become rich. As for any risk of environmental damage, well, that was nothing to worry about—fracking for gas was absolutely safe, industry representatives claimed. In fact, it was part of America's lucrative clean-energy future.

These sales pitches caught Americans off guard. Meanwhile, few independent studies existed to shed light on fracking's economic, environmental, or health impacts. Organizations like the Delaware River-keeper Network got busy documenting early instances of devastation unleashed by fracking, but we had a lot of ground to cover, and the industry had a huge head start. I, along with Tracy Carluccio, spent countless hours researching the latest science, seeking out experts, and talking with victims of the fracking industry. Grassroots organizations like Berks Gas Truth and Damascus Citizens for Sustainability were founded and began to raise awareness and sound alarm bells.

For the most part, however, people heard from the well-funded industry and their elected representatives that fracking was both safe and profitable. In fact, fracking seemed like a no-brainer. Why *not* allow it on your land or in your community?

More Dangerous Than It Looks

If you scrutinized the industry sales pitch, as my colleagues and I did, there was ample reason to suspect that fracking poses serious problems, especially as far as water is concerned. A traditional natural gas well (what regulators term a "conventional well") requires approximately one hundred thousand gallons of water to drill. At the time Terry was enduring fracking operations on his farm, a fracked shale gas well (or as regulators call it, an "unconventional well") required a stunning three to five *million* gallons. That water isn't simply used and then recirculated. It's infused with proprietary mixtures of chemicals, including toxins and carcinogens. These chemical-laden fracking fluids are then injected, at extreme pressures, through a borehole drilled deep into the earth, where they mix with naturally occurring (but no less dangerous) substances, including barium, strontium, benzene, toluene, and naturally occurring radioactive materials (NORM).

After passing through the Earth's geology, the already toxic frack fluid becomes even more contaminated and dangerous.[13] As the industry has advanced, drilling longer and longer boreholes, the volumes of water and toxic additives have dramatically increased. Soon, fracking a well required four times the amount of water—an astonishing fifteen to twenty million gallons for just one frack. Wells can be fracked multiple times, and 85 percent of that water, Pennsylvanians were learning, was fresh—natural water from streams and aquifers, not mostly reused frack water as the industry was suggesting.[14] That's an enormous volume of water, toxins, and irreversible devastation.

It's not just the water impacts that are a concern. Shale gas extraction requires devastating modification of the landscape. Every shale gas well requires heavy and polluting industrial equipment as well as access roads to accommodate thousands (yes, thousands) of trucks loaded with sand, chemicals, and wastewater. Each industrial shale gas extraction site, known as a well pad, requires up to five acres of land for the pad itself, but when you add in the access roads, pipelines, vast wastewater pits, and other infrastructure needed to support the drilling and fracking operations, each pad really requires the development and degradation of approximately seventeen to twenty-three acres of land, much of it forests, wetlands, and other natural habitats.[15]

As we consumed the scientific research and the constantly emerging stories of damage, our worst suspicions were confirmed.

Jenny and Tom Lisak had lived happily on their land since 1983. Their organic farm provided them, their three children, and their community with delicious fruits, nuts, vegetables, and berries. In 2009, when drilling in the Marcellus commenced in their township, the Lisaks noticed their water going bad. As they peered in their cistern, it was a grisly orange and smelled oily, with bubbles rising and white chalky matter floating on top. The Lisaks were horrified. Believing that the drilling company, their elected representatives, and the Pennsylvania DEP would be equally upset to learn about what was happening, Jenny began making phone calls. When she reached the drilling company, employees there denied any wrongdoing but offered to buy her bottled water anyway. Officials from the Pennsylvania DEP came and tested her water but then went silent—Jenny didn't hear anything back for months. As for her call to State Senator Joe Scarnati, Jenny shakes her head and simply reports that he offered "no help."[16]

Unable to rely on the water at their home, the Lisaks repurposed a large water tank they had for irrigating crops. Every day or so, a member of the family drove the tank in their pickup truck to a neighbor's house and filled it up with a garden hose—a two-hour process. It was hard living like that, but the Lisaks didn't know what else to do.

The Pennsylvania DEP finally called back with test results. Their water problems weren't caused by the drilling, the agency claimed. So what *was* causing it? The Pennsylvania DEP couldn't say. The Lisaks weren't at all reassured. "I knew that there was nothing else happening in the area," Jenny recounts, "and nothing between the gas well and our water."

Other horrors continued to mar the Lisak family. Under the guise of trying to suppress dust, trucks rumbled over the local dirt roads, spraying water. Among them was the road that ran right by the Lisaks's house. Jenny's collies, who enjoyed investigating the freshly sprayed roads, would come home and "lie around on the front porch, licking their paws." Within a few months, the male dog died of cancer at age five, and the female lost a litter of puppies. Jenny and Tom soon learned that the water sprayed was frack wastewater.

Over this same period, the Lisaks had been trying to decide whether to send their fifteen-year-old son away for school. A particularly smart kid, he had a chance to enroll in an early college program. For Jenny, the choice was clear: "In the end, I realized that I had to send him away in order to keep him safe. I wasn't sure what would be best for him, but I wanted him safe. I knew I had to let him go."

The parade of horribles continued. More wells were drilled in the township, their toxic emissions carried by the wind and fouling the air on the Lisak property. A well in nearby Clearfield County blew out. Horrendous traffic, day in and day out, disturbed their once-quiet community. Walking and driving around their property and the surrounding lands, the Lisaks passed massive impoundments filled with toxic frack wastewater. On one occasion, Jenny's throat seized up. She hurried away, coughing and wheezing. For three days, the coughing continued, accompanied by a sore throat.

Month after month, year after year, stories like these made clear the fracking industry was impacting every aspect of people's lives—their health, their peace of mind, their ability to sell their land and move away to safer spaces. It was ruining their present and compromising their future. And still the politicians supported it. And still the industry claimed it was safe.

The reason so many politicians cared so little soon became evident: oil and gas money deposited into their political coffers to support their personal and political aspirations. State Senator Eugene Yaw, among the Pennsylvania legislators working to defeat our Delaware River Basin protections from fracking, received over $58,000 between 2007 and 2018. Yaw also directly pockets income by leasing his own property for drilling.[17] Pennsylvania Senator Joe Scarnati—lead supporter of the infamous Act 13—accepted more than $693,000 during the same time frame.[18] Governor Tom Wolf, who has received a significant $149,500 in contributions, touts himself as pro-environment.[19] But Governor Wolf has been as supportive of fracking as his predecessors—Democrat Ed Rendell, who shepherded in the industry during his tenure, and Republican Tom Corbett, who signed Act 13 into law and had received $1.8 million from the industry as of 2013 (his term ended in 2015).[20]

Fortunately, not every public servant can be bought off. Mary Pat (MP) Tomei was a leading staffer for Pennsylvania Senator Daylin Leach, the one legislator who had the temerity to propose a ban on fracking in the state (a proposal that inevitably failed). From her perch in Leach's office, MP worked tirelessly to get impacted families the help they needed. Whether progress took the form of medical help, a ban on fracking, or at least more protective regulations, she just wanted elected leaders to actually do something.

Among the families MP had been working with was that of Lois Bower-Bjornson. Lois, a mother-turned-advocate, had been leading a frack tour to show legislators what was really happening to Pennsylvania families. MP and I, along with my daughter, Anneke—as well as Delaware Riverkeeper Network staff members Bridget Brady and Molly Atz, who were working to advance Green Amendment protections—convened at Lois's home in Washington County to take the tour. We spent the day inspecting a handful of the twenty-five active frack sites that surrounded her home. Whether they adorned their lawns with "Trump for President" signs or supported other candidates, to a person, everyone we met that day felt sacrificed.

At one point during the day, Bridget leaned over to me to quietly ask: "How can the government and industry get away with this? They just check the permit boxes and then look away? Children are literally getting sick; some are even dying."

She was right. It turned my stomach and twisted my heart to know this was the kind of world Lois's children—and my own—were growing up in: a world in which our government leaders were incentivized to ignore the plight of the people in service of their own cynical political agendas.

In 2020, just as the Covid-19 pandemic was descending on us, a new study came out. Environmental Health News had noticed a gap in the science and sought to answer an important question: Were fracking chemicals building up in the bodies of local residents? Five families were selected for the study, including Lois and her four children. The results were striking. Not only were the daily lives of Lois and her children being degraded by fracking trucks, smells, and noise and light pollution, but their bodies were being invaded as well. Among the most alarming findings: Lois's then-thirteen-year-old son Gunnar had benzene, toluene, naphthalene, and other chemicals coursing through him. The threat posed by this contamination is not benign; it ranges from potential organ damage to reproductive harm, increased cancer risk, and more. And it's not just hidden and future effects that Lois and her kids face: suffering nosebleeds and even coughing up blood clots have been part of her son's life since nearby fracking operations began.[21]

By 2021, there were 1,584 wells drilled or being drilled in the 861-square-mile landscape that is Washington County, where the Bower-Bjornsons live. As Lois recounted to *Environmental Health News*, "[fracking] just completely encompasses us. It's not like we can look to our right or left and say it's not there. And everywhere [my children] go, school or wherever, it's there too."[22]

Despite living with this reality, Lois maintains an extraordinary and passionate optimism about securing the protections her community so clearly needs. Far from giving up or giving in, she is determined to make sure government leaders take notice—and more important, take action.

My Wim is the same age as Lois's Gunnar. I can't help but worry about his future and what fracking is doing to it. What will the Earth be like when he grows up? What harms is industry already inflicting that we may not know about? I worry.

And I fight.

The Scientific Consensus against Fracking

Today, we know beyond any doubt that fracking isn't safe. Between 2009 and 2015, scientific research on fracking's health and environmental effects exploded, with at least 685 research studies appearing in peer-reviewed journals.[23] By 2020, this figure would balloon to over two thousand.[24] The evidence is damning.

A 2014 research study of Washington County, Pennsylvania, home to Terry Greenwood's farm and the Bower-Bjornson family, found that "within 1 kilometer of a gas well, residents had up to twice the rate of health problems per person compared to those who lived 2 kilometers away or further."[25] These include "higher rates of skin, respiratory, neurological and gastrointestinal problems." Other studies show increased asthma, heart problems, mental health problems, and more.[26]

Studies also find increased cancer risks among those inhabiting the gas lands. Researchers testing at fracking sites in Arkansas, Ohio, Colorado, Wyoming, and Pennsylvania documented the presence of eight toxic chemicals in the air, with levels significantly surpassing federal limits. In some of the samples, the concentration of the carcinogen benzene tested at 770,000 times over normal levels.[27] Dr. David Carpenter, the lead scholar on the 2014 study, lamented that only time would tell how truly bad the impacts were. "Cancer has a long latency," he explained, "so you're not seeing an elevation in cancer in these communities. But five, ten, fifteen years from now, elevation in cancer is almost certain to happen."[28]

Grotesquely on cue, five years later in 2019, journalists Don Hopey and David Templeton reported on an apparent child cancer cluster in a Pennsylvania fracking sacrifice zone spanning four counties.[29] Between 2008 and 2018, the two reporters counted twenty-seven cases of Ewing sarcoma in the region—about four times the number of cases that would be statistically expected. The cause of the rare bone cancer, which generally strikes children or young adults, is unknown, but it is not believed to be inherited. Joshua Potter of Fayette County was just sixteen years old when he died from the cancer; genetic testing showed he had no markers for being at an increased risk for the disease.

And Joshua is far from the only child afflicted. Seeing displayed in Don and David's article the beautiful, happy faces of those who have died or are suffering from this disease is heart-wrenching; at least, this was my reaction. What was the reaction of David Spigelmyer from the Marcellus Shale Coalition? That there are "no known lifestyle-related or environmental causes of Ewing tumors," and that efforts to link Ewing sarcoma to fracking in the region are without scientific or medical support. It's exactly the kind of galling, bad-faith statement that's impossible to take seriously when advanced by a fracking industry executive.

In point of fact, there is growing evidence that years of exposure are not required for the health of our children to be harmed by fracking. A significant and still-accumulating body of research demonstrates that pregnant women who live near fracking operations are having children with unusually high rates of premature birth, low birth weights, and/or birth defects, including defects of the brain and spine.[30] Scientists are even learning that babies born in communities with the highest rate of fracking expansion are more likely to die in their first month of life— 28 percent more likely—than babies born in the same region before fracking came to town.[31]

In addition to our health, the fracking industry takes from us other essential underpinnings of life—among them clean, healthy, fresh water. Only 0.5 percent of the Earth's water is fresh water available for daily human use.[32] We cannot afford to sacrifice this finite supply to an industry that uses it in ways that make it unavailable for human or ecological use. And yet with fracking, we are doing just that. Of the fifteen to twenty million gallons of fresh water sacrificed for every fracking well, as much as 90 percent is lost underground. In just nine states over a ten-year period, we have ceded at least 239 billion gallons of water to fracking.[33] Not only does this water become inaccessible for essential uses, but as the now-toxic water circulates through the Earth's geology, it can also contaminate additional underground water supplies, inflicting a "double whammy" of water loss.

The rest of the water returns to the Earth's surface (up to five million gallons per well) as wastewater. Fracking wastewater is seriously contaminated, containing barium, strontium, benzene, toluene, ethylbenzene, xylene, oil, and grease, along with incredibly high levels of salts.[34] Too often, it's also radioactive, with lethal amounts of radium—sometimes as high as 3,600 times the United States Environmental Protection Agency's limit for drinking water.[35] Frack wastewater is so toxic that generally only one of three things happens to it: the water is diluted and blended with additional toxic chemicals to be used for additional fracking, it is disposed of through injection deep into the earth, or it is stored in surface water impoundment pits. Impoundment pits are known to experience leaks, spills, off-gassing, and damage to pit linings—all of which can spread toxins into the environment. In addition, wildlife that sees frack wastewater impoundments as another innocent body of water to drink from, swim in, or gather food from, too often become unwitting victims of its contamination and harm. The same goes for residents living above frack wastewater disposed of in the earth via underground injection.

On November 6, 2016, a 5.0-magnitude tremor seized Oklahoma, ruining homes, canceling school, and causing widespread evacuations near Cushing.[36] Though such earthquakes are historically unknown in this region, the state experienced so many earthquakes from 2014 to 2017 that Oklahoma briefly overtook California's status as the nation's leader in seismic activity.[37] Oklahoma's recent influx of earthquakes owes much to the injection of fracking wastewater.[38] The subterranean frack fluid, explains geophysicist George Choy, is the culprit; it "fills pores in dormant faults, causing them to slip and unleash the quakes."[39]

While the number of quakes fell after state disposal rules were put in place in 2015, the damage had already been done—and quakes were locked in for years to come, as already-injected wastewater continues to travel through the geology, triggering ancient faults and new quakes. "I don't think people fully appreciate the scale, the amount of water that was injected over the years," explains the state seismologist, Jacob Walter.[40] Scarier yet, above-grade oil storage containers stud the landscape around the small town of Cushing, and beneath the surface a maze of pipelines crisscross, creating one of the largest confluences of underground energy pipelines in the country.[41] As a result, Oklahoma, and Cushing in particular, has "the potential for producing one of the worst environmental catastrophes in American history," notes Johnson Bridgwater, director of Oklahoma's Sierra Club chapter.[42] On May 25, 2021, Oklahoma communities were struck by a 4.1-magnitude earthquake—a quake so strong it was also felt in Texas and Kansas.[43] It is only a matter of time before a larger earthquake causes cataclysmic damage.

Contrary to widely circulated industry claims, fracking is also bad for the economy and erodes the fabric of our communities. While a few make money, entire towns are left to suffer. The 24/7/365 exposure to light and noise disrupts community peace and causes detrimental effects on health. Fracking operations are correlated with "steep increases in rates of crime, including sex trafficking, sexual assault, drunk driving, drug abuse, and violent victimization."[44] Though women disproportionately bear the brunt of such abuses, men have also suffered routine harassment and intimidation. No one is safe.

While fracking is damaging every aspect of our lives today, it is also threatening worsening harm for future generations. In fact, whether we continue to allow shale gas extraction to fuel our energy needs, and to tolerate the infrastructure that accompanies it (like pipelines), might well determine our planet's fate. That's because fracking is a significant cause of climate change. Numerous studies show high levels of greenhouse gases, volatile organic compounds (VOC), and other airborne toxins emanating from drilling sites.[45] An April 2016 study found that North Dakota's Bakken shale oil and gas field operations emitted a stunning 2 percent of the world's ethane. Until 2009, ethane emissions, among the world's top three sources of human-generated climate change, were decreasing. But emissions have increased since America's shale gas explosion, putting the world at greater risk for an imminent climate-change catastrophe.[46]

Likewise, between 2002 and 2014, we saw a 30 percent increase in US emissions of methane—a deadly greenhouse gas that is eighty-six times more potent at trapping heat in the environment than carbon dioxide.[47] Come 2018, NASA would unveil research demonstrating that methane is responsible for about a quarter of human-induced climate effects—and that the fossil fuel industry is responsible for the lion's share of this dramatic rise in methane emissions.[48] This means pro-fracking state and federal government officials are not just supporting an industry that is devastating people's health and taking young lives today, but also compromising the safety of our future generations by stripping the stability of our climate.

Experts reviewing the science and data are clear: there exists "no evidence that fracking can operate without threatening public health directly and without imperiling climate stability upon which public health depends," and furthermore the risks and harms of fracking are inherent to its operation and cannot be "sufficiently averted through regulatory frameworks."[49] You may be thinking that this is an overstatement, an exaggeration—that it can't possibly be true. But it is true. There is no way to regulate fracking and make it safe. To succeed, the industry quite simply requires the environmental desecration, toxic contamination, and consumptive misuse of natural resources. And quite simply, our nation's legal regime is ill equipped to just say "no."

The Fracked-Up Legal Landscape

Given the widespread scientific and medical consensus, not to mention the personal tales of destruction that activists like me hear about daily, one might wonder how fracking could possibly be legal. Sadly, fracking isn't merely legal: the fracking industry actually enjoys special exemptions from many of the environmental laws governing industrial activity in the United States. In 2005, President George W. Bush enacted the Energy Policy Act. This bill was a boon to conventional energy, providing tax incentives and other kickbacks to the nuclear and fossil fuel energy sectors. The bill also contains the so-called Halliburton loophole, which allows the oil and gas industry to keep its chemical fracking recipes secret and grants them exemption from Safe Drinking Water Act requirements.[50] The Halliburton loophole has hastened America's fracking-based energy boom, in the process contributing to the grievous injuries suffered by families throughout our country.

Witnessing the cascade of harms from this boom/bust industry, many US municipalities, cities, and states have responded by enacting moratoriums or outright bans on shale gas extraction and fracking operations. The Delaware Riverkeeper Network was one of the first groups to secure a moratorium against the industry, when we secured a de facto moratorium on drilling and fracking within the confines of the Delaware River watershed in 2010. In 2021, we turned the moratorium into a permanent ban on drilling and fracking operations in our watershed. But rather than put in place complete protection from the industry, the

DRBC is considering loopholes that will allow the import of toxic frack wastewater and export of water withdrawals to support fracking operations elsewhere, allowing these insidious parts of the fracking threat to bring unacceptable harm. And so, the battle for complete protection wages on in my watershed.

Fracking protections—to the degree they have been secured—have been a bipartisan affair. Vermont banned fracking in 2012.[51] Democratic Governor Andrew Cuomo banned fracking in New York in 2014. In 2017, when signing a bill that banned fracking in the state of Maryland, Republican Governor Larry Hogan announced, "Because of Maryland's position in the country and our wealth of natural resources, our administration has concluded that possible environmental risks of fracking outweigh any potential benefits."[52] Cities and municipalities in Florida, Ohio, California, and elsewhere have similarly enacted outright bans or moratoriums on unconventional methods until science can confirm that they do no harm.

Europe is also boldly headed toward a frack-free future. The European Parliament heralded fracking's decline at the end of 2015, when it issued a report confirming that unconventional drilling contributes to climate change. Scotland, Northern Ireland, and Castile La Mancha have also issued fracking moratoria, with Wales and Scotland now extending their protections indefinitely.[53] What's more, France, Ireland, Bulgaria, and Spain have banned fracking outright.[54] And Ireland is expanding its anti-fracking stance to include opposition to import facilities that would bring in fracked gas from the United States.[55]

By contrast, this country continues to eagerly tap its own shale oil and gas resources. Every time the industry or pro-fossil fuel politicians see an opportunity—such as the war in Ukraine—they advocate for even more fossil fuel extraction. While Ukranian families are being devastated by unwarranted Russian aggression, here in the US, Russia's attack on Ukraine is being used as an argument for more fracking to replace oil and gas no longer shipping from Russia. The right solution is to ramp up on clean and renewable energy creation, not more fossil fuel extraction that will devastate even more lives.

The weakness of regulatory regimes in the United States, coupled with the industry's immense power, are leaving many people vulnerable— even when public opposition to fracking is strong. Consider the city of Denton, located just north of Texas's sprawling Dallas–Fort Worth metropolitan area. In 2015, residents in this fossil fuel–friendly state decided to wage their own grassroots opposition effort against fracking. As Dr. Adam Briggle, a professor of environmental studies at the University of North Texas, explained, "It was when people saw . . . how close to homes they were drilling that we realized we had to look after each other here."[56] A chorus of concerned locals, donning "Frack-Free Denton" T-shirts, amassed enough signatures to force a vote on whether fracking should be banned locally. Despite the industry's stiff opposition, in 2014, Denton became Texas's first city to enact a ban.

"It felt like vindication," Dr. Briggle said, "an indication that grassroots democracy can still work in this country."[57] And yet Denton's victory proved temporary. Immediately, industry representatives filed legal challenges. In May 2015, the industry overturned Denton's ban on fracking. It also used this opportunity to preempt similar actions in other towns. There now exists a functional ban on banning fracking within the Lone Star State.

Denton's story has been replicated throughout our country. Concerned communities have joined together to secure protections, only to have them overturned or undermined by the courts, or through political misuse of procedural or bureaucratic obstacles. In 2016, the Colorado Supreme Court overturned one local fracking moratorium, citing its incompatibility with state law.[58] After the Ohio counties of Meigs, Athens, and Portage sought to strike down fracking in the 2016 elections, Jon Husted, the secretary of state, eliminated their anti-fracking ballot initiatives for technical reasons.[59]

In Pennsylvania, the biggest political step that's been taken to quell local opposition to fracking was that infamous Act 13 I first talked about in chapter 1. Brian Coppola, a Robinson Township supervisor in Washington County, had a front-row seat as the first wave of fracking swept his region.[60] He watched as the industry infiltrated the area, promising his constituents economic windfalls but instead contaminating the area's water tables, compromising soil quality, and destroying the quality of life for the residents of his community. Locals began complaining that they now inhabited an industrial wasteland and needed protection. So Brian tried appealing to the Pennsylvania DEP, only to find the government agency filled with industry apologists.

When Brian got wind of pro-fracking legislative proposals appearing in Pennsylvania's legislature, he joined with other elected officials in the county to lobby every representative and senator in Harrisburg to vote against those proposals. But he found that most of Pennsylvania's elected officials hadn't even read the legislation. When Dave Ball, a councilman and kindred spirit from Peters Township, joined with Brian to challenge their legislators on the substance of the bill, legislators merely recited industry talking points.[61] These were the legislators who would join forces with industry players to pass the new pro-fracking law—Act 13—putting their constituents and environment in grave peril.

But when Act 13 passed, threatening an unprecedented expansion of fracking in Pennsylvania, we had a tool Denton never possessed: our state constitution. With it, we overturned the most dangerous and damaging parts of Act 13 and stopped the exponential fracking increase the law sought to usher in. While our Pennsylvania Green Amendment is a powerful tool to help us take on the industry, the frackers got a strong foothold before we had a living and thriving constitutional right. So it's going to take more time and precedent to regain control. But now we have the constitution on our side.

The Perils of Pipelines

It's important to consider another outgrowth of the fracking industry: the pipelines and other gas infrastructure emerging as an added battlefront. Many are aware of a few iconic pipeline battles, such as the infamous Keystone XL Pipeline System, and the Dakota Access Pipeline that would run beneath the Standing Rock Indian Reservation. As a nation, we watched ranchers, farmers, Native American communities, and activists join forces to protect ancestral burial grounds, water supplies, environments, and property rights. We witnessed in horror as law enforcement officers in riot gear faced off with Native American activists and other protesters.[62] But outside the limelight, there are many other pipeline battlefronts—at street protests, in hearing rooms, and in courtrooms—where homeowners, environmental activists, and children worrying about their future join forces to protect all they hold dear.

Fracked gas requires a vast pipeline network to transport it to power plants, factories, and homes, and increasingly to export facilities so it can be shipped to foreign nations. As the web of pipelines grows, more families, communities, and environments across America find themselves confronted with threats to health, safety, and property rights these pipelines pose. In many ways, the laws for pipelines are even more unfair than for fracking.

The federal Natural Gas Act preempts state and local legislation and regulation when it comes to interstate natural gas pipelines, and entrusts most of the authority over pipelines to the Federal Energy Regulatory Commission (FERC). When natural gas pipelines are approved by FERC—an approval that is virtually guaranteed, given the over 99 percent approval rate of the FERC commissioners—the company gets the power of eminent domain.[63] That means private pipeline companies are empowered to take property rights and to force construction on homeowners, businesses, and farmers alike. Sure, they have to offer some cursory compensation in exchange for what they're taking, but the money is rarely, if ever, enough to cover the emotional and monetary costs that property owners suffer.

The Department of Energy and FERC also wield disproportionate power when it comes to liquified natural gas export facilities. While industry loves to tout fracking for oil and gas as creating an energy independent United States, in truth an increasing amount of fracked gas is being exported to countries where the industry can secure a higher price for its product.[64] So, it's not really about energy independence; it's about profits for industry executives.

Pipeline construction and operation come at a soaring cost. Approximately eighty-four acres of forest are lost or irreparably damaged for every mile of interstate pipeline laid therein. Rainfall—once absorbed by leaves and forest beds—now runs off the land, carrying pollution and causing erosion, while the loss of natural forest and healthy soils also robs wetlands and streams of the groundwater needed to sustain them. Streams and wetlands are literally carved through or under by heavy machinery and become deprived of essential shade, habitat, and pollution protection from waterside vegetation. Herbicides used during construction and follow-up maintenance introduce poisons that prevent vegetation regrowth. Construction crews compact the soil in what are supposed to be temporary construction work zones near pipelines. These areas end up being so damaged that the forest struggles to regrow. Forests, fragmented to make way for pipelines, lose the continuity needed to keep out invasive plants and animals, as well as to sustain the many flora and fauna that require an unbroken forest home. Pipelines are also a serious source of climate-changing methane emissions, and the compressors needed to move the gas through the line are yet another source of pollution. An estimated 7.6 percent of methane emissions in the United States come from pipelines, highlighting their part in the advancing climate crisis.[65]

Pipelines are just as devastating for businesses. Time and again, I've seen farmers testify that crop yields plummet once pipelines are laid under their property. Soil compaction and improper landscape restoration reduce farm yields, and according to numerous firsthand accounts, they never recover. At one public forum I helped convene to discuss the proposed PennEast Pipeline, a farmer from West Amwell, New Jersey, stepped to the microphone: "I have two pipelines that already run through one of my farm fields, and for years I have been monitoring the crop yield with an expert's help. What I can show you now," he said, holding up a colorful picture of his farm fields with bright red areas signaling where a pipeline lay, "is that the pipeline in my field causes a 30 percent reduction in crop production." I have also seen evidence of landscape operations bifurcated by pipelines unable to use the heavy equipment needed to manage their operations, spoken with maple syrup producers who've had their syrup trees callously cut down by pipeline companies, and heard testimony from real estate and tourism professionals discussing how their businesses suffer when a pipeline comes into town.[66]

Householders forced to live near a pipeline or compressor station, worrying about their explosive potential and burdened by both pollution and the limitations on how they can use their own property because of the pipeline right of way, are often unable to move away. People don't want to pay top dollar for a property with a pipeline running through. And the pipelines don't even have to be built before they start inflicting fear and harm. When Mark and Alycia Egan bought their dream home in Sullivan County, New York, it became their refuge and respite from bustling New York City, where they lived and worked full time. But then the Millennium Pipeline Company proposed to expand its existing line, including by constructing yet another new compressor right near their home. The Egans quickly joined forces with the community to try to stop the impending doom. But they also realized the odds were stacked against them, so they tried to put their self-described "dream home" up for sale.[67] After a year on the market, this fabulous house—located in a bucolic forest, on the bend of a beautiful stream whose running water makes soothing sounds day and night—still had no interested buyers. In fact, when the Egans left a map of the proposed compressor station on their kitchen table, a buyer touring their house took one look and immediately left, telling the realtor that she "loved the setting" but couldn't possibly take the risk. Many homes and farms proximate to pipelines languish on the markets like this, selling for fractions of their pre-pipeline values, if they can sell at all.[68] And when property values and local businesses decline, so too does the tax base upon which towns and cities rely.

Neighboring residents' fear of pipeline accidents is not unfounded. Gas pipelines are eminently hazardous. Accidents, incidents, and explosions do happen. On April 29, 2016, James Baker was at home in Salem Township, Pennsylvania, nursing an ankle injury. Shortly after his wife left for work, the nearby Spectra Pipeline exploded, setting both the family house and James himself on fire.[69] James couldn't maneuver too quickly due to his injury, but he managed to hobble outside. A Good Samaritan spotted him from a distance and dragged him away from the nightmarish scene. James's clothes were burning, irreparably damaging his skin. He suffered extensive damage to every part of his body and inhaled toxic smoke that caused his insides to burn as well. When doctors prepared to amputate his ear, which had been badly damaged during the fire, they unwrapped the bandage to discover that it had fallen off all by itself. James's tragedy seemed even more poignant in the following days, when, in reading the news reports, we all learned that his wife was pregnant. Where would his family live? What would his life with his new child be like, given the extent of his injuries? The answers were yet to be seen.

Energy companies claim that their pipelines are safe and getting safer, but the record speaks for itself. Over just two decades (2001 to 2020), the Pipeline and Hazardous Materials Safety Administration recorded 5,750 "significant" (i.e., those resulting in $50,000 or more in costs) pipeline incidents, which caused 256 fatalities, 1,142 injuries, and nearly $11 billion in costs and damages.[70] Recent research suggests that the rate of accidents and explosions is not improving; in fact, it's growing worse. The latest generation of natural gas pipelines has an annual average incident rate exceeding that of pipelines installed prior to 1940.[71] With industry poised to install countless more miles of fossil fuel pipelines, these safety concerns grow increasingly scary. And explosions are not the only harm suffered by those who are forced to have pipelines run across, under, around, and near their properties; day in and day out, fear is enough to take a toll on their hearts and minds.

Increasingly, industry is building pipelines that also carry the natural gas liquids—ethane, propane, butane, isobutane, pentane—used for a variety of purposes including to make plastics and synthetic rubber. The pipelines carrying natural gas liquids (NGLs) are subject to a different body of law, under which each state has more traditional environmental authority. But even then, the companies always seem to come out the winner.

Take the Mariner East II pipeline. Like others in the fracking pipeline industry, it wreaks havoc during construction and operation—and is known for its perpetual violations of law. Mariner East II transports NGLs from the shale fields in Ohio, West Virginia, and Pennsylvania to ports near Philadelphia for export to other nations, including for use in the manufacture of plastics, which are themselves creating a harmful environmental footprint. Energy Transfer Partners (successor to Sunoco Partners LP) committed so many egregious violations during pipeline construction that Pennsylvania Attorney General Josh Shapiro charged the company with forty-eight counts of environmental crimes for illegally releasing industrial waste in eleven counties and failing to take needed action, including failing to report pollution releases to agencies that could have responded.[72]

Spanning 350 miles and crossing through 17 Pennsylvania counties, tens of thousands of gallons of drilling fluids have contaminated streams, lakes, wetlands, fields, and people's backyards. On top of it all, the drinking water of at least 150 families was contaminated. Energy Transfer Partners went so far as to tell people their water was safe to drink when it in fact was not; unsurprisingly, the result was that people ended up in the hospital.[73]

For years, communities and organizations like the Delaware Riverkeeper Network and the Clean Air Council battled against permitting of the Mariner East II pipeline. Once it was approved (over our objections), Monitoring Director Faith Zerbe of the Delaware Riverkeeper Network worked with communities as a watchdog on construction, documenting and reporting violations. But it was an uphill battle to get the state to act on them. The attorney general's criminal charges vindicated our work, but they came too late—*after* the damage had been done to the environment and the future climate impacts were locked in.

While the attorney general cited the constitutional environmental rights of Pennsylvanians when announcing the criminal charges, communities are correct to say the constitution should have brought stronger protections earlier and helped us avoid these harms. Unfortunately, Mariner was proposed and began moving through the process in the early years of our having enlivened Pennsylvania's Green Amendment. And while we had secured our 2013 opinion and the law was changing when the Mariner East II applications were submitted to the Pennsylvania DEP in 2015, it would be another two years before a majority of the Pennsylvania Supreme Court confirmed our victory as unquestionable precedent.[74] And so Mariner, like so much of fracking, got in under the Green Amendment wire.

We are going to have to work harder and faster to make sure our Green Amendments become meaningful tools in the battle against fracked gas infrastructure. In Pennsylvania, the attorney general invoked the power of the state constitution to support criminal charges against a company after the pipeline was laid. But what we need now is for government agencies to invoke state constitutions to stop pipeline harm before it starts.

The power of Green Amendments in addressing pipelines is important for my watershed and for our nation, but also for my own family in a very personal way. My watershed is consistently targeted in order to get the fracked gas from central and western Pennsylvania to other parts of the United States and overseas. The more pipelines are built in our nation, the more fracking can advance. Remember in chapter 1, when I told you about the inheritance my mother left me—sixty-eight beautiful acres of forest in the Susquehanna River watershed? Since the fracking industry damaged our ability to enjoy that special place, my husband, Dave, began to explore other pieces of nature to protect in memory of my mother and my opa. After investigating properties for weeks, Dave announced one evening that he had found the perfect spot!

We contacted a local realtor and arranged to travel to New York to see the site. The following weekend, as we pulled onto the mile-long drive that took us to the property, we were excited but braced for disappointment. The seasonal gravel road led past idyllic forests, much of which were protected state wildlife lands. We came upon a small clearing with a dilapidated little house. Our hearts sank a notch, but we knew there was land with the property, and that was really what we had come to see. We told the realtor that she should go to her next appointment, for which we had already made her late, and we would meet her back at the parking spot in an hour. After she left, Dave and I, along with our then-nine-year-old son, Wim, took a walk.

We discovered a little trail behind the house and quickly found ourselves in a forest filled with beautiful trees, massive rocks, and acres of natural huckleberry and blueberry bushes, as far as the eye could see. As we continued to walk along this path, we saw off in the distance a mama bear with her two babies. Wim screamed at the sight, simultaneously exhilarated and frightened. It was a wonderful family experience, and in that moment, we knew we had found the perfect place to carry on my mother's legacy. Three weeks later, we signed the papers, and this special forest was all ours. Soon after, Anneke, Wim, and I took the earthen pot that had carried my mother's ashes and buried it in the center of the forest with song and prayer, hugs and tears.

When we purchased the property, I knew that the Millennium Pipeline ran through a portion of the forest located some distance down the road. It was admittedly a big mental hurdle to overcome, and I researched and analyzed the possible drawbacks at length. After considering the possible blast radius of an explosion, the environmental threat to our parcel, and the psychological effects of having this fracked gas pipeline proximate to our family's new sanctuary, we decided it was far enough away. We were wrong.

Within eight weeks of signing the papers, we learned that Millennium had a new project planned for the area, including a new compressor station slated for construction in our new town, a mere five miles as the crow flies from our forest home. We joined with the community, among them Mark and Alycia Egan, to wage a battle to stop the expansion project. But given the state of the law, our ultimate defeat and the expansion of the pipeline's capacity was no surprise.

Every time we walk past the gash through the forest that signals the Millennium pipeline, my heart sinks a little bit. I wish we had a federal Green Amendment to help us defend ourselves against this FERC-regulated pipeline. Failing that, I wish we had secured our New York Green Amendment just a few years earlier. It might have been a tool to help protect us and others in the community.

Toward a Frack-Free Future?

Fracking cannot be made safe, and associated pipelines inflict irreparable damage. No set of regulations will address the wealth of harms this industry inflicts. We need the US Constitution. At the federal level, a Green Amendment could well have prevented the fracked gas and oil boom from sweeping America in the first place. If the right to a clean, safe, and healthy environment were enshrined in the federal Constitution, the 2005 Halliburton loophole might have come under judicial review and been found unconstitutional. Without this piece of enabling legislation, along with others that have been implemented at the state and federal levels, significant portions of our wild, forested areas could have remained unfracked, allowing biodiversity to flourish and curious children and adults to explore. Our air and water quality would be better. We would be contributing far less to global climate emissions, and would be on track to achieving both the 2030 and 2050 emission reductions goals essential to protect our planet and our very existence. Absent exploiting local sources of natural gas and propping up the frackers with our tax dollars, the country might have focused instead on advancing truly clean and renewable sources of energy, while at the same time creating long-lasting and well-paying jobs.

Green Amendments at the state level, too, could have made a substantial impact. In Pennsylvania, with a living Green Amendment, we might have kept the frackers out, proving through science and the experiences of already-fracked states that intrusion of the industry into Pennsylvania would violate the rights of the people to pure water, clean air, and the natural and scenic values of the environment. Green Amendments in states across our nation would have provided us the tools needed to secure protection and exercise more caution.

And they still can.

A state amendment wouldn't guarantee that fracking won't exist, but state constitutional amendments similar to Pennsylvania's will strengthen grassroots anti-fracking struggles nationwide—and could give us the legal tool we need to just say "no."

Even at this late hour, the enactment of Green Amendments at the state level could still allow us to transform our communities and our mindsets. In some places, we could stop the proliferation of industry into as-yet untouched areas; in others, we could secure regulations to provide critical protections for our air, water, soils, and forests, not to mention for the health of ourselves, our children, and future generations.

Denton's mantra should be our own: We are all entitled to a frack-free future. Constitutional Green Amendments are a winning strategy, and that's what we need to get us there.

Terry Greenwood would have liked to have seen such victories. Yet he never will. In 2011, he abandoned his life as a farmer and became a full-time anti-fracking activist. The energy industry tried settling with Terry for the damage inflicted on his farm. As with others, they tried paying him off for an undisclosed amount, requiring a nondisclosure agreement as part of the settlement to prevent him from speaking out. But Terry refused to be silenced and instead devoted himself to educating others about the perils of fracking. Soon, though, Terry would contract an aggressive brain cancer, taking him in and out of the hospital for treatment. The diagnosis was shocking and painful, and those close to him say that nothing in his genetic history suggested he was predisposed to such an illness. Terry continued his advocacy despite the diagnosis. But on June 8, 2014, Terry succumbed to his illness. He was sixty-six.

We can't prove that exposure to fracking-based toxins caused or hastened Terry's death. But members of his community have little doubt. I will never forget Terry's dedication, passion for protecting others, or his personal mantra: "Water is more important than gas."[75]

Over the years, many champions have risen to combat the industry and protect communities. As powerful as we are when working together, these extraordinary people and countless others cannot effect change on their own. The industry is powerful. Constitutional Green Amendments that raise environmental debate and protection above partisan politics and industry dealmaking are powerful tools for preventing harm before it starts. But they are not limited to preventing damage yet to be done. They can also help protect us from ongoing harm; after all, you can't grandfather in a constitutional violation.

As we'll explore in the chapters to come, our greatest hope for combating environmental desecration and the loss of inalienable environmental rights isn't more piecemeal legislation and regulation. It's well-written Green Amendments in every state and in the federal constitution.

CHAPTER FIVE

WASTED

In the early 1950s, the DuPont corporation began using a chemical called perfluorooctanoic acid (PFOA) at its Washington Works chemical plant in Parkersburg, West Virginia.[1] Belonging to the family of perfluorinated chemicals (PFCs), also known as perfluoroalkyl and poly-fluoroalkyl substances (PFAS), PFOA became popular among industrial producers because of its ability to keep surfaces smooth and free of moisture. In particular, the chemical served as the key ingredient in Teflon, DuPont's highly lucrative, trademark product. Companies also used PFOA in many other consumer products requiring a nonstick surface, including Stainmaster carpets, food wrappers, microwave popcorn bags, and the surface coating of eyeglasses.[2] As PFOA became part of the fabric of everyday life in the United States and beyond, DuPont grew into one of the world's largest, most profitable conglomerates.

There was a dark side, though. PFOA was toxic—and the company knew it. Within a decade of using the substance, one of DuPont's scientists judged PFOA so dangerous that people had to handle it "with extreme care." The company's in-house scientific studies linked the toxin to genetic mutations, organ malfunction, cancer, and death in animal subjects. In 1962, DuPont experimented with human subjects, asking study participants to smoke cigarettes laden with PFOA and report their symptoms. These subjects became acutely ill, suffering diarrhea, chills, and body pain. Over the decades, DuPont's factory workers also exhibited a variety of short- and long-term health ailments. Colds were so prevalent among DuPont factory workers that the afflicted referred to their routine nausea, dizziness, chills, headaches, and fever symptoms as the "Teflon flu." These workers also suffered from higher rates of cancer and birth defects in their children. As peer-reviewed articles have since confirmed, PFOA is extremely harmful to human health. Even infinitesimally small levels of exposure have been linked to kidney and testicular cancers, thyroid disease, high cholesterol, pregnancy-induced hypertension/pre-eclampsia, ulcerative colitis, and decreased birth weight.[3]

Given this evidence, you would think that DuPont would have pulled Teflon off the market and notified workers of the risk. But the company didn't do that. For that matter, you would think that government officials would have required DuPont to prove the new chemical was safe before it was allowed to be used so prolifically, entering people's bodies and our environment. But the government didn't do that. Instead, DuPont kept quiet about the risks and *increased* the volume and scale of its PFOA-laden products, while the government sat on the sidelines and let it happen. As a result, DuPont employees and the public at large were exposed to the contaminant in even greater volumes. DuPont workers and chemists handled the substance every day. DuPont disposed of PFOA waste by dumping it straight into the Ohio River, where the Washington Works facility was located. Alternatively, the company loaded it onto boats and disposed of it in the open ocean. During the 1980s, the company acquired land from a West Virginia farmer and disposed of 7,100 tons of the chemical by dumping it in a landfill. The farmer became so sick from contamination that he had to discontinue cattle ranching.

After environmental attorney Robert Bilott decided to take on this humble cattle farmer's case in 1998, he became the DuPont Corporation's worst nightmare, exposing the company's decades-long cover-up and winning what was, at the time, the most lucrative settlement in the history of US environmental law. Based on information he revealed, the US Environmental Protection Agency sued DuPont for maliciously concealing the dangers of PFOA. A court fined DuPont $16.5 million, the largest penalty ever secured by the EPA for a case of this kind. Still, the fine represented less than 2 percent of the company's PFOA-based profits in a single year.[4] In 2006, the EPA acknowledged the grave risks that PFOA posed, creating a stewardship program and encouraging leading companies to reduce and eventually eliminate PFOA from their emissions and products.[5]

Meanwhile, DuPont became the subject of over 3,500 personal injury lawsuits. It cost DuPont $670 million to settle the class-action suit filed against it.[6] But let's be honest, no amount of money can alleviate the suffering of those who lost their healthy lives. Environmental journalist Sharon Lerner has christened PFOA "the tobacco of the chemical industry."[7] Big tobacco and DuPont both aggressively marketed their products for decades, knowing that as they reaped massive financial windfalls, they were poisoning and killing their consumers. Both now stand as enduring and hateful symbols of corporate greed and a failure of government to act.

In 2005, Tracy Carluccio, deputy director of the Delaware River-keeper Network, became aware of the chemical and its dangers to human health and the environment.[8] Having read about PFOA in West Virginia, she wondered whether it posed a danger in our watershed. Tracy was especially worried about DuPont's Chambers Works facility located on the banks of the Delaware River in Deepwater, New Jersey. This large manufacturing plant, which treated hazardous waste and manufactured Teflon, had discharged other toxins into the Delaware River. In fact, DuPont was one of the largest emitters of toxic compounds in the entire mid-Atlantic region. And it wasn't all that long ago that the Delaware Riverkeeper Network had fought and defeated a proposal concocted by the US Army and DuPont to receive and dispose of VX nerve agent waste at one of DuPont's Delaware River facilities, essentially treating the highly toxic waste through dilution in the river. Was the Chambers Works facility discharging PFOA into the river and nearby water supplies? We were determined to find out.

Exercising her characteristic vigilance and meticulousness, Tracy read every piece of science she could find about PFOA. Then, joined by her husband, Paul, she traveled to Deepwater, New Jersey, and went door to door to collect tap-water samples. Having heard rumors of contamination, many families were eager to have their water tested. They pointed Tracy to their cupboards, where they had stockpiled gallons of water. The Delaware Riverkeeper Network sent the samples Tracy and Paul amassed to a Canadian laboratory, one of the only scientifically reliable labs not connected to DuPont. The Canadian facility found measurable traces of PFOA and related chemicals in the New Jersey tap-water samples. PFOA exposure had indeed spread to the Delaware River and our watershed state of New Jersey. In due time we would learn that communities and waters in all of my watershed states, including Delaware, Pennsylvania, and New York, were being contaminated by chemicals in the PFAS family.

Eager to combat the PFOA threat, the Delaware Riverkeeper Network notified residents, the New Jersey Department of Environmental Protection (New Jersey DEP), and local water companies. Several New Jersey–based environmental organizations joined us in a working coalition, including key statewide leaders David Pringle with Clean Water Action and Jeff Tittel with the New Jersey Sierra Club. The United Steelworkers union at the DuPont facility eagerly joined the cause. Some employees at the Chambers Works factory had experienced frequent illnesses and were undergoing blood tests to reveal how much PFOA coursed through their veins. Tracy also contacted the attorneys involved in the Washington Works lawsuit in West Virginia. They traveled to the Delaware River watershed and held a town meeting at a local high school gym. Tim White, chief innovation officer for the Delaware Riverkeeper Network, led the organization's online effort to publicize the event, peppering the region with advertisements and notifying our members and community leaders. Our coalition lined the town with fly-ers. Hundreds of concerned residents showed up.

In time, our coalition would go on to host many organizing meetings, sharing information about the latest water-quality samples and spreading awareness about the dangers of PFOA. All this attention spurred the New Jersey DEP to investigate. What they found caused great concern: most of the sampled water supplies in New Jersey contained PFOA!

In 2007, the New Jersey DEP established a PFOA drinking water guidance level of forty parts per trillion (ppt). By 2009, the water experts and scientists at the New Jersey Drinking Water Quality Institute (DWQI), a panel that advises the state regarding drinking water standards, were deep into their study of PFOA and its health consequences. The New Jersey DEP conducted another round of water sampling and awaited the institute's findings so it could propose the adoption of a "maximum contaminant level" (MCL) and begin mandating the removal of the toxin from drinking water supplies. When the DWQI met in late 2010, it was expected to issue its PFOA recommendation to the New Jersey DEP. It issued no report, however, and the New Jersey DEP wound up taking no action.

How could this be? The answer is politics. Nine months before the DWQI convened, Republican Chris Christie became governor of New Jersey. Having already indicated that he wouldn't approve any new environmental regulations, he held true to his word. As if that weren't enough, Governor Christie went so far as to shut down the Drinking Water Quality Institute. It wouldn't reconvene for another four years.

Tracy was shocked but not defeated. At the Delaware Riverkeeper Network, we redoubled our efforts, submitting numerous public information requests for the PFOA study and water sample data that the DWQI should have issued. We finally secured the data and publicly exposed its findings: there was evidence of contamination in drinking water! One startling discovery was an astronomically high level of another member of the perfluorinated compound family—perfluorononanoic acid, known as PFNA or C9—in the borough of Paulsboro's water supplies. We rang the alarm bells and notified Paulsboro, afterward discovering that a large plastics conglomerate located nearby, Solvay Specialty Polymers, had employed and emitted more PFNA than any other company in the country. Indeed, DEP investigations couldn't find records of a higher quantity of PFNA in a water supply anywhere else in the world. Like DuPont, Solvay took no responsibility for contaminating local water supplies. Nonetheless, it temporarily paid for bottled water for some in the affected communities. DuPont also settled with Paulsboro by paying for the installation of a carbon filtration system on the borough's water supply after special counsel Bradley Campbell sent the company a Notice of Intent to Sue.[9]

But for many, the damage was already done. To this day, residents who drank contaminated water worry about whether their children or family members might get cancer or contract some other debilitating or deadly disease. Many towns demanded that their drinking water be tested and remediated. In addition, in 2014, the Christie administration succumbed to public pressure and finally reconvened the New Jersey Drinking Water Quality Institute. Its members in turn got to work researching PFAS, to develop safe drinking water standards that would remove PFAS chemicals from the state's water supplies.

The need for speed in protecting communities from the devastating health consequences of PFAS compounds was increasingly obvious, and with the political hurdle of Governor Christie's office out of the way, you would think protections were swift to come. But they were not.

The DWQI decided its first action would be to set limits for PFNA. With data showing that the people of Paulsboro were drinking some of the highest levels in the world, this seemed an obvious place to start. Surprisingly, given PFNA's prevalence in industry and the environment, there was little research for the New Jersey DEP or the DWQI to use in grounding their recommended drinking water standards. As a result, their efforts began with painstaking and groundbreaking research. In July 2015, little more than a year later, the results were in. The standard the scientists would recommend was thirteen parts per trillion (ppt) of PFNA in drinking water.[10]

At the Delaware Riverkeeper Network, we were pleased but still concerned. We knew that at even the lowest level PFAS compounds like PFNA are extremely toxic, can build up in the blood, and can have a negative effect on human health. We also knew that children are at even greater risk. As Tracy explained to the DWQI members, children drink more water per their body weight than adults, creating greater exposure. "At 13 ppt," Tracy clarified, "children will have proportionally greater exposure that can affect their physical and mental development and could mark them for life." Thus, for children and for fetuses developing in the womb, "we need to put in place even greater protections," she concluded.[11]

Ultimately, the decision makers at the New Jersey DEP did not accept the 3 to 5 ppt recommendation my organization was urging. But still, the 13 ppt proposal was tremendous progress. It would take two more years to move through the entire New Jersey DEP rulemaking process. While the rest of the nation was being guided by the US EPA to consider a health advisory level of 70 ppt (a shockingly high level that the EPA has since rejected), New Jersey had put forth the first safe drinking water standard in the nation for a PFAS compound (PFNA), at a level that offered significantly better protection.

As we would later come to learn, the technologies that communities began using to meet the new, lower New Jersey standard would work better than anticipated and would remove PFAS toxins from drinking water to a level that was undetectable by testing labs. So, while the law didn't require the lower levels the Delaware Riverkeeper Network was advocating for, in the end it seemed that technology was getting us there. New Jersey communities were on the way to getting needed protection from this man-made family of toxic contaminants.

While all of this is encouraging, the danger lingers. PFAS toxins are still in the environment, accumulating in our groundwater, soils, vegetation, environments, water supplies, food, and bloodstreams. And although the Biden administration is looking to advance the science with regards to PFAS—in direct contrast to the previous Trump administration, which routinely rejected even the most robust scientific findings when it came to environmental and health issues—the federal government is only advancing a voluntary program to reduce the use of PFAS chemicals. The government has put in place an *advisory* limit for exposure, not an enforceable one. In addition, failing to put in place regulatory standards and relying on government investment to test for and clean up PFAS is just another way of foisting responsibility for addressing the toxic devastation of PFAS onto the public, rather than the industry that has profited so handsomely from their use.[12]

And here's the next shocker: our government has failed to ensure the safety of the replacement chemicals that would be used by US companies—including Solvay, which has wreaked such toxic havoc on Paulsboro. Solvay was among the companies that had participated in the federal voluntary PFAS phaseout program. But it turns out that the chemicals they have been using to replace the phased-out PFAS toxins are even more toxic![13] And so the environmental justice communities in Paulsboro and the surrounding region, which have already been exposed to the highest levels of PFNA in the world, find themselves, yet again, on the front lines of toxic exposure that shamefully has been allowed by our government.

As this toxic health crisis continues, we must confront an uncomfortable fact: legislative and regulatory tools like the Safe Drinking Water Act, the EPA, and state agencies have an abysmal record of protecting our water. Corporate interests are simply too strong, the lure of profits too great. Members of the public—you and me, our friends and families—are left to pay the price. We'll need bigger guns—Green Amendments—if we are to protect our communities from the dangerous chemicals and toxins industry keeps bringing to market.

The Great American Dumping Ground

PFOA represents just one industrial chemical. What other substances might be poisoning us unawares? The answer is, quite a number of them. Across our nation, toxic waste products from industrial operations are ruining our water, land, and air, despite powerful legislation intended to curtail them.

Consider air pollution. Following President Richard Nixon's historic Clean Air Act (1970), air quality improved dramatically in our country's cities and communities. By 1990, this national air quality legislation had prolonged 205,000 American lives, preventing 672,000 instances of chronic bronchitis, twenty-one thousand instances of heart disease, and eighteen million childhood respiratory problems.[14] That year, President George H. W. Bush bolstered the Clean Air Act, putting in place even more rigorous emissions standards. And by 2010, when the nation celebrated the fortieth anniversary of the act, the improved Bush standards had brought us a 41 percent reduction in the six most hazardous airborne toxins; had significantly reduced emissions of volatile organic compounds (31 percent), carbon monoxide (46 percent), and sulfur dioxide (51 percent); and had led to dramatic reductions in diseases related to air exposure (like skin cancer and cataracts), less acid rain, and—it was predicted—some fifty thousand lives saved from particle pollution.[15]

Yet as gratifying as these improvements are, they obscure a more important truth: our air is still terribly polluted. According to the American Lung Association, over 40 percent of Americans are exposed to unhealthy levels of particle pollution or ozone.[16] As is often characteristic of the harmful consequences of pollution, this burden is not shared equitably among our nation's communities. Communities of color are three times more likely than white communities to be breathing the air that is most polluted.[17] Not only does this increased exposure to air pollution inflict direct harm, but it increases the vulnerability of people to other health threats such as the deadly Covid-19 virus; for this and other reasons, communities of color and Indigenous communities have been harder hit by the pandemic than the whiter communities that surround them.

As the story of PFAS highlights, by-products of industrial activity are also polluting our water. How much? That is hard to say. While the Clean Water Act requires states to fully assess the level of pollution contaminating all waterways, they still have not. Remember, it's not illegal to pollute here in the United States; you just need a permit that legalizes what kind and how much pollution you release. And so when we talk about assessment of waterways, that means assessing whether the level of pollution meets the legal limit, not to what degree the waterway is actually fouled.

Only about 30 percent of all streams and rivers have been assessed by government scientists to see if their pollution levels comply with the law; of those assessed, about half do not meet water quality standards. When it comes to lakes, reservoirs, and ponds, only about half have been assessed for the level of pollution they contain, and more than 70 percent of those are over legal pollution limits. When it comes to wetlands, less than 2 percent have even been assessed, so for the most part we don't know their pollution status; of those that have been tested, over 50 percent are too polluted according to the law.[18]

Too often, the data tells us that we are not just exceeding legal pollution standards, but have already allowed our waterways to become contaminated with toxins at dangerous levels. In 2009, a national EPA study of lakes found the presence of noxious toxins—including mercury and polychlorinated biphenyls (PCBs)—in fish sampled at all five hundred randomly selected locations nationwide.[19] Additional data shows that mercury is actually present in most US waterways.[20] PCBs cause cancer, liver damage, and birth defects. They're so harmful that Congress officially banned them in 1979. And mercury is a dangerous neurotoxin that is especially harmful for babies and nursing women, adversely affecting fetal and childhood development.

Kacy Manahan, a senior attorney with the Delaware Riverkeeper Network who has dedicated her career to preventing environmental harm, points out that it is we "the public—those of us who drink water and recreate in rivers, lakes, streams, and wetlands—who are burdened with the unknown risks of government-sanctioned pollution, including the potential synergistic effect of exposure to combinations of multiple pollutants."[21] Kacy is right: contamination of our waterways isn't just creating polluted water; it is contaminating our lives—including the food we eat, our bodies, and the way we feel about being in nature.

For many kids and adults, fishing is a chance to get away from it all—to spend time in nature, test one's skills, and enjoy a break from the bustle of life. In comparison to other hobbies, it can be relatively inexpensive to get started. I have often considered the serene and happy faces of children languishing on the banks of the Delaware River with family or friends, or just on their own, their fishing lines in the water as they await a catch or simply ponder the world around them. For some Indigenous communities, the ability to catch and consume fish is an integral part of their culture and way of life. In Alaska, the Yup'ik, Alutiiq, and Athabaskan peoples have been fishing local waterways for thousands of years, and to this day about half of their diet is made up of wild caught fish.[22]

People used to expect that you could eat any fish caught in our nation's waterways. Not anymore. The rate at which industrial toxins accumulate in fish—a process called "bioaccumulation"—makes them increasingly dangerous to consume. Sometimes toxins even affect the physical development of fish. Anglers can associate these "Frankenfish," as they are sometimes called, with specific waterways. "Oh, that must be a Hudson River fish, because it looks like that," some anglers say, indicating the historic New York waterway. "Oh, it has three eyes. It must come from the Raritan River," note others, referring to one of New Jersey's major watersheds.

Striped bass with offset spines are, unfortunately, a frequent occurrence as well in the New Jersey/New York region. So are pug-nosed bass. When fish have this genetic condition, their faces don't connect with the bottom of their jaws, leaving their lower jaws unnaturally and precariously distended. Few things are scarier for anglers than hooking a great catch only to find it physically deformed, riddled with unnatural growths, body lesions, bleeding ulcerations, or suppurating, cottage cheese–like growths. On second thought, here is something scarier: most chemicals don't produce visible physical effects. Unlike food going bad in your refrigerator, most industrial toxins found in fish—including some of those most hazardous to human health—are undetectable in terms of color, smell, and texture.

In response to dangerous contamination levels in fish flesh, state agencies routinely issue fish advisories, notifying people which fish are safe to consume and in what quantities. Consumers of sport fish in Pennsylvania, for example, are often advised to consume no more than one eight-ounce serving of fish per month so as to allow enough time for the body to naturally purge contaminants. Bottom-dwelling carp and American eel in Pennsylvania's Schuylkill River are so laden with industrial chemicals that the state of Pennsylvania recommends never consuming them.[23] In Washington State, in order to protect pregnant women, nursing mothers, children, and women who may become pregnant, there is a statewide "do not eat" advisory for northern pikeminnow.[24] In Missouri, you might find "do not eat" advisories for sunfish, carp, redhorse suckers, largemouth bass, smallmouth bass, or bottom-feeding fish in some waterways.[25] Additional advisories urge people to limit their consumption of a variety of species over the course of a week, month, or year, in order to prevent contaminants from building up in their bodies and threatening their health.

Search pretty much any state, and you will find such fish advisories. In 2018, for the first time, New Jersey added fish advisories because of PFAS contamination.[26] The ability of PFAS chemicals to cross the placenta makes them particularly concerning for pregnant women and those who might become pregnant, and was, in part, an impetus for the advisory.[27] In October 2021, Pennsylvania followed suit and issued a "do not eat" advisory for fish caught in the Neshaminy Creek, a tributary to the Delaware River, due to high levels of PFAS.[28] As toxins continue to proliferate in our environment and waterways, so too do the number of fish advisories essential to keeping fish-eaters safe.

Recreational anglers—as people who fish for fun are called—have the luxury of throwing back fish that are the subject of a toxic fish advisory rather than taking them home for dinner. But not everyone is so lucky. For subsistence anglers—people who rely on fishing to supplement their diet—much more is at stake. They often must either feed their families contaminated fish or go hungry.

As I've seen along the Delaware River and its tributaries, language barriers and cultural habits compound the problem by limiting understanding of, and compliance with, fish consumption advisories. One Delaware Estuary fish consumption survey revealed that subsistence fishers who fished from shore (as opposed to boats) were often Black, Vietnamese, Cambodian, and Puerto Rican. While white and Black anglers tended to cook their food in compliance with safety regulations (for example, removing belly and back fat, where chemicals concentrate), anglers of other ethnicities consistently consumed more than the recommended amounts of wild fish, thereby endangering their health.[29]

Something is clearly wrong. Companies put the toxins into the environment, generating a tidy profit while doing so. The rest of us pay the price. We pay with our health and with the lost enjoyment of healthy nature, but also through tax-funded cleanups and restorations. In some cases, as with water contamination and fish, the contamination is so serious, so enduring, and so deeply embedded in the natural world, that all we can do is warn people to stay away, as with fish advisories.

It's time to flip the script and focus our laws on preventing harm in the first place—which is, of course, where Green Amendments come in. We need to stop legalized contamination from occurring at such alarming rates that it damages our health. We also need to ensure that companies and governments operate transparently and responsibly to prevent both intentional and accidental harm.

The Making of an Industrial "Accident"

Industrial contaminants are not simply present in our environment because companies and municipalities deliberately and legally release them. They're also there because industrial actors of various kinds have adopted a dangerously cavalier attitude toward disposing of and handling these chemicals. The "accidents" that result threaten our safety and the ability of future generations to enjoy a safe and healthy environment.

On the morning of November 30, 2012, Trisha Sheehan was preparing to receive guests at her Woodbury, New Jersey, home, when she received a frantic call from her mother. "You need to turn on the news. There's been a bad chemical spill," her mom said.[30] A train had derailed in nearby Paulsboro, an industrial town with a marine port and a large oil refinery located southwest of Philadelphia. Unfortunately, the derailment occurred while the freight train was crossing a bridge, sending several of its cars plummeting into the Mantua Creek below, releasing approximately twenty thousand pounds of vinyl chloride into the atmosphere.

Vinyl chloride is the primary ingredient in polyvinyl chloride (i.e., PVC), which is used to create plastics, wire coatings, vinyl floors, and automobile parts. A colorless, highly flammable toxin, vinyl chloride causes neurological problems, respiratory illness, and cancer in human beings. Trisha's family lived downwind from the spill, her home abutting the tidal Mantua Creek where the train cars lay, half submerged. While most parents would shudder at the thought of their children's exposure to such a chemical, news of the spill inspired terror in Trisha, because her children already have chemical sensitivities.

When Trisha first discovered that her children were sensitive to allergens, she wasn't particularly alarmed or anxious. You don't have to be a scientist or public health expert to know that skin, food, and respiratory allergies are on the rise.[31] Most schools and restaurants are aware of the increased prevalence of environmental irritants and now offer an assortment of gluten- and nut-free menu options, nondairy foods, and chemical-free soaps. But in 2009, Trisha began realizing that her case might be unusual. Her sister had just recarpeted a new home. As Trisha left her sister's house after an impromptu housewarming celebration, she was stunned to find her toddler unconscious in his car seat. As she learned from her pediatrician, there were chemicals in rugs and carpeting that were toxic to her baby. For most children and healthy adults, everyday exposures to chemicals in consumer products and environmental toxins have little noticeable effect. But for chemically sensitive children and immunocompromised adults, such exposure is immediately debilitating and, if left untreated, even deadly. When Trisha welcomed her second son in 2011, history seemed to repeat itself, as he exhibited similar signs of sensitivity.

With two chemically sensitive children to care for, Trisha began learning all she could about environmental toxins, allergies, and irritants. When cleaning agents caused her children to break out in rashes, she made her own. She installed air purifiers in her home and spent hours at the grocery store, studiously reading the labels of all food items to ensure they were toxin- and allergen-free. Parenting her children sensitized her to the larger environment and the effect that certain airborne exposures had on her children.

In 2010, Trisha joined the West Jersey/Philadelphia chapter of the Holistic Moms Network (HMN), a national nonprofit organization that helps parents avoid chemicals and take a holistic and varied approach to health. As Trisha's parenting experience had taught her, human health is so much broader than regular doctor visits, dental hygiene, and our vitamin and mineral intake. Our health has larger environmental determinants, like the air we breathe and the chemicals to which we are exposed in our homes, workplaces, and communities. Trisha used HMN to empower her community and other parents; the network gave them access to nontoxic cleaning supplies and food recipes, as well as to the camaraderie of other parents facing similar child-rearing challenges.

On the morning of November 30, Trisha was preparing for an HMN gathering at her home, and she felt empowered. She had taken her knowledge of environmental toxins and transformed her home into a protective cocoon, free of toxins and irritants that might harm her children. But after news of the accident that morning, Trisha felt stunned and helpless. She sprang into action, canceling her plans and her children's playdates, taking every safety precaution and following every protocol to the letter. Community members had not been encouraged to evacuate but were instead instructed to shelter in place. Trisha followed the advice of the government agencies and professionals charged with protecting her community. She locked her doors, fastened her windows, and kept her children close. But she intuitively knew that there was nothing she could do to protect them from an accident of this magnitude.

Even for healthy individuals with no allergies or sensitivities, short-term vinyl chloride exposure is dangerous, causing eye and throat irritation, difficulty breathing, dizziness, loss of consciousness, and even death. Occupational studies on long-term exposure suggest that the substance accumulates in workers' livers, heightening their chances of developing lung cancer, a rare type of liver cancer (hepatic angiosarcoma), brain cancer, leukemia, and lymphoma.[32] Given that most vinyl chloride exposure results from workplace conditions, most research is focused on adults who work in PVC facilities or other heavy industries. There was little study indicating what Trisha's children and the larger Paulsboro community should have expected following such an extreme vinyl chloride exposure. According to the guidelines of the federal Occupational Safety and Health Administration (OSHA), the highest level an industrial worker should be exposed to is five parts per million, for no more than fifteen minutes at a time. Following the accident, a visible cloud of vinyl chloride encased the community, posing long-term health concerns to everyone there. Exposure rates were in the thousands of parts per million!

The derailment wasn't merely a tragic accident—it was the result of shortsightedness and negligence. As the freight train bearing toxic chemicals approached the movable bridge that November morning, the light was red. A red signal indicated that the rail lines weren't properly aligned and locked into place. As the National Transportation Safety Board report indicates, "The conductor inspected the bridge and erroneously concluded it was properly locked to prevent movement."[33] But the conductor lacked the expertise or qualifications to make such an assessment. On his command, the train barreled through the red light on misaligned train tracks and predictably swiveled, sending several freight cars plummeting into the water below.

The public health and safety response following the derailment was just as negligent as the original accident. Emergency response protocols dictated, for example, that following an accident of this magnitude, all people residing within a half-mile radius of the crash must be evacuated. And yet people residing in most parts of the contaminated zone weren't asked to leave. Perhaps given a false sense of security driven by this seeming lack of urgency coming from government officials, elderly residents tended to their gardens, and children played outside and walked home from school, with no breathing apparatus or other precautions. First responders, told they didn't need to take special precautions in dealing with the airborne toxin, worked without hazmat suits or breathing apparatus. On a street running parallel to Mantua Creek, police and health officials offered protective gear—but on one side only. Walking down that side, you had to put on a mask; if you crossed to the other side, no mask was proffered. They acted as if a detoxifying curtain ran down the middle of the road, providing a barrier of protection. Of course, that wasn't at all true.

Even downwind in a neighboring town, shuttered in her home, Trisha and her family began exhibiting the telltale symptoms of vinyl chloride exposure. "We were vomiting, our eyes were watering, and it felt like there was a band around our head, the pain was so severe," she recalls.[34] After the spill, people around Paulsboro coughed and wheezed for weeks. Local Paulsboro residents visited their local health providers for relief and were consistently told they had seasonal colds or allergies. "You have bronchitis. It's that time of year. It's seasonal," was a typical response. Trisha repeatedly called a nurse's hotline, asking for relief from her nausea, vomiting, and migraines. "You can go see your family doctor, or go to the hospital and they will treat you," the hotline nurse told her. After a week of ongoing symptoms, Trisha left her home to seek care at her family doctor. But she also fundamentally didn't understand what was going on.

Community air quality notices in the area showed that toxicity levels were well under safe thresholds. Environmental attorney Mark Cuker, who represented over a thousand people affected by the accident, confirmed that exposure levels advertised on the Paulsboro Response website were false. The website indicated that the highest detected levels were "hundreds of times lower" than what the EPA deemed to be harmful. In actuality, the levels were dangerously high.

To make matters worse, air quality was inconsistent. Approximately five thousand pounds of vinyl chloride remained submerged in one of the freight train cars in the Mantua Creek. In the two weeks following the accident, first responders and emergency professionals tried to dislodge the car from the creek. Each time this occurred, there would be an "evacuation" of vinyl chloride. Trisha recalls that each time this chemical evacuation happened (without warning to the community), her sore throat and respiratory symptoms flared. The repeated eruptions caused dizziness and confusion as those two weeks wore on. One evening when Trisha's husband returned from work, he looked at her blankly and asked, "Have you been drinking?" Trisha was intoxicated and delirious, but not from recreational alcohol consumption. That evening she passed out, only to wake up later, vomiting and with a migraine.

The Consolidated Rail Corporation (Conrail), which owned the train and the malfunctioning bridge, took action to shield itself from legal liability. Immediately after the spill, railroad representatives visited doctors, telling them that the train derailment couldn't possibly have caused the physical complaints they were seeing in the community. Medical officials heeded this "expert advice" and told clients like Trisha that they had a seasonal cold or bronchitis. For this reason, many were misdiagnosed.[35] Conrail also hosted meetings with pizza and soda, offering families $500 vouchers in exchange for signing a waiver promising they wouldn't sue the company. If you were in the small evacuation zone, the company offered $2,500 a head. Many in this hardworking, largely low-income community took the money out of need, perceiving it as a windfall. Local families collected these checks for themselves and on behalf of their children. But if they ever develop angiosarcoma of the liver or any of the long-term respiratory conditions associated with their exposure, they are prohibited from suing.

As time passed, more side effects of vinyl chloride exposure manifested. In the spring of 2013, about six months following the accident, Trisha's youngest son began suffering dangerous nosebleeds. As she later discovered, these were the same symptoms that the children who had walked through the vinyl chloride plume were exhibiting. In 2016, a kindergarten teacher asked Trisha, "Do you know your son has short-term memory loss?" A public health policy expert later informed her that memory loss was one of vinyl chloride's many side effects.

The chemical sensitivities of Trisha's children did not make them uniquely susceptible to the hazards of a vinyl chloride spill. It just meant that Trisha was more aware when things went awry, and that her family suffered the effects more acutely and quickly than others. Many people exposed that day suffer now and will continue to suffer in the future. Reactive airway dysfunction syndrome (RADS)—an unusual disease causing long-term, severe respiratory problems—and other chronic respiratory illnesses are among the health conditions experienced by first responders and residents alike. For many, it's a waiting game, to see if even greater hardship and disease manifest.

"Cancer is big on my mind, and whether or not we will end up with the rare form of liver cancer that vinyl chloride causes," Trisha says. "I shouldn't have to worry about my three-year-old getting cancer from a chemical that was released nearby that he breathed in, in his own home."[36]

The Paulsboro train derailment should never have happened. Conrail officials responsible for managing the bridge should never have acted with such nonchalance in the accident's wake, thereby elevating the cancer risks and long-term respiratory illnesses for community residents and first responders. The negligent company took advantage of the rampant misinformation, falsely reassuring the public and shielding itself from liability. Government officials failed to take adequate precautions. Health officials, firefighters, police officers, and school administrators weren't given the information they needed about the astronomical levels of vinyl chloride that had erupted into the atmosphere, and were therefore unable to protect the long-term health of the larger community.

Now, you might read the Paulsboro story and think, "How awful! But at least *my* community is safe." But is it? What kinds of industrial operations exist in and around where you live? And what kinds of chemicals do these operations handle? According to one estimate, about nine million Americans, including a disproportionate share of people of color, "live in neighborhoods within three kilometers of large commercial hazardous waste facilities," and "thousands of additional towns are near other major sources of pollution, including refineries, chemical plants, freeways and ports."[37] But as we explore throughout this book, you don't have to be located in an industrial corridor or in close proximity to hazardous facilities to be at risk. Remember James Baker from chapter 4, who—like Trisha Sheehan and her family—was just sitting at home one day when he was injured by a nearby "accident"? Given how lax industry routinely is in handling their chemicals and operations, and how lackadaisical government has been in regulating industry, such incidents might well happen in your community one day.

Foaming Up Our Water Supplies

I've pointed to the gross failure of government and our laws to prevent pollution. More disturbing? Sometimes government itself is the polluter.

In the mid-1960s, the 3M Company partnered with the US Navy to engineer an ingenious product that would help suppress airplane fires, making military personnel safer while fighting wars abroad.[38] They created aqueous film-forming foam (AFFF), which the US military has stockpiled in large quantities since the 1970s. Toxic PFAS chemicals were among the foam's key active ingredients. AFFF is used frequently when conducting military foam testing exercises, during which the military simulates an emergency, creating a huge fire on one of its bases and marshaling copious amounts of foam to suppress it. These exercises often take place in cavernous indoor airplane hangars, which become filled with AFFF from floor to ceiling. Throughout these drills, military personnel constantly release the foam until the fire is suppressed. Then they rinse it away, sending it down the drain and into the environment.[39]

For years, nearby residents were oblivious to the risks. Children residing just north of Philadelphia, near military bases located in Warminster, Horsham, and Warrington, used to look forward to the days when magical foam, resembling spools of white cotton candy, trickled down from the sky. As it accumulated throughout the town, children spent the day frolicking in the substance, staging mock foam battles, and using it as lubricant to slide down sidewalks and hills.[40] But make no mistake—the foam is anything but safe. The military has long known about its toxicity but, like DuPont, chose to expose its own people and the public at large in order to serve its own goals.[41] As one 2016 investigation revealed, "Studies by the Air Force as far back as 1979 demonstrated the chemical was harmful to laboratory animals, causing liver damage, cellular damage and low birth weight of offspring."[42] These studies revealed damage to the animal subjects' "thymus, bone marrow, stomach, mesentery, [and] liver, and testes in the male rats."

Later, research demonstrated that female rats and their young were also harmed, with some offspring suffering low birth weights and other pregnant females perishing before they could give birth. Throughout the 1990s, the Army Corps of Engineers, responsible for overseeing matters of environmental policy and regulation on behalf of the military, told the Air Force to stop using perfluorooctanesulfonic acid, or PFOS (a member of the PFAS family of chemicals), warning it was "harmful to the environment." "Despite alarming findings," details one news report, "the service kept using it, leading it to seep into drinking water in Colorado and around the globe."[43] In 2001, fire-foam specialists, manufacturers, and the military acknowledged that PFOS was "persistent, bioaccumulating, and toxic."[44] Thanks to the military's continuous usage of toxin-laden foam for decades after it knew of its toxicity, water in many local areas has been contaminated. And so too have the bodies of neighbors and military service members. Air Force base fire chief

Steve Kjonaas was involved in many foam exercises during his nearly thirty-year career at the Peterson base in Colorado Springs. His career ended in 2007 when he developed prostate cancer. Speaking of the foam contamination, he said that he did "feel like a lab rat."[45]

The number of known military bases causing problems for water resources is significant. According to the US Department of Defense and the US Government Accountability Office, as of the end of 2020, a known or suspected release of PFAS chemicals occurred at 687 military installations.[46] Those who are serving in our nation's armed forces find themselves exposed to this dangerous toxin at higher rates because of such prolific use. How can that be? When service members sign up to put their lives on the line for our nation, surely it is not so we can then sacrifice their healthy bodies and lives to toxic chemicals. (More to come in chapter 9 on this sad reality.)

Naturally, it is not just military personnel who are being invasively harmed by PFAS used on military sites. Communities near these facilities show some of the highest PFAS contamination rates in the nation. In Pennsylvania's Bucks and Montgomery Counties alone, more than eighty-five thousand people have been exposed to PFAS chemicals.[47] When faced with the emerging data of their exposure to PFOA, these communities started to connect the dots. They thought about all of the illnesses they had experienced in their families and communities and wondered if they now knew the reason: exposure to PFAS chemicals— and it was totally legal.

Residents began to demand answers and action. Inspired by our success in New Jersey, the Delaware Riverkeeper Network filed a petition with Pennsylvania's Environmental Quality Board—a body that played a similar role to the New Jersey Drinking Water Quality Institute. Our petition was later complemented by legal action demanding that Pennsylvania put in place enforceable drinking water protections from PFOA. Among our assertions: that the state is required to act under existing law, and that Pennsylvania's constitution, article 1, section 27, obligates the state to protect the people's right to pure water and a healthy environment.[48]

Nationwide, as more information emerges about the role of the military and industry in spreading this toxic chemical epidemic, public demand mounts for safe water and groundwater, and for environmental cleanup—as well as for blood testing, health studies, and meaningful government action. Yet while Canada and the European Union have outlawed PFAS chemicals because of their toxicity, many US military bases continue to employ the substances in their firefighting materials despite recent legislation requiring the military to begin phasing out use of PFAS chemicals in 2024.[49]

For far too many, awareness and action comes too late. Tracy Carluccio recalls getting a phone call from then-congressman Mike Fitzpatrick about the PFOA contamination now recognized in Bucks County. She recalls the congressman exclaiming, "Oh my God, my parents lived there, and I grew up there." Congressman Fitzpatrick had just won a battle with colorectal cancer and seemed moved to act powerfully on this issue. Colorectal cancer is among those illnesses linked with PFOA exposure. The congressman had vowed and worked to secure a stronger EPA response for his Bucks County constituents. Sadly, he would not see this work through. A few years later, he succumbed to yet another bout with cancer.[50] Was it due to lifelong exposure to PFOA in his water and community? We can't really know. But many think the answer is obvious.

Innocent until Proven Guilty?

Cynics might expect that large corporations would put profits over people, but how could the US government expose its people to toxic chemicals for decades? For that matter, how can it continue to do so? Isn't the military's mission to *protect* the safety and security of the American people? Aren't legislators elected and agency employees hired to protect and serve the interests of the people?

Given our country's troubling lack of environmental oversight, the answers to these questions are eminently unsatisfying. Despite compelling evidence that conclusively demonstrated the toxicity of PFAS and its harm to human health, the Army continued to use it and the US EPA failed to act with needed mandatory and enforceable protections. Even in the face of public fury and mounting water emergencies, it wasn't until major manufacturers voluntarily agreed to phase out the use of certain PFAS chemicals by 2015 that we started to see some action. In the intervening years, children kept frolicking in the magical foam—and Americans at large consumed infected fish, drank contaminated water, and served homemade dinners to their friends and loved ones using their sleek, PFOA-laden Teflon pans.

Dismayingly, the EPA's next step has not been to ban or regulate PFAS chemicals. Instead, it has only suggested health advisory limits to guide the actions of industry and state government. Until recently, the recommended limit for all PFAS chemicals was five times higher than the limit New Jersey has implemented to protect its population, and fifteen times higher than the levels that Delaware Riverkeeper Network experts said are needed to protect children. Although it has still not set enforceable protective standards, in June of 2022, EPA began the process of strengthening the health advisories for at least two PFAS chemicals. Based on scientific research, EPA has put forth updated health advisory levels of 0.004 ppt for PFOA and 0.02 ppt for PFOS, either singly or combined. And its updated advisories also include two compounds that some companies are using as replacements for PFAS: GenX compounds and Perfluorobutane sulfonate (PFBS). These strengthened recommendations send a message that stronger protections are needed. The update also confirms what communities, activists, and scientists have been saying for years: PFAS chemicals in drinking water have impacts at even miniscule levels. But notably, these advisory levels only apply to a small subset of the toxic family and are still just that—advisory. They are neither regulatory nor enforceable, and so whether they create change or not is left to the political will of state governments or the goodwill of industry.

Recognizing the absence of strong federal leadership, action has been advancing at the state level, but there, too, progress is painfully slow. As of June 2021, only five states had joined New Jersey in setting enforceable maximum contaminant levels for a handful of the top PFAS chemicals, although six other states are now in the process of considering and/or pursuing this option. Still, sadly, most states, much like the federal government, are only offering guidance or guidelines. Some are requiring notification of PFAS contamination. Others are taking no meaningful action whatsoever.[51] All the while, the scope of the PFAS problem grows and spreads through our water and our food.

In fact, PFAS is proliferating in unexpected ways. In Maine, the Tozier farm was among those that had used municipal sewage sludge for fertilizer as part of a state-sponsored program. The farm would later learn that the sludge contained not only helpful nutrients but dangerous PFOS contamination as well. (Recall that PFOS is a member of the PFAS family of chemicals.) In time, this PFOS contaminated the farm's water, and then its beef and dairy cows. By 2020, due to "very startling" levels of PFOS, ranging from 12,700 ppt to 32,200 ppt, the farm's milk and beef was deemed unfit for sale. A few years before, the Stoneridge Farm elsewhere in the state had faced a similar story and fate. No longer able to sell its products, the farm was ultimately forced to shut down altogether.[52]

It's not just farmers in Maine who are being affected. Wherever PFAS contamination exists, there is danger, harm, and heartache. Due to PFAS contamination, the Clovis farm in New Mexico was dumping fifteen thousand gallons of milk a day, reportedly enough to "provide a carton at lunch to 240,000 children." By March 2021, Art Schaap, the owner of the farm, calculated he had been forced to discard seventy-two million pounds of PFAS-contaminated milk—that's about "1,500 semi-loads of milk." "This has poisoned everything I've worked for and everything I care about," Mr. Schaap has reported. "I can't sell the milk. I can't sell beef. I can't sell the cows. I can't sell crops or my property." He estimates that by 2021, he had lost $11 million in revenue, all because of PFAS.[53] And the damage is not just to the farm; a spreading pollution plume now creeps toward the largest aquifer in the nation, the Ogallala Aquifer, which underlies eight states.[54]

Unbelievably, it doesn't end with beef, milk, fish, and drinking water. In 2021, Maine issued a "do not eat" advisory for deer in portions of the state due to PFAS contamination found in their flesh. Again, municipal and industrial sewage sludge contaminated with PFAS spread on farm fields was the culprit. Deer eating on and around the farm fields became dangerously infected—so much so that even deer killed prior to the advisory must be discarded. The flesh cannot be used to feed anyone's family; it's just trash.[55]

At this point, PFAS contamination is ubiquitous. As of 2021, the Environmental Working Group reports PFAS contamination has been found in all 50 states and two US territories.[56] Multiple European countries, the Middle East, and Asia are also contaminated. PFAS is even found "in the blood or vital organs of Atlantic salmon, swordfish, . . . Alaskan polar bears, brown pelicans, sea turtles, sea eagles, . . . and Laysan albatrosses on Sand Island, a wildlife refuge on Midway Atoll, in the middle of the North Pacific Ocean."[57]

With water pollution and toxic contamination, as with so many environmental issues, our legislative protections have consistently failed us. Indeed, they have provided us with only the illusion of environmental protection. Under current rules, the EPA must play regulatory defense, testing waterborne chemicals only if they have already demonstrated large-scale harm. In fact, as journalist Sharon Lerner describes, "In America, killer chemicals are essentially innocent until proven guilty."[58] While this might be a compelling standard for criminal justice, it doesn't work for water quality.

Part of the problem is "regulatory capture"—that is, when government officials or a government agency that is supposed to serve the public good instead sets about advancing the needs, goals, and desires of industry. This happened to the extreme in the DuPont case. We see it today in Pennsylvania, New Mexico, and Texas, among other states, where the fossil fuel industry reigns supreme in the halls of government.

It wasn't supposed to be like this. The Safe Drinking Water Act, for example, which passed in 1974 at the height of the global environmental

movement, provided the EPA with a strong mandate to proactively protect our country's drinking water.[59] The regulatory body went to work,
identifying the various microbes, chemicals, and carcinogens hidden in
our water. From 1986 to 1996, the EPA identified and monitored nearly
one hundred chemicals. Water utilities, however, complained about the
financial burdens and "red tape" that such oversight caused. In response,
in 1996, Congress curtailed the EPA's powers, making it difficult for the
agency to regulate any emerging toxins. Since then, the EPA has gone
from playing offense to defense, monitoring and determining it would
regulate only one hazardous chemical—perchlorate, which is used to
create explosives, and which infected the water of millions of Americans. Roughly one hundred other industrial substances that the EPA has
identified as toxins remain unregulated. And in 2020, the EPA decided
that even perchlorate was off the table and rescinded its decision to regulate it.[60] We have no knowledge of when the next PFOA-style outbreak
will surface, creating a public health nightmare and further degrading
our environment—although it's starting to look like the replacements for
PFOA and other PFAS chemicals could well be it. And sadly, our government is just as ill prepared to respond today as it has been in the past.

Making Precaution a Guiding Principle

As we've seen throughout this book, many victims of environmental
degradation face insurmountable odds as they try to protect themselves
or redress grievances after they've been wronged. At first, when environmental attorney Rob Bilott tried to initiate a class-action lawsuit on
behalf of individuals contaminated with PFOA, he was at a loss. How
could he demonstrate that people were harmed by something that the
federal government didn't even regulate?

The legislators who drafted the Safe Drinking Water Act, the Toxic
Substances Control Act, and other environmental laws may have had the
best of intentions. But over the years, industry has increasingly gained the
upper hand. They simply have more money and more access to experts

and lawyers willing to make their case. Furthermore, there are more legislators working to weaken regulations under false claims of economic
hardship, and more regulators willing to overlook enforcement needs or
to simply give industry a slap on the wrist when major penalties or even
criminal enforcement are warranted. Others, of course, deserve credit
for stepping into the breach. Under some administrations, the EPA has
filed lawsuits, some states and their scientists have worked for stricter
and stronger standards, and watchdog organizations like the Delaware
Riverkeeper Network have advocated and organized for needed environmental protection, filing lawsuits that try to stimulate change when
all else failed. But these efforts aren't remotely sufficient. Our waterways,
air, and landscapes remain contaminated, with more pollution being discharged legally and illegally every day.

To secure our health and the planet's future, we must turn to our
constitutions.

With a Green Amendment in place in New Jersey during the PFOA
debacle, we could have brought a compelling claim to the courts, arguing
that the government's failure to regulate PFOA amounted to a violation of its supreme mandate to ensure a healthy and safe environment.
We might have had the authority to prevent a gubernatorial administration from disbanding the New Jersey DWQI tasked with studying and
recommending drinking water standards that keep people safe. With a
Green Amendment, "when the people speak out and demand protection
of our rights, the government is required to take heed. The government's
ability to govern exists only because we granted it, and the government
may not act contrary to our rights," explains Delaware Riverkeeper Network attorney Kacy Manahan.[61]

In Pennsylvania, when we put forth the legal claim that the state's
failure to install protections from PFAS amounted to a constitutional violation of environmental rights, we didn't have to wait for a final decision
from the courts to spark government action. A year after our 2017 petition was filed with the state Environmental Quality Board, the governor
signed an executive order creating a PFAS action team, with the very first

clause of the order citing the Pennsylvania Green Amendment as foundational to the effort.[62] To keep the heat on, the Delaware Riverkeeper Network continued our advocacy and pursued our legal challenge to the slow pace of state-level action. The Pennsylvania DEP paid heed, and ultimately recommended new maximum contaminant levels for two PFAS compounds—PFOA and PFOS. Our advocacy and litigation, combined with the power of the Pennsylvania Constitution, forced the state to kick into gear, and we anticipate enforceable standards will be forthcoming.

With the help of our constitutions, we can secure use of the precautionary principle, avoiding action unless all potential environmental consequences are proven positive and safe in the environmental context, adding it to the government's mandate rather than turning our communities into testing grounds. With robust Green Amendments in place, we can go from leaving emerging toxins unregulated to treating them like new pharmaceuticals. Think about it: GlaxoSmithKline or Eli Lilly & Company can't simply manufacture a new drug and then advertise it to consumers. Pharmaceutical companies must perform rigorous scientific studies proving their products safe before bringing them to market. As anyone who has encountered drug advertisements knows, pharmaceutical companies must also disclose all conceivable side effects their products might produce. Shouldn't such rigorous science and protection apply to all industries?

Constitutional Green Amendments won't just create a tool for securing new protections; they will strengthen all the laws already on the books. Political and industry objectives will no longer reign supreme. Laws passed to protect our water and air will now be applied in service of constitutional rights. And not just to prevent pollution, but to protect nature in its entirety. As we'll explore in the next chapter, across our nation, we're rushing to build and pave over our natural spaces. Despite the laws and regulations ostensibly in place to protect the healthy nature we all need, we're literally paving over paradise to a frightening extent. This too needs to stop—and with Green Amendments in place, increasingly it will.

CHAPTER SIX

THE PAVING OF AMERICA

In 1987, a young couple—Kate and Larry Stauffer—were looking to buy a starter house. When they drove through General Warren Village, located in East Whiteland Township, Chester County, Pennsylvania, they knew they had found their new home. The village was a quiet neighborhood on a dead-end street with mature trees, where they could afford a nice-sized piece of land along with a quaint little house. Kate and Larry were planning to start a family, so the presence of other young couples with kids sealed the deal. What Kate and Larry didn't know was that they were moving in next to a toxic site, one that state officials had already flagged as a source of oozing and ongoing pollution.[1]

In 1972, government officials found elevated levels of fluoride in Little Valley Creek, the gentle stream that flows along the border of General Warren Village. Agency regulators, looking for the source of the contamination, traced it back to the Bishop Tube Company, a manufacturer of stainless-steel pipes located on a thirteen-acre parcel through which the creek flowed—a parcel that neighbored the home that would later become the Stauffers's.[2] Elevated fluoride was only the first hint that the Bishop Tube plant was spewing harmful contaminants into the environment and neighboring communities. In time, nearby residents would come to learn that the creek and their community were being infused with an industrial solvent called TCE and other contaminants oozing from Bishop Tube.

The federal EPA began studying TCE in the 1990s, querying its possible effects on people. According to journalist Ralph Vartabedian, who broke a two-part exposé on the chemical for the *Los Angeles Times*, EPA officials determined that "trichloroethylene, or TCE, was as much as 40 times more likely to cause cancer than the EPA had previously believed."[3] As the EPA planned to alert the public and control the substance, the US Department of Defense intervened. Apparently, over a thousand military bases were contaminated with TCE, and the EPA's actions would prove onerous from a financial and public relations standpoint. The EPA, under the stewardship of President George W. Bush administration officials supportive of the Defense Department, was powerless to continue its work. "As a result," notes Vartabedian, "any conclusion about whether millions of Americans were being contaminated by TCE was delayed indefinitely."[4]

But ignoring TCE didn't make it go away. According to TCE expert and Boston University epidemiologist David Ozonoff, it just meant more unexplained birth defects and cancer in the country. "It is a World Trade Center in slow motion," noted Ozonoff. "You would never notice it."[5]

University of California San Francisco environmental medicine expert and Natural Resources Defense Council scientist Dr. Gina Solomon concurred. "The evidence on TCE is overwhelming," she said. "We have 80 epidemiological studies and hundreds of toxicology studies. They are fairly consistent in finding cancer risks that cover a range of tumors."[6] The White House provided a large grant to the National Academy of Sciences to study the substance in 2004. In 2007, it linked the chemical to many human diseases, and in 2011, the EPA belatedly classified TCE as a "human carcinogen."[7]

Unbeknownst to Chester County residents, including those in General Warren Village, Bishop Tube was using TCE all along—lots of it. During the manufacturing process, the company "pickled" its pipes, bathing the stainless steel in an acidic chemical bath laced with TCE. The toxin also figured prominently in the final part of the pipe preparation, known as degreasing, when the finished products soaked in a giant vat of TCE.[8] Keith Hartman, a longtime company employee, angrily describes TCE's ubiquity on company grounds and notes that people interfaced with the substance without covering their skin, utterly unaware of any danger. David Worst, a seventeen-year Bishop Tube veteran (1972 to 1989), likewise describes seeing open-waste pits, spills, and other "hot spots" of TCE contamination.[9] He and his coworkers were shocked to learn that while the company was purchasing clean water for communities nearby to use (concerned that water in these communities had been contaminated), it failed to take similar protective steps for its own workers.

Other residents of East Whiteland Township interfaced with the site, too. Paula Warren lived nearby since she was born in 1951—the same year that Bishop Tube began its operations.[10] She still vividly remembers the day in 1972 when she and her cousin Dale swam in Little Valley Creek, located approximately ten thousand feet from her home. As they wound their way down the stream, they gazed in disbelief at the fluorescent blue-green water issuing from a nearby culvert. They traced the water to its source—a place called Bishop Tube. They excitedly told their family about it, and no one even considered that it could be deadly. "If only," Paula says, shaking her head in regret.

In 1990, Paula received notice that her family's well water, which they had been innocently consuming since 1953, was contaminated with dangerous levels of TCE and many other carcinogens. The Philadelphia Suburban Water Company told her family to thereafter "minimize consumption." Paula's small family of two parents and three children, who had no predisposition for cancer, developed five different types. Her brother and mother ultimately died of the disease. Twenty-seven years after Paula's initial contamination notice arrived, the groundwater still tests positive for high levels of TCE.

Besides rendering her family's beautiful 1.1 acres practically worthless, the toxic groundwater has taken a physical toll. Memory loss, chronic vertigo, headaches, decreased mental function, brain fog, and liver failure—her family has experienced them all. These are precisely the kinds of illnesses that the scientific literature has associated with TCE exposure.[11]

Living approximately a hundred yards from the plant over years of its operation, Kate and Larry Stauffer noticed intermittent chlorine-like smells around their property, but thought little of it.[12] "We were busy raising a family and didn't pay too much attention to what was going on," Larry remembers.

The plant closed in 1999, when the couple's oldest son, Nicholas, was in high school. He often joined his friends to hang out in the facility's abandoned buildings. The Stauffers's daughter, Liz, who was born in 1990, played in nearby Little Valley Creek—the same creek that was later found to be heavily contaminated from the site. All three Stauffer children collected rocks from the creek for a geology unit in their middle-school science classes. On his daily walk with the dogs, Larry sometimes noticed overwhelming chemical smells coming from the buildings. He and Kate discouraged their children from playing in these areas, but as they later learned, people didn't have to enter the buildings to be exposed to toxins from Bishop Tube's operations.

Since 2006, Liz has been diagnosed with three brain tumors. Kate and Larry aren't positive whether they can blame Bishop Tube for their daughter's cancer. Because of the many toxins and contaminants in our environment, medical and legal professionals often can't conclusively link individual toxins and specific health outcomes. The Stauffers nonetheless find it eerie that so many in nearby neighborhoods have suffered serious illnesses, including other children. Five neighborhood children received cancer diagnoses within a year of each other, including Liz's friend from down the road. After conducting their own research, the Stauffers found TCE exposure has been linked to central nervous system defects. Although Liz is thankfully in remission now, many others in the small community continue to suffer from life-threatening illnesses.

David Worst is one of those individuals. He suffers from an incurable cancer, and many of his former coworkers have died from cancer or other neurological diseases. After retiring from Bishop Tube, Keith Hartman, like his father who also worked at the plant, experienced increasingly debilitating symptoms similar to those of Parkinson's disease. Research has shown strong evidence linking TCE with a group of nervous system disorders called parkinsonism, which have symptoms like Parkinson's. Although he often struggled to walk and even breathe, Keith would come to community meetings to talk about the Bishop Tube site—until he died at the early age of sixty-two. Keith made it clear until his last days that he believed his crippling illness, and his ultimate death, were related to his years working at the site.

Desperately Seeking a Clean, Green Oasis

Given its toxic history, what should become of the Bishop Tube site?

In 2005, developer J. Brian O'Neill began surveying the property, hoping to entice another commercial operation to move in.[13] When that didn't materialize, he flirted with the idea of converting the site into an athletic complex.[14] O'Neill eventually discarded those plans, applying to rezone the site as residential space, where his firm envisioned building over two hundred townhomes. Lacking a full appreciation for the level of contamination at the site, and without help from the state Department of Environmental Protection to understand either the site's supersaturated toxic condition or how incredibly difficult it would be to secure a meaningful and safe level of cleanup, the township was persuaded by O'Neill to rezone the site for residential development. O'Neill was quick to act on the change in zoning and pursue his residential development plans, including applying for a variance from the township needed to accommodate elements of his building proposal. According to the proposed plan, O'Neill's firm would cut trees and excavate the natural areas that cover much of the site to accommodate homes, roads, driveways, and lawns.

As contaminated as the land may be, the Bishop Tube site and its surrounding woodlands and wetlands are the only open space available to this segment of the East Whiteland community. It's the only place where residents can hear the birds, see the trees, and enjoy nature's serenity. Residents weren't happy about the prospect of losing their oasis of natural green space to a development project. Community members became increasingly alarmed as they learned about the site's toxic condition, a situation that started to emerge only as the development proposal advanced through the township approval process. Alarm turned to anger as they discovered the inadequate cleanup measures that O'Neill planned to undertake before breaking ground. But the community was positively outraged when it became clear that both township officials and the Pennsylvania DEP were going along with O'Neill's development plan.

The site's contamination extends through saturated soils, down to bedrock, and infuses toxins into groundwater supplies and the Little Valley Creek. TCE compounds have been found at fifty, two hundred, and even more than three hundred feet below the ground's surface. O'Neill planned to remediate contamination from only a portion of the site, and these efforts would extend only to soils approximately seven to twenty-five feet below the Earth's surface.[15] At one community meeting, Larry Stauffer asked O'Neill's lawyer if the company had tested the whole site for contaminants. As community members recall, the lawyer said the company was testing only what the state DEP required—not the entire site. O'Neill remained adamant that he would only address identified hotspots. There was also talk of vapor barriers to prevent potentially harmful fumes from entering the new town houses to be built. But the actual plan remained unclear.

O'Neill continually referenced other wealthy corporate entities responsible for cleaning up the site contamination, including the deep layers that—if left unaddressed—would continue to endure and release contamination over time. But there was no clarity on who these folks were and no recognition that, up until that point, the Pennsylvania DEP had done little to advance their cleanup responsibilities. O'Neill would reference these other unknown entities and characterize their obligations and his own as he saw fit, all in an effort to secure township approval of his development regardless of the ongoing site contamination.

Missing from the township meetings were Pennsylvania DEP staffers to help fact-check what was being said, and to explain the mandates of the law for ensuring site cleanup. Johnson Matthey and Whitaker Corporation were among the former owners of the site that, under state law, shouldered obligations for cleanup. But their obligation did not require them to clean the site up to what is known as a "residential standard" to ensure its safety for homes and families. Rather than secure plans from all responsible parties to clean up the toxic contamination, Pennsylvania DEP had spent its time negotiating an agreement that opened the door for the site's development by O'Neill regardless of its contaminated condition. This meant that if O'Neill's development was approved, it would be for a site plagued by contaminated groundwater and tainted soils, including areas of contamination so deep that even the fractures in underground bedrock were saturated. It would mean that government had approved the construction of homes for families on a site known to be highly contaminated and for which no remediation plan yet existed. To David Worst, the Stauffers, and the other residents of East Whiteland, this outcome was a betrayal of trust in their government.

It was clear to the community that the site would remain dangerously contaminated, and not fully cleaned up, as part of O'Neill's development plans. They also realized that no one could answer the question of when they might expect full remediation, or anything close to it. It seemed that Pennsylvania DEP was helping O'Neill advance his development, and allowing responsible parties—including O'Neill, Johnson Matthey, and Whittaker Corporation—to evade the full cleanup the community was legally and morally entitled to. For those at the decision-making table, protection of the neighboring residents seemed like an afterthought (if it was a thought at all).

Further questions arose about how O'Neill's development plan would impact future attempts to remediate groundwater, Little Valley Creek, and other contaminated areas associated with the site. At public meeting after meeting, residents expressed fear that limited remediation efforts would further expose the community, including children, to toxins. What would happen when children were playing in a nearby backyard and the company started digging into the contaminated ground? Would more toxins be released into the air or the creek as the site was developed? What about the health of the children in new families buying homes built on a still-contaminated site? Could O'Neill, his representatives, and the various government officials imagine (community members would ask) raising their families in that kind of environment?

When residents raised their questions, fears, and concerns, O'Neill and his spokespeople were defiant, telling the community that no one would be willing to do a better job than he would.

When the residents of East Whiteland contacted me in early 2017 about the contamination and proposed development of the Bishop Tube site, they felt besieged. It's hard to understand the state and federal laws that deal with toxic contaminated sites—even environmental advocates and attorneys like me who work 24/7 on environmental protection issues have difficulty. In this case, layered on top was another rigmarole of land development regulations. The community had little experience organizing itself, and it couldn't secure the expensive scientific and legal expertise necessary to pursue its interest in a healthy environment. Further, residents felt as if government officials charged with serving the community either weren't listening or weren't prioritizing the community's best interests. They weren't wrong.

I and my Delaware Riverkeeper Network joined forces with the community to fight for site cleanup and its preservation as natural open space. Brian O'Neill was not happy about my intervention or the community's increasingly organized and effective response to his plans. O'Neill went so far as to file a legal action to try to silence me, my organization, and other "to be named" members of the community, asserting we were spreading misinformation that was causing him harm. At each round of this litigation, however, the judges sided with us, protecting our rights to free speech and confirming that our assertions were true and accurate. Still, the filing of the suit was scary for the residents. Had the Delaware Riverkeeper Network not been there to defend their rights, O'Neill may very well have gotten his wish: that they sit down and shut up. But I had faced these strategic lawsuits in the past and would face them in the future, and I was not going to allow our efforts with the community to be silenced.

In the spring of 2017, when the zoning hearing board granted portions of O'Neill's variance request with limitations, he scaled down his proposed footprint but still crammed in dense development of residential homes. From there, the question of whether or not to approve the development went to the township's Board of Supervisors. The Stauffers and Peggy Miros, a close neighbor, along with a dedicated band of residents, urged the township to hold off on offering approval, at least until the full plan for site remediation by all responsible parties was developed and known. But the township solicitor told the community that the law allows the developer to press for a decision, and O'Neill was doing just that. They had to vote.

"What does it say about the developer's intentions that they are not willing to wait for all the information to be in?" Peggy asked township officials. Just minutes later, they approved the proposal, albeit with conditions.

And so the battle continues for full cleanup of the Bishop Tube site and the preservation of this little patch of nature. The communities around and downstream from Bishop Tube have suffered tremendous harm because of this site's toxic history. As Bill Coneghan, another longtime resident of the neighboring village, recounted at a public hearing in 2021: "My son was three when we moved here, and since then my son and any other children who moved into, [have] grown up [in], or were born in [our] village have had that aura of danger, knowing that in some way—either through the water in the area or vapors coming down the street—they could be affected by these hazardous chemicals." Bill concluded his remarks by expressing that his "frustration and resentment toward DEP stems personally from that" and from the regulatory agency's failure to put forth a plan that will make this site less hazardous.

The East Whiteland community deserves to keep their trees, creek, critters, and ecosystems, and to enjoy these valued natural treasures for the beauty, health, and healing they provide. This is their little piece of natural paradise. But instead, as is so often the case, the developer and the state are using the site's contaminated condition as an excuse to try to force development. They fail to recognize that protection and restoration of this pocket of nature will bring far more value to a community that has suffered irreparable harm from both the site's toxic condition and the failure of local and state government to act.

"The Township Supervisors asserted that they were counting on the state DEP to ensure proper site cleanup before development could take place. But the state has shown no urgency in resolving the significant environmental contamination issues at the site and has made clear that the legal authority regarding site use belongs to the township," says Mark Freed, senior legal counsel with Curtin & Heefner, and one of the lawyers representing the Delaware Riverkeeper Network in our legal challenges regarding Bishop Tube's development.[16] "So while everyone has an excuse for why they are allowing this site to remain contaminated and development to advance, the community suffers. This is a classic case of 'justice delayed is justice denied.'"

Among the most important insights the Delaware Riverkeeper Network has brought to this battle are the confirmation that residents' concerns are justified, and the realization that town and state officials have a constitutional obligation to protect their environmental rights—to protect the water and air that flow through their towns, and to protect the scenic, aesthetic, and natural values of the environment that residents treasure. "I don't think most people in Pennsylvania realize that a clean environment is a constitutional right," says Kate Stauffer. But now that she knows, she and her neighbors have a renewed determination to fight hard for what is theirs. They understand that they are defending an entitlement that rivals, and arguably even surpasses, any property rights that the owners of the Bishop Tube site might claim.

In November of that year, the Delaware Riverkeeper Network filed a legal challenge against the state. In part, we were arguing that the state's failure to take action and clean up the Bishop Tube site after so many decades—despite the overwhelming evidence of contamination, the scientific understanding of threatened harm, and the legal foundations on which to hold responsible parties accountable for cleanup—was in fact a violation of its constitutional duty to protect the environmental rights of the people of East Whiteland. Of course, the state's first response was to try to shut down our legal challenge with a request that the court dismiss the case. But the court sided with us, agreeing that our assertion of the state's failure to diligently pursue cleanup of the site was legally and constitutionally relevant. And so the case continues in the courts, and the Delaware Riverkeeper Network continues to support East Whiteland residents in their fight. As with our PFAS petition and action, our legal challenge was the kick in the butt the state needed to get active on seeking site cleanup.

The decision-making table is unfairly laid when it comes to sites like Bishop Tube. But with the constitution, we are starting to create some equity. While our advocacy and legal challenges for cleanup and protection from development at Bishop Tube rely in no small part on existing laws in the state, the constitutional right to a clean and healthy environment has created a balance of power that otherwise doesn't exist under the lower laws. The constitutional right of the people to pure water, clean air, and the natural values of the environment has provided grounds for our call for government action. At the same time, this right has strengthened our claim that the state's failure to enforce existing laws mandating site cleanup is legally indefensible. The residents of General Warren Village and East Whiteland deserve their natural piece of paradise to be cleansed of toxins and protected as natural open space for the families of today and tomorrow. With the help of the Pennsylvania Green Amendment, we expect to get there.

Still, it's costly to undo the harm of environmental degradation after the fact. The mere attempt to clean up the toxins at Bishop Tube will cost many millions of dollars. More important than the cost of attempted cleanup, however, are the incalculable human costs suffered. Liz Stauffer won't get back the childhood years she lost to brain tumors. David Worst won't recover his health from the incurable cancer he battles. Paula Warren can't get her family members back, and Keith can't get his life back. But moving forward, we can use Green Amendments to prevent this kind of harm, and the many other harms that result from environmental degradation, so other people don't have to suffer unnecessarily.

The Theft of Nature's Crown

The ability to resort to the courts to remedy an environmental inequity and secure needed government action to protect environmental rights is one benefit of the Pennsylvania Green Amendment. An even better one is when our government leaders rely on the constitution to protect pockets of paradise and elements of nature without being forced to do so. We are already starting to see this shift in Pennsylvania.

Remember the old-growth beech tree forest known as the Don Guanella woods, which you read about in chapter 3? The community relied in part on the Pennsylvania Green Amendment in its call for township officials to protect the woods from deforestation and development. Their words, together with the higher power of the constitution resonated, as evidenced by the statement of Commissioner Michael Molinaro: "This is the last little piece [of woods] that we have . . . . I believe this is our duty to protect these woodlands for not only us, not only Delaware County, Pennsylvania, but also for future generations." The people didn't have to appeal to the courts for protection; they just needed to appeal to the duty of their local government to uphold the state constitution.

In addition to the pockets of nature held so dearly in the hearts of our communities, we also need to work on the big picture: protecting natural ecosystems in order to avert the catastrophic losses that otherwise result. Since the dawn of civilization, the number of trees in the world has decreased by nearly half, reflecting a commensurate decline in the number of forested acres.[17] The pace of destruction is only increasing. Beginning around 1990, we've destroyed, on average, a thousand forested football fields per hour—a loss that roughly equals the surface area of South Africa![18]

The United States has the fourth-largest number of forested acres in the world, trailing only Russia, Brazil, and Canada. Like these other countries, we've been poor stewards of our precious resources. When Europeans arrived in North America, relates Christopher Roddick, chief arborist at the Brooklyn Botanic Garden in New York, "it's said that squirrels could travel from tree to tree from the Northeast to the Mississippi without ever having to touch the ground."[19] At that time, old-growth forests were still intact on the East Coast, with chestnuts, hemlocks, and other New World staples soaring hundreds of feet into the sky, providing a protective canopy to sustain the rich biodiversity below. After Europeans arrived, massive deforestation occurred, which in turn created conditions for tree diseases and parasitic infestations to take hold. The trees that remain today are more vulnerable than ever.

Forested areas are hardly the only kinds of wild lands that are disappearing at alarming rates. Since the turn of the twentieth century, the world has lost 64 percent of its global wetlands.[20] And the rate of their loss is increasing every year.[21] The contiguous United States, between the 1780s and the 1980s, lost an average of sixty wetland acres per hour—a staggering 53 percent total loss.[22] People throughout the world tend to view wetlands as worthless and disposable, thinking it doesn't matter if developers pave them over or if farmers clear them for agriculture. But nothing could be further from the truth! Wetlands are vital to a healthy landscape because they capture carbon, support biodiversity, purify and recharge water supplies, and constrain floodwaters. Because of massive wetland loss, according to international conservation group Ramsar and the Wetlands Extent Index, "access to fresh water is declining for one to two billion people worldwide."[23]

The vital role of wetlands in helping stave off a climate crisis is also becoming increasingly clear. Peatlands, for example, are waterlogged wetland systems where plant decomposition dramatically slows, and as a result the carbon they hold is naturally sequestered.[24] Peatlands actually store twice as much carbon as forests. So while they make up just 3 percent of the world's surface, protecting their carbon storing power is vital for meeting worldwide carbon reduction commitments to address climate change.[25]

Whether it is forests and wetlands, or tundra, grasslands, and savannahs, all the primary classes of wilderness in the world are fast disappearing. A 2016 report found that since the 1990s, we've destroyed 10 percent of our global wilderness, defined as environments largely untouched by human development.[26] This wholesale destruction of an area twice the size of Alaska has left a mere 20 percent of the world's wild ecosystems intact. South America (with 30 percent declines) and Africa (with 14 percent declines) witnessed the most staggering losses, leaving the globe's remaining wilderness—an area a little over thirty million square kilometers—largely concentrated in Australia and the northern reaches of Asia, the Americas, and Africa. Researchers were particularly alarmed to discover that remote and largely uninhabited areas like Siberia, the Sahara, or the Arctic tundra weren't self-sustaining wild areas, as many specialists had previously assumed, but were instead imperiled.[27]

The amount of wilderness loss in just two decades is "staggering," noted forest scientist Oscar Venter, PhD, of the University of Northern British Columbia. "We need to recognize that wilderness areas, which we've foolishly considered to be de-facto protected due to their remoteness, [are] actually being dramatically lost around the world." Venter concludes, "Without proactive global interventions, we could lose the last jewels in nature's crown."[28]

In the United States, we might debate the merits of converting our wild lands over to agriculture, livestock, and housing for an increasingly populated planet. After all, we need places to live, recreate, and grow our food. Businesses, shops, and roadways all require spots on the landscape to operate, as do the solar panels and wind turbines that will power our future. Despite these many development needs, there is no question that we have unnecessarily sacrificed many of the "last jewels in nature's crown" and deeply and irreparably harmed ourselves in the process. Dick Riseling, who owns the sustainable and energy independent Apple Pond Farm located in the Catskill Mountains of New York,[29] offered a frank assessment during a presentation we gave together: "Nature gives us life. It gives us special places to enjoy. Nature is beautiful. And we are giving nature a kick in the heart. We all came from nature. We need to start taking care of nature."[30]

You would expect kindred spirits like Dick and me to feel that way, but the extent of overdevelopment is becoming increasingly obvious to many others, including some in the real estate industry itself. Consider the problem of excessive mall space. From 1970 to 2015, malls multiplied at double the speed of the overall population.[31] According to Derek Thompson, an economics and labor markets specialist, "The US has 40 percent more shopping space per capita than Canada, five times more than the UK, and 10 times more than Germany."[32] After the Great Recession, cash-strapped Americans stopped frequenting these malls, shopping plazas, and retail complexes, converting what was previously thriving mall space into abandoned, boarded-up wastelands, with grass and weeds sprouting through the asphalt parking lots. As commercial real estate expert Ethan Rothstein relates, such overdevelopment means that "most of the United States is left with hundreds of millions of retail square footage that no one appears to want."[33]

The Covid-19 pandemic has contributed to the exodus. Mall vacancy rates in 2021 have climbed to 7.2 percent, up from 4.9 percent, since the pandemic's onset in 2020.[34] Twenty-five percent of malls across the United States are anticipated to shutter by mid-decade (2025), and while some spaces are looking to diversify the way they could be used—for example, as apartments or other commercial uses—for many there won't be an alternative use other than bankruptcy and/or vacancy.[35] And now it is not just malls and retail stores that are finding themselves standing vacant, but increasingly office buildings as well. Stay-at-home work models driven by Covid-19 notably are providing some support to neighborhood shops, while at the same time devastating some inner-city shopping areas now starved of workday shoppers taking a midday break. Many former retail and commercial businesses will remain vacant, and acres of unused parking lots and development-blighted land will stand empty for some time yet.[36] Yet developers still can't resist cutting down forests and filling in wetlands in order to build new retail spaces. It's crazy!

When George van Amelsfort moved to Hamilton Township in Mercer County, New Jersey, in the early 1990s, he encountered quaint neighborhoods with homes nestled amid trees, wide-open spaces, and free-flowing creeks.[37] Harkening back to an old magazine article, local politicians affectionately refer to Hamilton as "America's favorite hometown." In recent decades, however, development has exploded. As George notes, rather than repurposing shuttered strip malls, city officials have green-lighted the construction of new ones. "Since I have moved to Hamilton, the loss of trees means a loss of nature to enjoy, a loss of shade as you walk down the sidewalk," George says. "I now hear the interstate, whereas years ago a mitigating natural buffer significantly dulled the noise."

In addition to the sprawling development that continues to engulf Hamilton, the town has also adopted poor practices for managing the stormwater that runs off of developed landscapes when it rains. Best practices dictate that municipalities require preservation of natural areas within and around development, and that they limit the development footprint as much as possible. Woodlands and natural meadows naturally absorb rainfall, soaking it into the soil and replenishing groundwater supplies. Trees, soils, and root systems filter out pollution like fertilizers, road salts, herbicides, and garbage that otherwise would surge into local creeks and water systems. Rather than benefit from nature's sponge and contaminant filter, Hamilton Township allows developers to use engineering strategies that make problems worse. Unadvisedly, the township encourages detention basins designed to capture runoff in a large landscape depression, from which it is discharged directly into local streams through a system of pipes, overloading waterways with an unnatural volume of water. And to prevent erosion, developers armor stream banks with concrete or riprap. Such measures don't protect the environment, but rather push floodwaters and erosion farther downstream.

Because of the township's overdevelopment and irresponsible stormwater practices, Hamilton now experiences increasing floods during small, frequent storms, with large volumes of water flowing from town streets and lawns into local creeks. Because less and less rainfall is allowed to soak into the ground, groundwater supplies are unable to provide local streams with healthy base flow on those days when it's not raining. The creek that George once enjoyed has diminished in beauty and biodiversity. "Pond Run, the stream near my house, is dying a slow death," laments George. "Because of development, there is more pollution, fewer fish, fewer amphibians, fewer birds, and an overall collapse of the ecosystem."[38]

One day George noticed that Pond Run began drying up in the summer, leaving only small pockets of water where fish struggled to survive. George scrambled to rescue as many as possible, transporting buckets of stranded fish to where water was more plentiful. He has had to repeat this rescue mission in following years. George can't rescue all the fish, and most of them die, their rotting carcasses serving as a sad (and odorous) reminder of the perils of environmental destruction, overdevelopment, and poor stormwater management. This is not the kind of scene you would expect in America's favorite hometown.

In 2004, the New Jersey state government had had enough of such self-destructive environmental mayhem and implemented progressive stormwater regulations. These rules modestly restrained development practices, encouraging protection of natural buffer areas and the use of water infiltration strategies so that rain could seep naturally into the ground instead of surging off impervious surfaces. But much of the power to implement and enforce these new standards was entrusted to towns like Hamilton. Despite the state's environmental mandates, Hamilton continued to allow detention basins, armored stream banks, and ill-advised development projects—often in flagrant violation of its own stormwater mandates.

The state of New Jersey also failed to hold Hamilton and other similarly situated towns accountable. Sometimes the state claimed it didn't have the financial resources to enforce compliance. In truth, New Jersey's government officials didn't prioritize environmental protection. Year after year, George and his neighbors advocate for smarter development decisions and better stormwater management practices at their township meetings. Township officials consistently disregard them. Such regulatory oversight isn't, unfortunately, unique to the township of Hamilton. New Jersey's stormwater rules are frequently overlooked throughout the state; no matter what political party is in charge at City Hall or the statehouse, somehow the developers always have the edge over local residents and the environment when it comes to development decisions.

Compounding the greenfields development pressure in communities across the nation is an expanding need for warehousing to feed the frenzy of overnight deliveries that are demanded, day in and day out, by online purchasing. It's been estimated that an additional one billion square feet of warehousing will be constructed by 2025.[39] And this modern-day warehousing descending on communities does not consist of small, midsize, or even large buildings; we are talking about megasized complexes. For instance, the Jaindl Land Company is fighting to build one of the largest warehousing facilities in the United States on prime agricultural farmland in White Township, New Jersey. The project will start with the construction of two buildings: one warehouse that is 1.9 million square feet and a second that is 800 thousand square feet—together, the equivalent of about forty-seven football fields! Once complete, the project will have brought an estimated six million square feet of warehousing to the township, turning this relatively rural agricultural community into a mega industrial site.[40]

The chosen construction site is near the Delaware River. The location is served by small roads used to light traffic, not the continuous onslaught of big trucks the warehousing will require. Massive paving projects to replace the absorbent farmland will cause rainfall to run off the landscape. As happens in Hamilton and in developments across the nation, when the rainfall washes over the now-developed landscape, it will pick up oil, grease, degraded brake padding, wintertime de-icing salts, and other pollution. Ultimately, this onslaught of harmful contaminants will infect local ecosystems and the ecologically and recreationally valuable river. Truck diesel engines will spew noise and air pollution, impacting quality of life and the health of nearby residents. The industrialization of the community is garnering strong and growing community opposition. Signs opposing the warehouse pepper the region.

"Warehousing that blights our natural areas and urban communities is not the right path forward," says Faith Zerbe, monitoring director with the Delaware Riverkeeper Network, which is a major opponent of the Jaindl warehousing project.[41] "Communities have worked tirelessly to protect the Delaware River. The warehousing projects we see advancing are too often on the wrong side of these key community issues and sacrifice our healthy ecosystems to inappropriate development practices and business models."

In addition to environmental protection being at stake, so too is environmental justice for many communities. According to an investigation by Consumer Reports, Amazon built three hundred new warehousing operations in 2020, with numbers the following year estimated to be just as high. Of the hundreds of communities across the nation where Amazon is building its new warehouses, 69 percent are in areas that are predominantly home to people of color and where concerns about air pollution and domineering industrial traffic and operations are already a serious concern.[42] In addition, 57 percent of these communities are disproportionately low-income. Small-particulate air pollution emitted from diesel engines and industrial operations has serious health consequences for surrounding communities, and particularly for small children, causing asthma, stroke, heart attacks, and even cancer. "Communities that host delivery facilities end up being the losers. They get more traffic, air pollution, traffic jams, and pedestrian safety problems, but they don't receive their fair share of the benefits that accrue from having the retail nearby," explains Sacoby Wilson, director of the Center for Community Engagement, Environmental Justice, and Health (CEEJH) at the University of Maryland in College Park. "You can treat this pattern as a form of environmental racism."[43]

This sense of injustice is deeply felt by those experiencing it. "Our communities are being sacrificed in the name of economic development," offers José Acosta-Córdova of the Little Village Environmental Justice Organization in Chicago.[44] Yes, a lot of online purchasing is being serviced. But given the development and operation practices used by companies like Amazon and Jaindl, it's also true that a lot of environments, ecosystems, and communities are being unjustly harmed.

Reining in Real Estate

Such stories of inappropriate or excessive land development appeal to many people's concerns about fairness or justice. Likewise, they hit me especially hard. When I was growing up, my town of Villanova in the Philadelphia suburbs formed part of a swath of communities known affectionately by many as the Main Line. While most people on our street lived in modest single-family homes, my family inhabited a duplex that was also the last house on our street. Through the walls on one side of our house, we could hear our neighbors. Through the walls on the other side, nothing but nature's music filtered through.

Our house sat next to an enchanting patch of forest. I spent countless hours as a child having adventures in those woods. My friends and I found special places, navigated massive rocks, and marveled at the large trees whose mangled roots jutted up like knots above the moist dirt floor.

The forest canopy covered a small waterway called Ithan Creek, where we played, fashioning moon pies out of wet soil. At a bend in the creek, a sediment bar served as a little beach, the perfect place for us to build muddy sandcastles, draw pictures with sticks, and wriggle our feet into the soft, wet sand. On warm spring and summer days, my best friend, Cecily, and I reveled in nature's beauty, searching for animals and little gnomes we were convinced lived in the forest.

With my friend looking on, I tested my agility, trying to balance on rocks without toppling into the water, or using fallen trees as balance beams. Sometimes my mother joined in the fun as we wandered the twists and turns of the well-worn forest paths we had created over years of use. She was just as excited about seeing an orange mushroom or Indian pipe popping up from the forest floor as she was to catch a rare glimpse of a deer, a fox, or other wildlife. And sometimes my adventures were solitary. When I was sad, angry, or just puzzled by life, I ran down to the creek and nestled into the folds of large, sprawling, radiating tree roots to sit, cry, ponder, and heal.

What I didn't realize as a child was that a new six-lane highway was being built, and the plans called for it to run straight through my enchanted playground. The community fought the new highway as best it could, just like the Stauffers fight the Bishop Tube project. But like so many development projects, this one was approved. Years later, when I was in college, I returned to my childhood home and was shocked to find the massive highway under construction. The trees were gone, the soil was bare, and heavy construction equipment and debris blocked all access to the creek. A few years later, the construction was finished, and the area was blasted night and day with noise and air pollution from the continuous traffic. I still feel devastated at the loss of my once beautiful forest. And I still recall my mother's sadness and anger. She had heard the buzz saws cutting the trees and had watched the bulldozers scraping the soil. For her, the sudden absence of the birds and wildlife she had so enjoyed was devastating. For many years thereafter, she would work to restore a little patch of nature for her own benefit and that of the area's suddenly homeless creatures. Within eight years, she created a small natural habitat bountiful with color and life, which was a treat for the eye. But this small stand of nature could never drown out the noise of the highway beyond.

With the highway came still more development, an influx of homes and shopping centers, and a dramatic reduction in open space. The fever to build in Radnor, Pennsylvania, (where Villanova is located) was so great that it proceeded without proper care for the environment. Rather than gently nestling homes into still-standing woodlands, developers (with the government's blessing) clear-cut the trees and moonscaped the land, creating massive homes with lots of lawn, oversized driveways, and wide roads to accommodate increased traffic. Rather than building away from the creeks and wetlands, volunteering a buffer of vegetation that would protect both the natural habitat and the community from flooding, erosion, and pollution, developers built as close to the water's edge as possible.

Radnor, like Hamilton, New Jersey, constructed vast detention basins that collected and delivered stormwater directly into local creeks. The predictable result: endemic flooding, erosion, and pollution problems across the region. But those living downstream bear the brunt of the resulting environmental assault and struggle to find ways to protect themselves. Among those communities is Eastwick, Pennsylvania, located near the John Heinz National Wildlife Refuge, the Philadelphia airport, and the Darby Creek that flows downstream from Radnor Township. When it rains, the flooding situation in Eastwick gets so bad, so often that many residents must store rows of sandbags so that they're ready to use them as a wall of defense from rising floodwaters when a storm passes through.

As community action coordinator for the Delaware Riverkeeper Network, Fred Stine finds it commonplace and unfair that a wealthier upstream community like Radnor would fail to fully consider the harms its development strategies are inflicting not just on its own residents but on downstream Eastwick, where residents tend to be poorer and mainly people of color who already face disproportionate environmental harms.[45] "Even though these communities are twelve miles apart as the crow flies," Fred says, "the unnecessary level of impervious cover associated with development in Radnor—as well as other upstream communities—along with the practice of dumping their runoff into local creeks contributes to the chronic, catastrophic flooding and pollution problems which the residents of Eastwick must face every day." Of course, Radnor is not the sole cause of Eastwick's environmental problems. Eastwick was built on top of a six-thousand-acre tidal marsh, of which only 285 acres remain, rendering the community far more vulnerable to flooding. But Radnor compounds the ravages of flooding for Eastwick with its cavalier disregard for the ways it makes things worse for its downstream neighbors.

Residents who had organized as the Eastwick Friends and Neighbors Coalition in order to challenge inappropriate development that was harming their community took their message upstream—to Radnor. I hosted a forum at which Terry Williams and other members of the coalition explained to their Darby Creek neighbors upstream how flooding impacted their downstream community of Eastwick, saying, "While most people worry about whether they left a window open in their house during a rainstorm, Eastwick residents wonder if they'll need to leave work to stack sandbags before the Darby Creek overflows its banks." Hearing these concerns, Radnor residents reacted positively—they really seemed to care. But did they?

Upstream Marple Township, home to the Don Guanella woods development proposal discussed in chapter 3, received a similar upstream-downstream neighbor message from the people of Eastwick. When given the chance, the Marple Township commissioners acted unequivocally, denying a development proposal that would have cleared a natural woodland for residential and commercial development, causing more polluted runoff to pour onto—and into—a tributary of the Darby and eventually contributing to the floodwaters faced by the residents of Eastwick. But in Radnor? I'm not seeing much change. A new house is right now (seven years after the Eastwick-Radnor forum) being built near the banks of a Darby Creek tributary—bringing a new source of polluted runoff to add to the Darby Creek floodwaters.

The real tragedy of situations like Eastwick's is that they don't need to happen. In this country, we know how to develop communities in ways that don't inflict so much harm. All too often, we simply don't do it. Under the current system of legislative environmentalism, real estate developers nearly always have carte blanche to undertake projects, with little concern for the effects on nature. Municipal officials approve development projects on a piecemeal basis and fail to put in place, or enforce, legal mandates that ensure best practices. While some development projects require initial community planning, developers inevitably argue that exceptions to environmental prohibitions should be made for their projects. Because approval processes tend to be piecemeal, any regulator or government official can accept a developer's rationale and grant relief while still claiming to comply overall with regulatory standards and zoning ordinances. Although a single development project—like Bishop Tube townhouses, a Hamilton Township strip mall, or another Radnor McMansion—may seem to contribute relatively little to water pollution, flooding, or land despoliation, cumulatively these projects have devastated our environments and endangered our communities.

A constitutional provision can bring about meaningful improvements in US real estate regulation by compelling government agencies to change the way they think about development—and to think about the cumulative impacts of legislation, regulation, and decisions that impact how development advances in our communities and states. Decision makers would start to consider whether a given project would exacerbate pollution in already overburdened environmental justice communities, would cause or contribute to the ravages of flooding, or would deprive nearby residents of the healthy river and fish they fought for decades to save. With a constitutional provision in place, government entities would be empowered to look beyond short-term economic benefits and instead consider the cumulative impacts of all the projects they approve.

Recall those powerful words spoken by Marple Township Commissioner Michael Molinaro when voting to reject the development project that would devastate the Don Guanella woods: "I've listened to people, and I've heard what they said, and I'm not going to say anything different because we have a duty, I believe, under article 1, section 27 of the Pennsylvania Constitution, to protect and preserve the Commonwealth's natural resources." Imagine if every government official in every state were bound by such a constitutional code of conduct: an obligation to protect natural resources and environmental rights for generations to come. Not only would we prevent destructive business operations and development projects—and encourage protective ones—but we also would be giving government an essential tool for protecting us from a looming climate crisis.

CHAPTER SEVEN

CONFRONTING THE
CLIMATE CRISIS

The Elbe is one of the great rivers of central Europe, flowing from high in the mountains of the Czech Republic through Germany to the North Sea. The waterway itself spans just under seven hundred miles, connecting the deep interior of northern Czechia with the Port of Hamburg. Its basin, which encompasses Prague, Dresden, and Berlin, is home to roughly twenty-five million people. Today, just under a third of the basin's land area is forested while nearly 40 percent is used for agriculture, though these percentages would've been much higher in centuries past.[1]

How would the Elbe river basin's coniferous, deciduous, and mixed forest habitats fare if such a significant, life-giving artery happened to run dry? What about the crops sustained by the Elbe and its tributaries, or the millions of people whose lives and livelihoods have, throughout history, depended upon them—and still do today? Unfortunately, we don't have to wonder.

Situated along the banks of the Elbe and other rivers in central Europe, submerged except when water levels fall dangerously low, ominous warnings from the past—known as "hunger stones"—are emerging. A 2018 drought exposed more than a dozen of these large natural rocks and boulders bearing hand-carved inscriptions, some dating as early as the 1400s—in the vicinity of Decin, a Czech town of fifty thousand just a short distance from where the Elbe crosses the border into Germany.[2] One especially prominent hunger stone presents a chronicle of woes stretching back centuries. Its carvings record "that drought had brought a bad harvest, lack of food, high prices, and hunger for poor people. Before 1900, the following droughts are commemorated on the stone: 1417, 1616, 1707, 1746, 1790, 1800, 1811, 1830, 1842, 1868, 1892, and 1893."[3] Etched like scars into the natural rock, these inscriptions are accompanied by a heart-wrenching lament and warning: *Wenn du mich siehst, dann weine*—in English: "If you see me, weep."

Tree-ring analysis supports the climate history that's etched into the hunger stones, confirming that the region has been subject to devastating "megadroughts" for hundreds of years. Scientists have found that the repeated central European droughts of the twenty-first century, while shorter in duration than those of the past, are still extreme—and ominously, the more recent droughts have been accompanied by skyrocketing temperatures. The result has been soil drying trends that are having devastating impacts on crops and ecosystems—which, according to researchers, "raises concerns about the consequences of extreme . . . droughts" caused by lack of rainfall as the effects of climate change continue to intensify.[4]

In 2018, the same rolling drought that exposed hunger stones along the Elbe also sent water levels plummeting across other parts of northern and central Europe—setting record lows, impeding the flow of cruise and freight vessels down the Danube,[5] and exposing previously sunken munitions from World War II.[6] By 2022, due to exceptionally low water levels caused by climate change (and also, in part, due to a downriver dam that altered the river's flow), the large hunger stone near Decin, Czech Republic—the one inscribed "if you see me, weep"—was visible so consistently that it had become a tourist attraction.

I hope the visitors are leaving with more than memories of their photo op. I hope they are taking with them the stark and sobering message our ancestors intended: danger is coming, and it is time to plan and act.

Reasons to Weep

Human history and climate have always been closely intertwined—from the ice ages and other natural phenomena that shaped early human migration patterns and evolution to the accelerating present-day effects of human-caused climate change, which threatens our future. You don't need me to recap the well-established science; my main point is simply about what separates us today from those who carved the hunger stones: agency.

During the fifteenth century, our ancestors were powerless to prevent megadroughts, because those megadroughts were naturally occurring. By contrast, modern science has equipped us with the knowledge that the extreme and more frequent droughts of today, as well as the increased flooding and unprecedented temperatures, are not natural. Their causes are linked directly to the accelerating climate crisis. This is a crisis created by human activity, and one that only concerted global human effort can address, by reducing human-induced, climate-changing emissions and restoring the ecologically healthy habitats that can naturally capture and sequester carbon. Green Amendments are, in some ways, an ideal expression of the agency we the people can exercise to achieve these aims.

As the recent reappearance of the hunger stones suggests, the current state of the climate crisis provides plenty of reasons to weep. It's not just that 2021 was the fifth-hottest year in recorded history; it's that the past seven years have been the seven hottest years ever recorded—by a considerable margin. Over 300 million people are expected to be on the brink of starvation within the next decade because of food access issues caused by climate change.[7] Climate change is contributing not just to death by starvation but to death by heat. The heat wave of June 2021 killed at least six hundred people in Oregon and Washington—one month, two states, six hundred people![8]

Climate change is also responsible for increasing wildfires. The number of acres burned in the twenty-first century to date is double what was seen, on average, in the 1990s.[9] In some forests in parts of the United States, it is projected that a 1-degree-Celsius annual average increase in temperature will increase the median of the area burned in wildfires by up to 600 percent.[10] While naturally occurring wildfires can have beneficial ecological effects, the growing climate crisis is causing wildfires to an extent that is deeply concerning—increasing the number, size, and impacts of those fires beyond natural conditions. Of course, when a wildfire roars through, it is not just nature that is burned; fires can also have serious consequences for people, consuming homes, devastating businesses, and destroying lives.

Climate change is wreaking havoc, from the spread of disease to habitat destruction to species loss and tremendous economic harm. The list of deleterious impacts is long—and getting longer.

Despite the death and damage, our governments aren't merely incapable or unwilling (or both, depending on the day) to take even the most basic steps to confront the climate crisis; they're actively leading us in the wrong direction. Just take a look at New Mexico, a state of abundant wind and sunshine that could be at the forefront of the clean energy revolution. Yet the oil and gas industry, with all of its environmentally devastating operations, reigns supreme in the state—including in the halls of the state capitol building ("the Roundhouse"), where lobbyists liberally and successfully spread their money around to keep environmental protections at bay. New Mexico is the third-largest oil producer in the nation, and is among the top ten natural gas–producing states.[11] It also happens to be home to the Permian "climate bomb" that could tip our reality from climate change to climate catastrophe.

The Permian Basin, home to over two million people, spans western Texas and eastern New Mexico.[12] It is characterized by the Energy Information Administration (EIA) as the most "prolific hydrocarbon production region in the United States." While the EIA intends that description as a positive, in the real world of facts and science, this "unchecked" growth makes the region a ticking climate bomb.[13] In 2020, about 30 percent of US crude oil was produced from the Permian, along with 14 percent of natural gas.[14] As of June 2021, the government was already reporting 44,990 operating fossil fuel wells in the Permian. A vast proportion of the oil and gas extracted is not for use in the United States; it is being drilled and fracked so it can be sent overseas.

Given the long-known and well-established climate-changing impacts of fossil fuel extraction and use, you would think curbing drilling in the massive Permian basin would be our shared goal, particularly in a state like New Mexico that—with its abundance of alternative energy options—could be pursuing a vibrant clean energy path. But the reality on the ground is just the opposite. Over the past ten years, oil development in the Permian has increased by five times. Over the next ten years (2021 to 2030) it is planned to grow by another 50 percent.[15] These are the very years when we need to be ramping down climate-changing emissions—with a goal of zero—not increasing them.

Drilling, fracking, and burning Permian oil and gas will release so much climate-changing methane and carbon dioxide that the United States will likely be unable to meet its international commitments regarding greenhouse gas emissions.[16] If the United States is going to abide by its obligations under the Paris Climate Agreement to "limit global warming to well below 2, preferably to 1.5 degrees Celsius, compared to pre-industrial levels,"[17] we need to cut our carbon emission levels by at least 50 percent by 2030. Instead, with increased drilling in places like the Marcellus and the Permian, US emissions are on the rise. As Kate Larsen (a partner at the independent research provider Rhodium Group) told National Public Radio in January 2022, instead of seeing reductions in greenhouse gas emissions the previous year, "We saw emissions grow over 6 percent."[18] While other nations are also falling behind in their commitments when it comes to climate, there is no doubt that the United States is top of the list for great rhetoric but lack of meaningful action.

The cost of inaction is getting higher by the day. If policymakers had listened to science back in 2010, governments around the world would have been able to limit global temperature rise to 1.5 degrees Celsius through collectively reducing greenhouse gas emissions by 3.3 percent each year. By 2020, however, their stubborn apathy and inaction meant the Paris Agreement's central objective had receded even further: it would now take an aggressive (but still achievable) 7.6 percent reduction in emissions every year. If we wait until 2025 for our governments to take meaningful action, that figure will be 15.5 percent—nearly five times the target we would've needed to hit a decade ago.[19] With each passing day, our agency over the Earth's climate future slips a little further out of reach. We can't say the scientists, or the hunger stones, didn't warn us.

The consequences of such a reckless, shambolic, and short-sighted approach to the climate crisis are not abstract—and their toll and impacts are escalating, as the increase in droughts, floods, wildfires, and heat waves prove. As Americans begin to experience the climate crisis in a real and visceral way, many are striving to awaken others to the scale and urgency of this emergency. Increasingly, concerned activists are not just protesting the reckless disregard and inaction of too many in government; they are mobilizing for enforceable change. In New Mexico, for instance, where oil and gas has such a significant stranglehold on government leadership on both sides of the political aisle, a growing powerhouse of legislators—following the steadfast leadership of Senator Antoinette Sedillo Lopez and Representative Joanne Ferrary—are working to advance a Green Amendment as part of their solution. Aware of our success in Pennsylvania to prevent the massive proliferation of fracking that Act 13 had promised to invoke, many in New Mexico are eager for this constitutional change. The proposed New Mexico Green Amendment will provide the legal strength to check the rampant pro-fossil fuel interests that seem to drive government action (and sometimes inaction) regardless of the ramifications for climate, people, and environments.

Green Amendments will do more than just allow us to realize the enforceable and as-yet unfulfilled promise of climate protection; they will create a foundation on which to secure needed change on a broad scale. When government acts, climate science and impacts will become obligatory considerations. Any law that unleashes a new wave of fracking, with its demonstrated impacts on the environment and climate, will be constitutionally suspect. On the flip side, government officials who want to advance good climate decisions—for example, a protective buffer from fracking for natural environments sacred to Native Americans, a permit limitation to protect the air quality of an already disproportionately burdened environmental justice community, a limitation on water withdrawals to protect natural resources or communities, a fee on vented natural gas that is otherwise spewed into the atmosphere with little limitation, or a prohibition on the misuse of toxic frack waste for agricultural irrigation or as brine on roads—will be able to better withstand industry challenges. A duty to address climate disruption caused by greenhouse gas emissions becomes an accessible legal argument. Laws or mandates that prohibit government officials from taking action to address climate disruption will be constitutionally infirm. There are many ways that a Green Amendment can transform the legal landscape, strengthening the power of the people to avert climate catastrophe.

The Nexus of Climate Change

When I think about climate change and all the industries that have brought us to our current precarious reality, I don't think about it as a stand-alone problem. I think of all the different ways that industry damages our environment and communities. And I recognize that often, when we address environmental damages of one kind—such as polluting emissions to our air, water, and landscapes; or the devastation of the wetlands and forests that absorb and purify our water—a happy side effect is that we also find ourselves reining in climate-changing emissions. The breadth of environmental rights protections that Green Amendments provide can help secure a number of pathways to argue for the reduction of industrial activities that are a source of climate harms. For example, advocating to mitigate industrial air pollution and protect human health in communities like Port Arthur, Texas, will simultaneously help reduce emissions contributing to the climate crisis. It's what politicians love to refer to as a win-win. Port Arthur needs these kinds of win-wins.

Port Arthur lies along the short stretch of the Texas–Louisiana border that runs through Sabine Lake, just north of the lake's outlet into the Gulf of Mexico. Home to nearly fifty-five thousand people, the city is enveloped by the fossil fuel industry: refineries, tank farms, pipelines, liquefied natural gas (LNG) export facilities, and more. In fact, Port Arthur is home to the largest concentration of petrochemical facilities in our nation, among them the largest oil refinery in the United States.[20] Petroleum refineries, fossil fuel power plants, and oil and natural gas operations are among the top sources of climate-changing emissions in our nation and world.

John Beard, who is now "60-ish" (in his words), was born in Port Arthur, and has lived there all his life. I first crossed paths with John at an event in Washington, DC, in 2021. As part of the Build Back Fossil Free campaign, we were joining with frontline and Indigenous communities from across the nation to demand that President Joe Biden live up to his promise to firmly address the climate crisis by creating a fossil-free future—one where people are given priority over industry and corporate greed. In addition to holding signs, chanting, and singing with grassroots leaders and protesters on the sidewalk in front of the White House, invited speakers like John and me were telling our stories of how the fossil fuel industry devastates the lives of today and tomorrow. Soon, I found myself among those taken away by police to be arrested for our audacity. Imagine that: singing, chanting, and speaking truth to power, on a sidewalk outside the White House, was an arrestable offense! As a result, John and I didn't have the chance to meet that day, but I sought him out afterward.

When we caught up via Zoom later that year, John told me about his hometown. We talked about his decade of service (from 2003 to 2012) on Port Arthur's city council. John shared that after serving in local government, he dialed back his public persona for a while. Then, on August

29, 2017, Hurricane Harvey made landfall in Port Arthur. The aftermath led John to conclude it was time to once again be of public service, but this time in a different way: as an activist.

"I felt that I had to do more on the people side of the equation," John says now. "And that led to the creation in 2018 of the Port Arthur Community Action Network, or PACAN." John likes to say that Port Arthur is "at the nexus of climate change." He explains: "It's at the intersection of the petrochemical industry we have here, and the buildout of that industry—whether it be pipelines, the largest refinery in the country, the founding of related industries, or the export of fossil fuels—as well as the result of those [operations], which is climate change."[21]

Despite the area's long history of hurricane and tropical storm activity, extreme weather events hitting John's home community have been increasing in both frequency and power. In 2005, Hurricane Rita brought some flooding and lengthy, widespread power outages to the region. Over the next few years, hurricanes Gilbert, Humberto, and Ike hammered Port Arthur, with Tropical Storm Edouard in between. Then, in 2017, came Harvey.

The storm was devastating. It deluged Port Arthur, dropping twenty-six inches of rain in a single day. It caused flash floods that left three thousand people scrambling for shelter—and the streets coursing with six feet of water.[22] As the water filled homes, people fled to the upper reaches of their houses to await rescue, and some waited so long they ran out of food and water. At one point during the storm, Port Arthur's Mayor Derrick Freeman, trying to let frantic families know they had not been abandoned to the floodwaters, posted to Facebook: "Our whole city is underwater right now but we are coming!" People trapped and in need of rescue were asked to "hang a white towel, sheet or shirt outside to alert rescuers."[23] The civic center, where more than one hundred evacuees from the floods had gathered, itself succumbed to flooding.[24] Flood victims forced from their homes were now standing around in knee-high water at the center as they waited for help—and to learn what might be their after-the-storm fate. Eventually, those flood victims would have to be rescued again, this time from the civic center. Nearby Houston and beyond also felt the wrath of Harvey; in Texas alone, thirty-seven people died from the storm.[25]

In the grip of Hurricane Harvey, John was forced to watch the government flail and fumble its way through yet another slow, inadequate recovery effort. "In 2005 they had Hurricane Rita, and there were flaws. Three years later, Hurricane Ike, and there were flaws in how they handled it," he continues. "There were several other storms in between . . . and then you had Harvey. And on each occasion, it was a total screwup!" John had done what he could as a political leader. Now, it was time to don the mantle of activist—and take on these challenges using a different approach. John knew he needed to come at the problem from multiple angles. He would have to advocate for clean energy operations that would provide clean and healthy energy, as well as jobs, as opposed to dirty fossil fuel operations; ensure the full enforcement of anti-pollution laws, in an attempt to blunt the health harms created by existing industry; and make sure that when catastrophe did hit, his community got the assistance to which they were entitled in order to deal with the damage.

John recalls one Port Arthur resident—let's call her Nara—who filed for assistance to get her home rebuilt after it was severely damaged by Hurricane Ike in 2008. At first Nara was led to believe there was enough money to rebuild or restore fifty or more homes. Given she was number twenty-three on the list, she didn't need to worry. Or so she thought. As John remembers it, the Regional Planning Commission, which was responsible for overseeing the management and disbursal of recovery funding, left her with the impression that all was well—before announcing abruptly that it had run out of funding.

Nara was devastated. She was not just out of luck; she was out of a home.

In the aftermath of Hurricane Harvey, in 2017, another tranche of recovery funding was directed to the Port Arthur area. That's when an audit discovered that the Regional Planning Commission was still sitting on funds from Ike, nearly a decade earlier—and federal authorities declared that those resources would need to be disbursed before any new funding was released. "And that's when they went to [Nara], knocked on the door," says John, "and they said, 'Hey, sign this document right here. We're going to get started building you a house.'" But it took Nara eleven years—from 2008 until 2019—to get the assistance to which she was entitled for repairing the damage caused by Ike. Heartbreakingly, during that interval, her husband passed away.

As John tells the story, it's not just exasperation in his voice. It's outrage—the kind that fuels a certain flavor of fed-up-and-not-gonna-take-it-anymore resolve and determination with which I'm quite familiar. Why does the natural environment of Port Arthur, along with so many of its residents, suffer such devastating climate impacts? John doesn't mince words: "Why? So America can have the lifestyle it likes, which is hopping on jet planes and getting in cars and trains and automobiles . . . . *We [in Port Arthur]* fuel that." But that's not good enough for John, who continues to urge action to reduce climate-changing emissions as a way to protect the health and safety of his community.

John remembers another incident, about two weeks after Harvey hit, when "there was a massive tank fire in Valero's refinery, less than half a mile from my home." John was outside his house, talking with a reporter about the fire, when he overheard a radio report saying that the Texas Commission on Environmental Quality, which had people on the scene taking air samples, had pronounced that "there was minimal exposure and there was nothing wrong with the air." Meanwhile, John recalls, "We're standing outside my home, virtually gagging from this stuff." Government agencies reporting no danger when, less than half a mile away, John is gagging from the pollution spewing into the air—to me it's unfathomable.

Days like that, combined with everyday exposure to Port Arthur's petrochemical emissions, have taken a toll on the city's residents. John remembers a public EPA meeting where it was disclosed that "Port Arthur had twice the state and national average for cancer, as well as heart, and lung, and kidney disease." And he doesn't need a study to validate his lived experience. "If you come to Port Arthur, and you meet someone on the street, and you ask them, 'Do you know anyone who has ever had cancer, or died from cancer, or had treatment for cancer, or is in remission from it?,'" John points out, "you will not find a single person of adult age that can tell you no."

As these stories demonstrate, the emissions spewing from Port Arthur's oil and gas industry hit its host community many times over, poisoning the health of residents and overwhelming them with the repeated ravages of the climate crisis in the form of rising floodwaters, lost homes, and ongoing economic harm. It's not an overstatement to say that the oil and gas industry in Port Arthur is among those causing and contributing to the climate crisis—helping to fuel the extreme weather events that hammer the Texas coastline, cause massive flooding in Louisiana, hit the Pacific Northwest with unprecedented heat, and contribute to drought conditions so severe that the hunger stones are reemerging.

John is not asking for regulations to hurt the industry. But, as he observes, "government also has an obligation to protect not only Texas, but Texans. And all we're asking is for government to do more to protect us, to shield us from those dangers. We're not trying to put industry out of business. We just want them to do better." That is exactly what a Green Amendment can help John achieve: it's a chance to force government to require industry to do better and operate in a way that will not devastate the environment or people's lives.

With the laws as they are, and with government agencies working so hard to help industry expand or avoid repercussions for its pollution discharges, the options for people to secure needed protection are too often "too little, too late." But a Green Amendment brings the law to the side of the people—so they can hold government accountable when it fails to use its authority and the laws on the books to provide equitable and protective change.

In addition, because a Green Amendment speaks to the rights of the people to all aspects of a clean and healthy environment, the multiple pathways of harm inflicted on communities like Port Arthur by industry are mirrored by multiple pathways to secure powerful protections from those harms. While one grassroots effort might focus on reducing climate-changing emissions to protect environmental rights, a constitutional action that addresses, for example, the health-harming pollution from surrounding industry will inevitably address the climate-changing emissions at the same time. Furthermore, to ensure the greatest strength when tackling climate issues, many Green Amendment proposals—like the one in New Mexico—explicitly recognize the right to a stable climate and strengthen that protection by clearly recognizing environmental rights as being generational. In this era of climate crisis, we don't have much time. Having multiple pathways to a solution is important, so if one path fails, we still have others to follow.

Breaking our nation's dependence on fossil fuels will not be easy. It's going to take resilient communities like Port Arthur and determined people like John Beard to redirect our climate future. But as long as industry is allowed to prey on the Port Arthurs of the world under the guise of income and jobs, not only will local suffering continue, but we will also be creating planetary catastrophe. We need to join with John and his community in advocating for a clean, safe, and green future; given that frontline communities are already more deeply impacted and disadvantaged, they can't be expected to do it alone.

And certainly having only the tools of public protest and political advocacy isn't going to be enough. As long as government is allowed to silence our voices by arresting respectful protesters on the sidewalks outside public buildings, denying the funds needed to rebuild lives, and empowering the petrochemical industry to spin the definition of "green," we will continue to walk the plank into a scary and uncertain future. But with the right legal tools, among them a Green Amendment, we can still turn things around. Although we are on the brink of climate crisis, we have not yet crossed the threshold of no return.

Knowledge with Power

Knowledge is power. When it comes to addressing climate change, it's important to make sure we fully understand what we know—and how we know it.

Before 2009, questioning the hypothesis that shale gas is better for the climate than coal was almost outlandish. Everyone from President Barack Obama to big green organizations like the Sierra Club and the Environmental Defense Fund (EDF) believed we should close dirty, coal-powered power plants and substitute natural gas. After all (they would say), natural gas produces less carbon dioxide than coal—and carbon dioxide is the world's leading greenhouse gas, trapping energy in the atmosphere and leading to climate change. With that rationale, natural gas was declared the "bridge fuel" to a cleaner, safer, and more sustainable future. But in 2009, two scholars at Cornell University—Dr. Anthony Ingraffea, an engineering professor, and Dr. Robert Howarth, an Earth and atmospheric scientist—noticed a flaw in the logic of the natural-gas-as-clean-energy party line: what about methane?

The entire bridge-fuel argument was based on the presumption that all methane pumped from natural gas wells was burned off. Bob and Tony suspected that an unknown quantity was actually being released into the atmosphere. They deduced that such fugitive emissions were responsible for higher concentrations of global methane in the atmosphere.[26]

The question of fugitive methane emissions has dramatic implications for climate change, but to appreciate this we need to understand how methane differs as a greenhouse gas from carbon dioxide. Ultimately, to halt catastrophic climate change, we must reduce our emissions of carbon dioxide. Carbon dioxide we emit today will continue to influence the climate and warm the planet for hundreds and perhaps even a thousand years. But methane is an important part of the problem, too. While it remains in the atmosphere for only a decade or so, methane is a more potent greenhouse gas than carbon dioxide in the short term.

Over a twenty-year period, when comparing an equal weight of the two gases, methane is eighty-six times more powerful than carbon dioxide in trapping heat in the Earth's atmosphere. While there is more carbon dioxide in the atmosphere than methane, and it is longer lived in terms of climate impacts, the Earth's climate system responds more quickly to changes in methane emissions. So by reducing methane emissions today, we can slow the rate of global warming in the near term.[27] So, while society must reduce emissions of both gases, only the reduction of methane can slow global warming in any meaningful way between now and 2030, the critical near-term target for significant climate change emission reductions we need to meet.

As Tony and Bob investigated and tested their hypothesis, the scientists discovered that no one had ever measured fugitive methane emissions from the fracked gas life cycle in a comprehensive or systematic way. So they surveyed all available literature, ran the numbers, and compared the climate-changing potential of shale gas, non-shale gas, coal, and oil. In 2011, the prestigious journal *Climatic Change* published their paper and its startling conclusion: natural gas, harvested from shale, was worse for the climate than coal.[28]

In subsequent years, dozens of peer-reviewed papers have followed, and the emerging consensus firmly supports the conclusion of Tony and Bob's paper: *Natural gas is not a bridge fuel to a cleaner future.* On the contrary, it is exacerbating global pollution and climate change.

Despite this now well-established scientific consensus—and the catastrophic effects wrought by our nation's disastrous embrace of fracking as a means to realize the mirage of "clean" natural gas—Pennsylvania's elected leaders are not among those who have learned the lesson. Or perhaps they just don't care.

Karen Feridun and I have worked together since the early onset of the fracking industry in Pennsylvania. Karen began her anti-fracking activism by founding an organization called Berks Gas Truth, which took on the industry on a local level. Her effort soon expanded to cover a broader region; she worked with Tracy, me, my Delaware Riverkeeper Network, and other partners on our watershed moratorium. As her knowledge and expertise grew, Karen expanded her efforts to span the entire state of Pennsylvania; she soon founded the Better Path Coalition to bring together organizations and grassroots leaders from across the state to work together on non-fracking and clean energy solutions. And so I was listening when, in the autumn of 2021, Karen sounded the alarm bells: Pennsylvania was at it again, advancing a false climate-change solution that was really all about advancing fracking.

It was with a stomach-turning sense of déjà vu that we watched Pennsylvania policymakers become enamored with yet another unproven (and supposedly green) technology. Once again, a new industry was about to come crashing down on Pennsylvania—and we'd have to get organized quickly to oppose it.

Karen had learned that a company called Nacero was proposing to build a $6 billion plant in Luzerne County, Pennsylvania.[29] The plant would turn natural gas into gasoline using a two-step process: first, they'd convert it into methanol, and from there—using a proprietary step—into gasoline.[30] In announcing plans to construct its first such facility, in Texas, Nacero boasted that "all of the plant's electricity will come from renewable sources," much of it produced using solar panels on-site at Nacero's 2,600-acre manufacturing facility. "The plant will be the first in the US to make gasoline from natural gas," the company claimed, "and the first in the world to do so with carbon capture and sequestration. Sequestered CO_2 will be transported via an existing on-site pipeline."[31] The trouble is, although Nacero touts all of this as proven technology, there's little or no evidence that's the case. Nacero's claims that it creates clean and renewable energy that will help address the climate crisis are similarly dubious.

Despite the dearth of meaningful information, Pennsylvania legislators were falling all over themselves to incentivize Nacero to bring its miraculous new industrial technology to the state.[32] Alex Bomstein, a staff attorney with the Clean Air Council (one of the leading organizations to oppose Nacero) emphasizes that "the greenwashing is really more blatant than I've seen before for any other proposed facility. . . .

And at the core of the problem, no matter how they were gift-wrapping it, this new operation in Texas and proposed for Pennsylvania was all based on continued fracking for gas from shale—with all of its devastating environmental and climate-changing consequences."[33]

As Karen would ferret out with her research, Nacero didn't even exist until 2015, and the company has absolutely no track record that can be assessed by any metric: what's involved, how it works, how compliance functions. "It's not just, 'Here comes this new thing that's untested,'" Karen says. "You could write that off to ignorance—not really, but you could—the first time around." But as she points out, we've been down this road. "We've seen what happens when you allow Pennsylvanians to be live test subjects in a laboratory experiment. Why would we go down that road again? [We know] what the petrochemical business in the state is all about: keeping fracking going."[34]

Indeed, the state legislature could hardly be more enthusiastic about the prospect of Nacero's unproven technology. Legislators worked intently, swiftly, and secretly to pass legislation that would provide significant subsidies for Nacero's proposed plant. If Nacero takes advantage of the full subsidies available, it adds up to a $6.7 million tax break they can give themselves each year.[35] "It happened so fast," Karen explains, "that it was just a done deal." Sadly, the same northeastern Pennsylvania legislators who were so quick to vocalize their enthusiasm about bringing Nacero to their region will be the ones whose constituents suffer the most if the plant is allowed to move forward. It's unclear precisely where the plant's intended site will be, and both Nacero and state officials have (so far) been tight-lipped. But according to Karen, locals in Luzerne County have heard rumblings it may be located not far from an elementary school. "So, here we go again with these things being planted in the middle of communities," Karen says, shaking her head. I can only shake mine along with her.

What we need, in this moment, is more information. Nacero's claims can only be refuted with hard facts and evidence, but both are in short supply. What we do know, looking at the Nacero website and reports in the press, is that at its core, the Nacero plan is to take fracked shale gas and use it to make gasoline for your car. Nacero claims it will also capture gas that would otherwise be lost to the atmosphere via venting or flaring, and asserts it will capture methane emissions from landfills and other sources, but the details to evaluate such claims are lacking. And in the end, what is becoming increasingly clear is that any captured gas will be mixed with fracked shale gas. No matter how you look at it, their plan obviously means more fracking. That fracking, Nacero's industrial process, and the burning of the gas in cars will all release climate-changing emissions, exacerbating the climate crisis, taking us away from needed pollution reductions, and diverting resources from the renewable energy technologies we should be building.

In addition, one of the key technologies Nacero touts for its planned facilities, which is getting a lot of buzz as the latest and greatest new weapon in America's supposed clean energy arsenal, is "carbon capture and sequestration." Laying aside the patent absurdity of a supposedly green technology that simply diverts emissions rather than reducing them, and looking at and beyond Nacero, carbon capture and sequestration actually appears to inflict more harm than it mitigates.[36] The idea, in its most basic form, is that carbon dioxide and other greenhouse gases that are produced by industrial processes would be captured (hence: carbon capture) rather than released into the atmosphere. The carbon is then transported and supposedly stored somewhere indefinitely (hence: sequestration), ingeniously sidestepping any need to reduce or limit the production of harmful climate-changing gases. But more often than not, the "storage" part of the equation actually allows companies to use captured greenhouse gases in other climate-changing operations, such as fracking for more oil or gas. On top of it all, many of the ambitious carbon capture projects that have been announced, stretching back to the 1990s, have been abandoned due to cost or insurmountable technical challenges. Despite bold, head-spinning claims, barely two dozen carbon capture facilities even exist. Even worse, more than 80 percent of captured carbon has been used to support more fracking. It's almost comically cynical how the industry uses supposedly green tech as a smokescreen to distract from its compulsion to destroy and degrade.[37]

In 2019, Mark Jacobson, a professor of civil and environmental engineering at Stanford University, released findings from a study he conducted into the efficacy of carbon capture. While proponents claim the technique can remediate 85 to 90 percent of carbon emissions, Dr. Jacobson found that the real number (on average, over twenty years) was closer to 10 or 11 percent. What's more, he discovered that carbon capture actually *increases* air pollution. "Even if you have 100 percent capture from the capture equipment, it is still worse, from a social cost perspective, than replacing a coal or gas plant with a wind farm," Jacobson explains. That's because carbon capture equipment cannot reduce air pollution—and what's more, it always comes with a notable cost: greenhouse gas emissions from operating the facility. By contrast, he adds, "Wind replacing fossil fuels always reduces air pollution and never has a capture equipment cost."[38] As a cure for climate change, carbon capture is not merely snake oil—it's worse: it doesn't just fail to protect the environment, but actively inflicts harm. As with fracking, breathless claims that carbon capture projects could be our bridge to a cleaner future need a reality check. One of the few data points we've been able to uncover about Nacero, thanks to Alex Bomstein of the Clean Air Council, supports this: the company's air permit applications for the model Texas operation show that the very same plant built in Pennsylvania would be the state's third-largest climate pollution emitter.[39] "If one plant is the third-biggest emitter in the state, what happens when they start building these all over the place?" Karen asks. "If it's their intention to replace [traditional] gasoline with Nacero gasoline . . . all of a sudden, we'd need about ten more plants, each one emitting at a dangerously high level." Alex adds that "we can't afford to keep permitting facilities like that in Pennsylvania, [in] our tiny little neck of the woods, having such an outsized impact on climate change."

And yet Pennsylvania politicians seem more intent than ever on repeating the grievous betrayal of public trust that has already mortgaged our state's future to the fracking industry. In legislators' zeal to hype Nacero and carbon capture to the voting public, Karen has noticed the use of inflated, fictitious promises about jobs, exaggerating above and beyond even Nacero's flimsy claims, and the tendency to wax poetic about the increased commerce and restaurant traffic that will flow when an exciting new industry comes to town. "It's very important for the environmental community to speak with one voice in a way that did not happen at the beginning of fracking," Karen concludes, recalling this very mistake as one big reason we are in such a difficult position now. "We can't have this be the thing that we're fighting for the next couple of decades. This has to be over before it starts."

As we strategize, Karen and I reason that—since lawmakers are already on board—our best bet for keeping Nacero out of Pennsylvania is to raise awareness to the point of inspiring a massive public uprising that forces legislators to remember their consciences. But of course, in Pennsylvania, the people also have another incredibly powerful tool at their disposal.

Years ago, we should've been able to use the state constitution to stop fracking before it started, but of course, the provision wasn't alive at the time. This time, though, we have a living, breathing constitutional right to pure water, clean air, and a healthy environment—and all Pennsylvania government officials have a clear obligation to protect natural resources for present and future generations. If we can't defeat false climate-change solutions with facts, science, and passionate advocacy, this time around we may have to turn to the Pennsylvania Green Amendment.

Knowledge is power, but in my mind knowledge *with* power is even better.

Clean Energy: Pitfall or Progress?

My phone rang one day in the spring of 2019 with a call from Michelle Henkin. Michelle had read the first edition of my book and was moved to get in touch. Right off the bat, she expressed her enthusiasm for the power of the Green Amendment movement and wanted to know if it was advancing in her home state of Maine. It wasn't. But it soon would be—thanks to Michelle.

She was unsure how to get things started, so we talked about the value of reaching out to potential partners and just starting to spread the word. We ended the call agreeing to touch base soon; she wanted to consider our conversation. A few weeks later, she sent me an email. It was now May. Michelle had been talking to professors and environmental advocates she trusted, and she felt it was time to bring us together in conversation. Andy Burt, a well-regarded social justice activist in Maine with years of experience, joined the leadership circle. We soon planned that I would come to Maine to sit with Michelle and Andy to talk strategy.

Our first meeting, on the porch of a Quaker meeting house in Damariscotta, Maine, was between Michelle, Andy, and me, but we were also joined by a young state legislator, Representative Chloe Maxmin. Chloe was a newly elected powerhouse who had garnered support from both conservatives and liberals because of her earnest interest in listening and finding solutions. In 2018, at the age of twenty-six, Chloe had trounced her opponent in the state House primary, defeated a Republican in the general election, and become the first Democrat ever to represent her home district—as well as the youngest woman serving in the state legislature. Chloe would go on to win a state senate seat in 2020, becoming the youngest woman ever elected to Maine's upper chamber. She was intrigued by the Green Amendment concept and would soon become our champion in the Maine Legislature.

Michelle, Andy, and I quickly developed into a cohesive team as Maine advanced as a leader in the Green Amendment movement. We worked in partnership to develop messaging, hold educational talks and trainings, and reach out to people of all ages, interests, and political stripes. As we hammered out what would be the best language for Maine and carried out our Green Amendment work, we did so in consultation with Wabanaki tribal leaders and youth climate leaders, with whom we continue to collaborate.

Before formally proposing the Maine Green Amendment, which would be known as the Pine Tree Amendment, Chloe wanted to secure nonpartisan support. Senator Richard Bennett, a respected Republican who had served in the state legislature already for thirteen years and a former chair of the state Republican Party, soon emerged as a leading sponsor of the effort. Senator Bennett immediately recognized that there's nothing political about protecting people's right to a clean, safe, and healthy environment and became one of our most compelling messengers. At the first legislative hearing on the Maine amendment, Senator Bennett would testify: "The proposed Amendment is predicated on the fact that a core condition of human life and a core to our state's identity is a healthy environment and a clean outdoors. This amendment will hold our government accountable to protect these as basic rights."[40] We also worked with Chloe to engage other conservative Republican leaders and took great care to be responsive to their input. As it has advanced, the Pine Tree Amendment has inspired sponsorship from Democrats, Republicans, and Independents alike.

On a side note, I am struck that our legislative champion in Delaware, Representative Madinah Wilson-Anton, the first practicing Muslim elected to the Delaware state legislature, is another young legislator who is similarly dedicated to an all-party, all-voices process as part of her early efforts. Madinah has invited conversation with conservative voices in the legislature and the agricultural community, while simultaneously engaging in outreach to environmental, youth, and faith leaders. This early and earnest outreach, while not always successful, invites meaningful respect for the effort—and is certainly worth the extra elbow grease.

As the Maine effort was first unfolding, questions about how the Pine Tree Amendment could help address climate change were often at the forefront of the conversation, including how it might impact a potentially game-changing discovery for Maine and efforts to advance clean energy technologies. That discovery, in western Maine in late 2021, was a massive deposit of lithium ore, weighing an estimated eleven million tons and worth approximately \$1.5 billion—the "richest known hard rock lithium deposit in the world."[41]

Lithium plays a significant role in modern society. Its most prominent use is in batteries, not only for cell phones and laptops but now also for electric vehicles—cars fueled by true clean energy (like my 100 percent electric Tesla that is powered by the solar panels on the roof of my all-electric house), not by Nacero's fracked gas-to-gasoline promises. Lithium is also important for solar and wind energy storage. Because of its light weight, combined with its high electrochemical potential, the US Geological Service predicts that "lithium is expected to play a key role in efforts to reduce carbon dioxide emissions that are responsible for global warming." Interestingly, once secured, lithium can be repeatedly recycled, giving it a long life span and reducing the need for an endless supply of new source materials. Once you have it, you have it—as long as you treat it right and recycle.[42]

Given lithium's potential for helping advance a clean-energy, clean-car future, would the Pine Tree Amendment prove counterproductive by preventing its extraction? Mining laws in Maine already raise questions about the future ability to secure the lithium find for any of a myriad of uses. Would the amendment be an even more unyielding hurdle to harnessing this lithium find for clean-energy progress? Or would it ensure that as we travel into a brighter clean-energy future, we do so in a way that avoids the pitfalls of our energy past?

The proposed Pine Tree Amendment is not going to prevent clean energy or economic progress—that is not its goal. Instead, it should help ensure that if the lithium extraction happens, it will be in a way that's protective of the environment—and that avoids costly harms that inflict irreparable damage along the way. Environmentally protective extraction is important not only for the health and safety of all Mainers, but also for the state's economy. The state's primary industry is tourism, and ecotourism is nearly twice as popular in Maine as the national average.[43] The Pine Tree Amendment would ensure that all these interests are considered, balanced, and protected—not that we repeat history by allowing extractive industries to profit while the rest of us suffer from the many facets and costs of the resulting environmental degradation.

In this regard, the Green Amendment approach is a bit like the Clean Water Act, which was crafted to be technology-forcing—that is, to drive the development of more effective pollution prevention technologies in order to meet the high environmental standards specified by the law. A Green Amendment can operate the same way when needed. For instance, if a destructive method like open-top mining proves to be the only known way to extract lithium from Maine's newly discovered deposit, the Pine Tree Amendment could inspire the pursuit of new methods. And if there turns out to be no safe extraction method available today, the amendment could provide the incentive necessary to develop newer, safer, and more successful technologies to ultimately allow for extraction in an environmentally safe manner in the future. At the very least, the amendment would ensure that there has been a careful, thorough, and meaningful process for considering all the harms and benefits as part of government decision-making on the matter, and that all efforts to minimize harm have been pursued. After all, it's not just about making money—it's about saving money, too.

Remember Maine's PFAS problem, discussed in chapter 5? It has contaminated water, shut down farms, led to "do not eat" advisories on deer, and inflicted other harms on life and business in Maine. The out-of-pocket costs to respond to that contamination are mounting for Maine taxpayers. Early in 2021, the government allocated $30 million for PFAS testing—and for the installation of water filtration systems where tests showed that contaminants were present. Meanwhile, the state's Department of Environmental Protection expanded its workforce to the tune of seventeen permanent and temporary staff members and also hired subcontractors to allow for more widespread PFAS testing.[44] The ultimate costs to Mainers will almost certainly be more significant as Maine comes to fully appreciate the extent of the contamination and resulting harm, but already we can see how costly just this one environmental problem is proving for the state budget. Clearly, solving the climate crisis in ways that do not burden us with a new set of environmental harms and problems is the best path forward—and it is a path that can, and will, be forged with the strong backing of environmental constitutionalism in the form of Green Amendments.

Mary Freeman and her husband, Gary, owners of the property where the lithium now lies, appreciate Maine's natural beauty. In fact, they found the lithium because of their love of Maine—quite by accident while enjoying their explorations of Maine's landscapes and geologic deposits. The Freemans are in no hurry to mine the lithium out of the ground. They are excited by the potential of being part of our nation's clean energy future, but they also want to be good stewards of Maine's beautiful nature. As Mary told the press when talking about their plans for the lithium and their land: "If we could do something positive toward green energy, I'd be honored to do that." But she is careful to add, "We're also very interested in making sure the forests and the land are maintained."[45]

Clearly, the Freemans and all those who support the Pine Tree Amendment—Maine's Green Amendment—are on the same page: let's address the climate crisis through clean energy in a way that doesn't dirty up and devastate our natural landscapes. Imagine if Pennsylvania government had been so careful when the fracking industry came knocking on its door, and if we'd had a thriving Green Amendment to ensure this kind of careful decision-making! Perhaps we would be close to hitting our targets for reducing climate-changing emissions by 2030—and our nation would be an international leader on the clean energy stage.

We are at a critical moment in the history of the world. As the UN Secretary-General António Guterres has urgently warned, because of the quickly accelerating climate crisis, we are in "a code red for humanity."[46] The World Health Organization (WHO) names climate change as "the biggest health threat facing humanity"—and projects that between 2030 and 2050, its impacts will result in roughly a quarter of a million additional deaths every year "from malnutrition, malaria, diarrhea, and heat stress."[47] Should this projection be borne out during each of the twenty years specified by WHO, it would amount to five million lives lost unnecessarily. And climate is far from an equal-opportunity offender: Indigenous communities, along with Black and brown people and low-income communities, are on the front lines of impact due to the increased pollution they are more likely to experience day to day. And it is not just people at risk: all of nature teeters on this same precipice.

Ultimately, future generations will bear the brunt of our lack of effort—or instead will enjoy the safety, security, and beauty of our forethought in taking swift and meaningful action to protect our planet. But it is important that, as we address the climate crisis, we do so in a way that does not sacrifice other essential foundations of life. We must protect water, air, native ecosystems, and the species that enrich our lives and with whom we share this Earth.

Protecting Sacred Mother Earth

I have long believed that my Green Amendment vision is just as much about protecting Mother Earth as about protecting her people. Often, during my talks to audiences far and wide, I have to respond to concerns that the Green Amendment approach is only about people—that it fails to recognize the rights, respect, and protection to which nature also is entitled. As someone who feels a deep connection to nature—I always stop and connect with a tree, plant, or stream before my talks, seeking the power of the natural world as I prepare to speak for its defense and protection—I find these moments of questioning difficult. It can feel as though my loyalty to and love of the natural world are being challenged. But then I patiently explain that the role of a constitution is to lay out the rights of people and the limitations they are placing on their government—and that I believe this pathway for protection does as much for nature as it does for people. After all, what is the value of giving nature access to the courts to argue for enforcement of an environmental law, if the environmental laws we have in place are all about accepting pollution and degradation rather than about preventing desecration in the first place?

Perhaps looking at such questions through a lens imbued with the dire consequences of climate change can help. While there is social and moral value in recognizing the rights of nature, if we can better protect nature's future through an anthropocentric right, isn't it possible that nature is better served through environmental constitutionalism? And certainly, these two approaches for protecting nature are not mutually exclusive—there is importance and value in pursuing both.

I think the positive synergy of enforceably recognizing environmental rights for nature, people, and future generations shines brightly in the testimony of Maulian Dana, the Tribal Ambassador for the Penobscot Nation, when she spoke on March 8, 2021, about Maine's Green Amendment proposal:

> *The Wabanaki Nations have been stewards of the lands and waters now called Maine since time immemorial. The environment is not a separate issue for us; it is woven into our culture, values, life ways, and how we view our place in the world. This speaks to the deep ancestral connection we have to our homelands but also to the modern day work we do in our natural resources departments and policy making in every level of tribal government. The proposed amendment to the Constitution of Maine would ease in part the place in our spirit that aches when we see desecration and polluting of Mother Earth. We, collectively, have a long way to go when it comes to treating the environment as a sacred being but this [constitutional amendment] is a great step in the right direction. A healthy environment is a human right. For our generation and the next.* [48]

CHAPTER EIGHT

ENDING
ENVIRONMENTAL RACISM

Gina Burton lives on Herbert Lane in Millsboro, Delaware. The land has been in her family for generations; the street itself is named after Herbert Burton Sr., Gina's grandfather.[1] Like many Black farmers of his era, Herbert made a living as a sharecropper—reputedly the very first to settle in Sussex County. Apart from 1998 through 2002, when Gina moved to a town called Felton, about forty-five minutes north of Millsboro, she has lived on Herbert Lane her entire life.[2]

It was a wonderful place to grow up, surrounded by family: aunts and cousins, grandparents and siblings, nieces and nephews who also lived on the lane. The Burtons had put down deep roots in Millsboro, carving out their own little haven that everyone hoped would remain in the family for generations to come. Before Gina's grandfather passed away, a company called Townsend, one of the area's major employers, approached him about purchasing some of his land for a poultry processing plant. He agreed to sell, but not before making sure there would still be enough land for each of the children, grandchildren, and cousins to live there, so the family could always be together. Townsend built its poultry plant, and the Burton family coexisted with its new neighbor for decades without serious issues.

It wasn't until 2002, when Gina moved back into her mother's house after four years away, that she began to notice alarming changes. In 2000, while she'd been living in Felton, Townsend sold its Millsboro facility to another company: Mountaire Farms, the fourth-largest chicken producer in the United States.[3] Not long after, people in the neighborhood—many of them Gina's close relatives—started to notice a foul smell in the air. By the time she moved back home two years later, she was horrified to find that the stench had grown even more suffocating.

"I think we weren't really realizing too much where it was coming from until we started seeing different stuff. . . . We constantly had molds and other stuff on the sides of our houses and our vehicles . . . . And that's when my sister made a video and took pictures of green [chicken] body parts coming out of [the] irrigation unit," Gina says. Soon, it became obvious that the Mountaire Farms poultry plant was the only possible source of this pollution—and it just kept getting worse. "Just living beside them and dealing with the smell on a constant basis, we never put up our windows. We never had a clothesline to hang up clothes [and] get their fresh smell. We [were never] able to breathe fresh air."

Along with the stomach-turning stench came bugs: swarms of flies and other insects that descended on Herbert Lane and the surrounding area, attracted by the smell of Mountaire Farms' waste—and eager to prey on the feces, blood, and other rotting poultry by-products that the plant regularly dispersed onto the toxic spray fields that now straddled the Burton family's land. Before long, the pollution and its malodorous side effects had invaded every aspect of life for those who lived along Herbert Lane. Even the simplest daily and weekly activities and community rituals, like going to church on Sundays, became not merely unpleasant but unbearable.

In fact, it was on the way home from a worship service one Easter Sunday that Gina's sister captured the video and photos of putrid green waste, including pieces of chicken carcasses, being sprayed by Mountaire Farms onto one of the fields near the Burtons's homes. In retrospect, this affirmative step toward documenting the plant's pollution, and the harms the plant's neighbors suffered as a result, marked something of a turning point. Not long afterward, other family and community members began keeping meticulous track of the many ill effects they were experiencing. Together, the evidence they assembled painted a damning picture of the practices at—and negative impact of—Mountaire Farms.

Maria Payan became one of the first people from outside Millsboro to review this evidence when, in 2017, the Mountaire Farms plant proposed an expansion—and community members asked Maria's organization, a nonprofit called the Socially Responsible Agriculture Project (SRAP), to intervene. Maria went from house to house on Herbert Lane, talking about water contamination and getting to know community members for the first time. Although SRAP specializes in protecting communities from industrial-scale agriculture and production, Maria was still shocked by what she found. "I was really alarmed, because it was like going to Walter Reed Hospital," Maria recalls, referencing the terrible, violent illnesses and injuries common to a hospital that provides care for servicemembers.[4]

In the first house lived Gina's sister, Donna, who had tumors all over her body, and Donna's daughter, who was pregnant and repeatedly suffering inexplicable seizures. The next house belonged to Patsy, Gina's cousin, who'd had a basic water softener system in place for a decade. The system itself, along with the shipments of salt that kept it running, was provided by Mountaire Farms—which had agreed to install them in a handful of nearby houses after a 2003 EPA investigation found unacceptably high levels of nitrates, which cause cancer and birth defects (among other harms), in wells and groundwater.[5] The water system was working properly but clearly inadequate: the result of a $4 state-provided test of Patsy's drinking water found nitrate levels of 25 mg/L—two and a half times the safe drinking water standard of 10 mg/L.

Next was Gina's house, where she lived with her mother. Gina was sick constantly, experiencing frequent gastrointestinal issues and hair loss that left her with permanent bald spots. Gina's daughter had been born with an extra ear.[6] But no one had endured greater suffering, or paid a higher price for Mountaire's callously destructive actions, than Gina's son, Kiwanis. Like Gina, Kiwanis had been born with asthma. His case was particularly severe. "When your asthma is at its worst, it's like somebody put a plastic bag over your head and just pulled on a string and cut off all your air circulation," says Gina. "[H]e really suffered. He just suffered."

When Kiwanis left Millsboro for a year, to attend school, his condition seemed to improve significantly. But then he came home, and his asthma was once again a daily source of hardship; despite nebulizers, inhalers, prescription steroids, and an EpiPen, he struggled to keep it under control. On March 5, 2014, Gina got a frantic call. While hanging out in a house full of friends, Kiwanis had suffered an extremely severe asthma attack. They were calling an ambulance; she needed to drive immediately to the hospital.

By the time Gina arrived, Kiwanis had passed away. He was just twenty-four years old. "I checked [with] his job, and he went to work early that night and he stayed until the time to get off," Gina recalls. "And he wasn't sick. He didn't tell me he was sick or anything." It was an incomprehensible loss. Just as incomprehensible was the official cause, confirmed by an autopsy that took Gina four months to get ahold of. "It said he died from an acute asthma attack," she says. "And I was like, who dies from asthma anymore?"

Another heart-wrenching reality was that the very same pollution that likely caused Kiwanis's death had also likely affected him from the very beginning of his life. One evening, Gina sent Maria a form and asked her to take a look. It was a form for Supplemental Security Income (SSI), a type of Social Security assistance for people with disabilities, which Gina had been receiving for Kiwanis. "The SSI form said that he could not be educated because of a lack of oxygen to the brain," Maria recalls. "Now, there is no bigger crime against humanity than a child who . . . because of exposure issues, cannot develop to be the person that they ought to be. To be a mother myself, and to hear Gina cry because her son wanted to be so many things and couldn't be any of them—that's an unforgivable sin."

And Kiwanis was almost certainly not the only victim: when Maria and her SRAP colleagues dug further, scrutinizing local statistics, they noticed immediately that relative to neighboring areas, special education rates were elevated in Gina's community—the one in closest proximity to the Mountaire Farms plant.

One of the possible effects of prolonged exposure to high levels of nitrates is inadequate blood oxygen levels. In infants, this manifests as a condition known as "blue baby syndrome," because of the visible discoloration the lack of oxygen causes. The impacts for young adults are consistent with the health impacts and learning difficulties that Kiwanis suffered.[7] In older adults, like Gina's aunt Martha—who lived next door to Gina and Kiwanis—it can take a similarly appalling toll. Maria recalls, "Aunt Martha had one of her legs amputated, [because of a] lack of oxygen going through the body." Ultimately, both of her legs would be taken.[8]

The more time Maria spent in Millsboro, which is predominantly a community of color, and the more residents she spoke with, the clearer it became that Mountaire Farms was responsible for countless life-altering harms. And the harms weren't limited to Herbert Lane. Maria explains, "We had neighbors having miscarriages. We had animals having seizures. We had three people in the same community with a very rare birth defect—with a risk assessment that should have been [roughly] one in . . . ten thousand." And Maria wasn't just canvassing the area for information; she was carefully documenting the egregious harms she was seeing, along with the staggering pollution that was happening in plain sight. "I was taking pictures, sending them to a guy in DNREC"—Delaware's Department of Natural Resources and Environmental Control—"and I would say, 'Here's a picture. Is this a violation?'" Maria recalls. He would respond, with sincerity, "Maria, we're looking at it. I'll get back to you." In the end, she wound up sharing a Dropbox folder filled with videos showing how Mountaire Farms pollution was devastating the surrounding community.

In one note, Maria asked her DNREC contact: "Do you know why

I do what I do?" She went on to share photos of her son, at the age of eight or nine, covered in palm-sized blisters after coming out of the bathtub—the result of chemical burns from contamination caused by a different poultry plant near where her family lived years before. Gina's story, and Maria's emotional investment in Millsboro, seemed to strike a chord with the DNREC official. "He emailed me and said, 'Maria, I promise you, we're going to get this right.'" He seemed to nudge the agency into action—shortly thereafter, agency testing in the area verified there was significant contamination.[9]

Around this same time—in 2017—Maria first crossed paths with a community organizer, US Senate candidate from Delaware, and (according to *Vogue*) "the next Alexandria Ocasio-Cortez": Kerri Evelyn Harris—the same Kerri that honored me with a foreword to this book.[10] Kerri learned of a public meeting Maria and the community had organized to discuss the DNREC data. The government agency wasn't publicizing its findings or taking needed action. When things like this "happen in poor Black and brown communities, it's in the best interest of local, state, and federal governments to ignore it . . . . [So] we were desperately trying to get attention," explains Maria.

"There was a panel, and I was there literally just to listen. My mind was blown," Kerri recalls.[11] "And it was the fact that nobody knew this was happening, throughout the state. We're a very small state, and everything happens in silos," she explains, pointing to the failure of the different branches of government to communicate effectively with one another or to consider the impacts of their decisions beyond those they are specifically charged to address. "The more you're in it, the more you realize that's not by accident, it's by design." Somehow, she recalls, a microphone wound up in her hand, and that night—on the spot—she became a vocal champion for the Herbert Lane community.

Afterward, Kerri approached Maria and Dr. Sacoby Wilson of the University of Maryland's CEEJH (discussed earlier, in chapter 6) to learn more. She says she knew environmental justice—which recognizes that communities of color and low-income communities are burdened

with disproportionately high levels of pollution and environmental degradation—"was important, but it wasn't *my* justice issue." But through
learning about the Burton family's plight in Sussex County, Kerri "really
started to understand the intersection of environmental justice and so
many other justice issues. And I used my platform during that time to
actually highlight Sussex."

Maria recalls Kerri throwing herself into the work, investing hours
knocking on doors to hear about people's experiences and learn their
concerns. Kerri visited with the people on Herbert Lane, in Millsboro,
and across Sussex County, and then shone a light of awareness as she was
alerted to each new issue. The more people heard about what industry
was doing to families like Gina's, the more they began to draw connections between other afflicted areas of the state. "When I would talk about
what was happening in Sussex . . . we started to realize we were having
the same nitrate problems in Kent County," recounts Kerri. "We'd go
up to New Castle, and while nitrates aren't so much of a problem there,
PFAS are. And so people started to see, 'Wait, how is this happening?
How didn't any of us know about it?'"

The fact that Mountaire's devastating operations inflicted harm on a
community of color with limited economic resources is no surprise. This
story is a clear example of environmental racism, advanced by systemic
inequities in laws and governance. "Environmental justice overlaps with
social justice," observes Maria. "I mean, it's not by accident that communities that are in environmental justice areas also have no access to good
education, no access to good food, no access to good health care. And
believe me, they don't have access to clean air and clean water." Despite
the vindication delivered by the DNREC-collected data and the growing awareness of harm, state officials still weren't acting.

Recognizing that the government wouldn't be riding to their rescue,
Maria, Kerri, and the community continued to do their work, uncover-
ing a history of violations by Mountaire Farms going back more than
a decade.[12] Armed with their years of documentation and discovery,
and refusing to be deterred by the hopelessly inert response of the state

government, some Millsboro residents took to the courts—one of the few routes of recourse that remained open to them. In 2018, Gina Burton and some eighty of her neighbors filed suit against Mountaire Farms, seeking medical compensation—and justice for Kiwanis, in the form of wrongful death damages.[13] Their court filings documented years of appalling transgressions, including the fact that "in August 2017, Mountaire had already exceeded its permitted total amount of nitrogen for the year on nine of its 13 fields. On six of those fields, Mountaire had disposed of over 320 pounds per acre—its annual limit—in August alone." This was in addition to a 2017 fecal coliform concentration test that revealed 5,500 times the amount permitted under law, among other violations.

The lawsuit was soon accompanied by a class-action suit involving nearly eight hundred Millsboro residents. After years of winding their way through the court systems, the people of Millsboro achieved two resounding, landmark victories—a result that signified a rare and remarkable rebuke of powerful industry. Mountaire Farms settled the lawsuit in which Gina took part for an undisclosed sum, and later agreed to a class-action settlement totaling $65 million—plus an additional $120 million in remediation and facility improvements.[14] "In the end, the people won everything," says Maria. "Which was monumental."

It is both just and right that those who were harmed by Mountaire Farms received compensation and solutions for the contamination of their lives and homes. But no legal outcome or settlement agreement, however righteous and well justified, can undo the irreversible health effects suffered by so many Millsboro residents—let alone bring back Kiwanis or restore Aunt Martha's legs. In truth, it should never have come to this. It shouldn't have taken years of advocacy and evidence to spur the powers that be to care, and to act. The government should have been accountable to the people to prevent harm in the first place—and when its failures became clear, there should have been a lever of power the people could pull to end the systemic inequities that were allowing Mountaire Farms and delinquent government officials to inflict such devastation.

You might be thinking this is just one bad actor—one polluting industry that slipped through the cracks. You may ask how I can call this "systemic racism." My answer is simple: across our nation, laws are written and implemented in a way that allows communities of color to be targeted by highly polluting industries and disproportionately impacted by environmental degradation—and then ignored when there's a problem. This isn't one bad actor, this is one example of a myriad. And more often than not, it isn't just one bad operation causing harm. There is a confluence of actions and decisions that *alone* may be in compliance with the law, but whose cumulative impacts inflict tremendous injustice and damage.

The View from Tsoodzil

Mountain View is a rural, working-class community in the South Valley area of Albuquerque, New Mexico. Largely located outside the city limits, it's home to vibrant Hispanic, Mexican, Chicana/o, and immigrant populations; 74 percent of residents identify as Latinx. This lower-income area is also home to widespread subsistence farming. Thanks to engaged and organized residents who refused to allow a former dairy farm to become the site of a sewage treatment plant, Mountain View also hosts the Valle de Oro National Wildlife Refuge.[15]

Despite the community's best efforts, Mountain View—like a handful of other North and South Valley communities with similar demographics—is also home to a disproportionate number of polluting industries. The fact that residents were able to spark the creation of the American Southwest's only urban wildlife refuge, but are still unable to overcome the structural barriers presented by the framework of regulatory laws and rules that continue to allow industry encroachment, is not a coincidence. It is evidence that the system is biased against them. According to Eric Jantz, a veteran staff attorney at the New Mexico Environmental Law Center (NMELC), "This is a clear case of environmental racism. The structural barriers to this community being able to ensure its own ability to breathe clean air, drink clean water, [and] walk on clean land are pretty stark."[16]

Due, in part, to an inexplicable quirk in New Mexico's framework for regulating air quality, the City of Albuquerque bears authority for regulating Bernalillo County, where Mountain View is located, while the New Mexico Environment Department is responsible for the rest of the state.[17] The ramifications of this altered structure are impactful and serious for Mountain View. The city's Environmental Health Department (EHD), Eric explains, has marginalized community voices time and again as it grants permits for air pollution. "One could even say it's been a rubber stamp," he says. "The community has consistently fought this sort of conveyor belt [of] industrial pollution permit applications and grantings from the City of Albuquerque. [But there's a] big structural barrier to these communities participating in this process in a meaningful way, and that is the statutory and regulatory framework."

Especially in places where many household incomes hover near or below the poverty level, it's unconscionable that people's ability to breathe clean air depends upon their capacity to hire experts and legal counsel—spending "money they don't have and tak[ing] time they don't have," in Eric's words—to appeal permit approvals and regulatory rulemakings to the relevant authorities. "It basically perpetuates this cycle of heavy industrialization in low-income communities of color," he says. Eric was therefore shocked, but not surprised, when he discovered that despite having roughly 1 percent of the total population of Bernalillo County, Mountain View had close to 28 percent of the total polluting industry.

Fortunately, this is where Eric and the NMELC come in: providing pro bono legal representation to people like the residents of Mountain View.

"It's always a struggle to find the resources to actually prosecute a case," Eric says—particularly when the level of resources required, and the barriers to access that are built directly into the legal system, seem inordinately (even deliberately) high. For instance, in 2007—the first time the community challenged an air pollution permit granted by the City of Albuquerque—NMELC discovered that the Environmental Health Department had imposed a $750 filing fee for any such appeals. "In order to get through the front door, people had to shell out almost a thousand dollars," Eric says. Finding no statutory or regulatory basis, or rational justification, for imposing such a fee, NMELC threatened to sue—and has been working with the people of Mountain View ever since.

The area's history is replete with examples of government inaction, neglect, and (even worse) outright abuse, much of it stemming from a 1970s rezoning process that allocated a large share of the neighborhood for industrial use. Over the years, dozens of companies and other industrial interests—from fertilizer suppliers to automotive recyclers, paint facilities, and sewage treatment plants—have come to Mountain View as a result, spewing toxins into the air, land, and water supply. Among people who live in the neighborhood, according to NMELC, rates of cancer and asthma are elevated—and the local life expectancy is ten to twenty-four years shorter than among the mostly white inhabitants of more affluent Albuquerque neighborhoods.[18]

Despite these and a litany of other well-documented harms, the city government continues to treat Mountain View as the textbook definition of a sacrifice zone. In late 2020, the EHD issued a permit for yet another industrial activity: an asphalt batch plant.[19] "There are a lot of problems with it," says Eric. "It's located several hundred feet from a subdivision in the Mountain View community, so those folks are going to be exposed to asphalt fumes, particulate matter, volatile organic compounds." The site is also quite close to the Valle de Oro Wildlife Refuge, proximity that both acutely threatens the natural environment and seems to pile insult and indignity on top of injury, spoiling the unique stretch of acreage that local residents have fought so diligently to protect. With NMELC's support and advocacy, however, people are translating their eminently justified outrage about this latest development into action, by challenging the permit—and along the way, exposing some truly bewildering self-justifications and inconsistencies on the part of government decision makers.

For one thing, the proposed asphalt plant would be located in one of the relatively few parts of Mountain View that is zoned not for heavy industry, but for agriculture—a fact that should have prevented the city from approving any such permit in the first place. Yet local officials ignored this inconvenient reality with impunity. When raising this fact regarding zoning during the pre-appeal process, Eric says, "The position of the Environmental Health Department (EHD) for the City of Albuquerque was: zoning is not relevant." This willful blindness isn't the only thing that's so enraging. The city clearly has the authority to say "no" to this facility but is simply choosing not to. The zoning issue is just one example of how the EHD is ignoring relevant laws intended to protect the environment and human health.

There is also an issue of federal law. National Ambient Air Quality Standards are set by the EPA, under authority granted by the Clean Air Act, to limit the concentration of certain harmful pollutants. One of Albuquerque's five monitors for ozone levels has established that the city is exceeding these federal standards, while another monitor shows Albuquerque is at the maximum allowable level of ozone as a result of current emissions, and so adding more pollution is likely to tip the city over the edge into more violations. As Eric explains, the law says a permit can be denied if the emissions from the proposed operation will cause or contribute to an act's violation. "We've got that already," he says, "but it's something else that the city has decided isn't a relevant issue." In addition, the asphalt manufacturing process results in significant ozone precursor emissions, so adding this new facility all but guarantees increasingly egregious violations of air quality standards. This is yet another fact that the city decided to ignore.

If local leaders' dereliction of duty weren't so appalling, it would be almost cartoonish. To Eric, the NMELC, and the entire community, the EHD's position—that it doesn't have to abide by any laws except for the State Air Quality Control Act, and can ignore any other laws (for example, zoning and federal air quality protections)—seems "insane." To demonstrate the egregiousness of this legal posture, Eric used an illegal facility as an example: "Suppose somebody wanted to apply for a [state] air pollution permit for a methamphetamine operation," he says. "The Environmental Health Department's position is, that would be fine. They would go ahead and expend resources analyzing an air pollution permit for a methamphetamine house."

For Mountain View, and for NMELC, endless delays in permit appeals and other regulatory matters are routine when working to protect residents, wildlife, and the environment from industry. Quite simply, it suits the local government's strategy and allows industry time to adjust. Perhaps most striking in the battle to protect Mountain View, which in my experience is not uncommon in battles of this kind nationwide, is the fact that the industry has not even bothered to involve legal representation—nor participated at all, for that matter. As Eric explains, "They let the City of Albuquerque Environmental Health Department carry the water for them, which it happily did. It's this weird proto-fascist setup, where industry and government . . . are skipping down the lane hand in hand [while] frontline communities are left to fend for themselves."

Eric observes that the very same dynamic has played out on the slopes of Mount Taylor, less than a hundred miles west of Albuquerque, where a dormant uranium mine was allowed to lie fallow for twenty-seven years after the precipitous decline of the uranium market in the 1980s. Rather than incur the considerable expense required to clean up the mine, its operator—a company called Rio Grande Resources, which in turn is a subsidiary of the massive San Diego–based defense contractor General Atomics—allowed it to fester like an open wound. "They were able to convince, or coerce, the state regulator that planning to mine sometime in the indeterminate future was essentially the same as doing actual, physical ore removal," Eric says. In New Mexico, according to Eric, mines can only be on "standby" for up to twenty years, after which they need to take action to clean up and shut down or actually produce minerals. So getting the state to join in on this imagined characterization of the Mount Taylor mine as being in perpetual preparation for more mining meant the company could avoid cleanup and remediation.

The direct environmental impact of this long neglect is only compounded by the fact that Mount Taylor is better known throughout the Navajo Nation as Tsoodzil, or the Turquoise Mountain—one of the four sacred mountains that mark the four cardinal directions and delineate the boundaries of the original Navajo homeland. Also found there are the headwaters of critical natural water sources for the nearby communities of Laguna Pueblo and Acoma Pueblo, where its Native name translates as "Place of Snow."

"The community, of course, was livid," Eric says, "because their position was, and is, that the mine should have been reclaimed decades ago, but it hasn't [been]." The good news is, on the slopes of Tsoodzil, things are finally (albeit gradually) improving. The bad news is that this is due not to some legal ruling or newly unearthed legislative language that can be marshaled to help impacted communities elsewhere in the state. "This is one we actually won [because] it became clear even to General Atomics that the uranium market wasn't going to bounce back anytime soon, if ever," said Eric. "The mine closed at the end of 2019, and now we're just making sure that the mine gets reclaimed in a way that's appropriate for the cultural sensitivity of the place where it's located."

Eric and the rest of the New Mexico Environmental Law Center have been among my key partners in advancing passage of a New Mexico Green Amendment. As a result, Eric has become very familiar with the values of this constitutional approach. If there had been a Green Amendment on the books in New Mexico, Eric suggests it would have been a very different prospect for the Navajo people and those of the Laguna and Acoma Pueblos. "They wouldn't have had to endure, ad nauseum, all that ongoing pollution and exposure," he suggests. "Because it's unquestionable that there is contamination, both radioactive and otherwise, at this mine site." With a Green Amendment in place, rather than argue over the definition of an "active mine," these communities could have simply demonstrated before a judge that the mine was contaminating their water and natural lands. The ambiguities in the law that General Atomics was able to exploit for so many years would have been completely irrelevant. "While this may have been deemed in compliance with the laws on the books, it [would be] causing a constitutional violation," explains Eric, "and so the court could [have ordered] the state to take action to restore the natural resources and environmental rights being trampled upon."

Across the country, we repeatedly see how Black, brown, Indigenous, immigrant, and low-income communities are left to suffer from pollution and degradation where richer and whiter communities are not. It may anger some that I state this so plainly, but we have to be honest. Environmental racism is real, and it is perpetuated under our current system of laws.

Recall John Beard's Port Arthur. In addition to bearing the brunt of the climate crisis, in the form of flooding, the community is surrounded by pollution-spewing, health-harming, and climate-changing industry—and in fact that is one of its defining features. Throughout this book, I have written about the health, environmental, and safety hazards associated with fossil fuel operations and heavy industry. Well, they all come together in Port Arthur—not just because there's a great deal of industry in the area, but because there are also, as John describes, "serial polluters" that contribute to the health harms inflicted on his community.

What makes the nearby Valero refinery and the Oxbow plant (owned by one of the infamous Koch Brothers) serial polluters? It's simple: they pollute a lot, and get away with it under the law. As John explains, the Valero refinery—which processes heavy crude oils into gasoline, diesel, and jet fuel—has, in just a five-year time frame, "had over six hundred unregulated environmental incidents, including flaring and leaks" that release harmful pollution into the air. If incidents are unregulated, it means polluters are not violating any law—meaning the government is free to ignore the harms they are causing.

The other serial polluter is Oxbow, which takes raw petroleum coke from domestic and international oil refiners and turns it into calcined petroleum coke used in the manufacture of metals such as aluminum. I'm not sure anybody without a PhD has any idea what that means, but the bottom line is that it's an intensive manufacturing operation owned by an obscenely rich man—a man who could most certainly ensure that Oxbow does better by the people of Port Arthur, but chooses not to. Instead, Oxbow releases twenty-two million pounds of sulfur dioxide into the air each year.[20]

Sulfur dioxide is "very toxic" and "corrosive" to the respiratory tract, not only causing severe irritation of the nose, throat, and lungs, but also accumulation of fluid in the lungs that can be life threatening. At the right exposure levels, sulfur dioxide can be fatal.[21] Those who live closest to the Oxbow facility suffer from higher rates of respiratory illness—such as asthma, shortness of breath, and difficulty breathing—in keeping with the sorts of health harms these kinds of emissions inflict. The amount of sulfur dioxide released from Oxbow alone has been calculated at ten times greater than the three refineries that surround it.[22] Yet these pollution releases are, quite unbelievably (at least to John and me) completely legal.

A loophole in the law that has required other industries in the area to upgrade their operations and reduce pollution has not required the same of Oxbow. In fact, Oxbow has been operating in the same highly polluting manner for over eighty years—without violating the law. In my experience, this kind of high-polluting industrialization, in which life-threatening levels of pollution go unaddressed—and are even legalized—would never happen in an affluent community of white people. That's racism. I won't be shy or apologetic about calling it what it is.

Across our nation, communities of color disproportionately live in environmental sacrifice zones, where industrial contaminants, pollution, and other poisons degrade water, air, and soil, causing heart disease, asthma, cancer, compromised immune systems, and other serious illnesses.[23] Black people in America are 1.54 times more likely than their white counterparts to breathe the fine particulate matter that leads to heart attacks, cancer, low birth weights, high blood pressure, and even premature death.[24] Over half of people living within 1.8 miles of hazardous waste facilities here in the United States are people of color, and they must endure the health, quality of life, and economic harms that result.[25] In neighborhoods with multiple hazardous sites, this percentage soars to as high as 69 percent. Dangerous air pollution levels around public schools disproportionately affect Black, Hispanic, Asian/Pacific Islander, and low-income children, leading to higher rates of exposure to neurotoxicants like lead, mercury, and cyanide compounds.[26] This burden has enormous ramifications for the physical health of these children, causing and contributing to illnesses that can plague them for their entire lives. But it is also the cause of deficits and disabilities that impact not only a child's ability to learn, but—as a result—their entire future, including job opportunities, income, and their relationship with the world around them.[27] The evidence is undeniable—and it requires us to take action.

It is hard to stand by and just accept the injustice of environmental racism. It is hard to hear people, especially politicians in a position to do something about it, deny that environmental racism is real. It is harder still to have to live this truth. The people of Millsboro, Mountain View, Port Arthur, and Tsoodzil know that environmental racism is real. I know it's real. And now—if you didn't already—you do, too. The question is: can we do something about it?

We most certainly can. One big thing we can do is secure Green Amendments, which ensure that all people have the same constitutional right to a clean, safe, and healthy environment. A constitutional Green Amendment would provide communities like Mountain View, Tsoodzil, and Port Arthur an important foundation for the environmental justice inequities they face—one that no longer lets industry players use government as a shield for their injustice. With Green Amendments in place, all government officials, at every level, would be duty bound to equitably protect the environmental rights of all people. Government officials would have to look at the cumulative impacts of existing and newly proposed industry actions as they assess the implications of their anticipated decision-making. There would be no need to prove racial intent if a community of color or Indigenous community were to be disproportionately impacted by pollution; the fact of the inequitable burden itself would be enough to secure constitutional consideration. Quite simply, with Green Amendments, environmental sacrifice zones and environmental racism will be constitutionally prohibited. And it will no longer be good enough to prove that you've complied with the law precisely as written; government would need to prove they've complied with the constitution, too.

Walking on the Backs of Salmon

Debra Lekanoff is a member of the Tlingit tribe of southeast Alaska, where she grew up in a town of three hundred people called Yakutat. As a young girl, she recalls playing in the woods with grizzly bears roaming nearby, though neither the bears nor Debra and her friends exhibited any fear of the other. "My summers were spent putting up all five species of salmon with my grandma and my aunties while my mom and dad fished," she recalls. "My whole youth has been wrapped around the timing of natural resources: we knew it was springtime because the candlefish were coming, the eulachons were coming, the sockeyes were coming, the silvers were coming. We had king salmon all year round."[28]

Debra clearly carries these lessons in her bones and her soul, but also in her very name: Debra's Tlingit name, Xixch'i See ("Frog Daughter-Doll"), passed down to her through generations, means "where there's a change in the springtime." Debra explains, "So, it's those tiny little baby frogs that are coming to life in the instream flow, where the cool grasses, where the baby salmonoids come. It's that time of change."

For decades, Debra has worked closely with Native American communities. In her thirties, she made a home in the Skagit Valley, which lies in the northwestern part of Washington State just ashore of the San Juan Islands. In 2018, Debra won election to the Washington State legislature, where she was the only current (and just the second ever) Native American woman to hold office.[29] She has listened and learned how Washington tribal leaders are "fighting for their treaty right, fighting for their salmon, fighting for their eulachons, fighting for their halibut, fighting for their deer, their elk—facing the impact and growth of pollution-based industry." In her work, Debra has followed both the science and the experiences of communities. "My heart was completely broken [to learn] that western Washington had no wild fish," she recalls, and that only a handful of rivers support a few small wild salmon runs, while virtually every river system in Washington State has a hatchery.[30] In fact, the Skagit River is the only river that still spawns all five species of wild salmon.[31]

Today, the patterns of Washington river systems are changing, along with their ecosystems; more and more, the salmon aren't returning. Decades of commercial and recreational overharvesting have decimated wild salmon populations. Dams and habitat degradation have disrupted long-established breeding patterns. Unrestrained agricultural and industrial growth—along with the pollution that inevitably accompanies both—has depleted surviving populations and hampered salmon recovery. Russ Hefner, the vice chair of the Lower Elwha tribe, which holds treaty rights in the vicinity of a river by the same name, has been a colleague and friend of Debra's for decades. He once told her that he recalls a time, many years ago—before the dams and the relentless encroachment of industry—when that river system was full. "The elders, our stories, our songs, our values, our memories, our summertime, we knew that we could walk on the backs of salmon. The backs of six-foot salmon . . . in the Lower Elwha River," Debra reports Russ saying. "This is who we are; this is where we come from. We are king salmon. This is who our culture is built upon. And when the dams came and the growth came, all of our king salmon were gone."

Washington State policymakers like Debra Lekanoff are in the unenviable position of needing to right past wrongs that have caused devastating environmental and cultural outcomes. And not all of the deleterious impacts of years of unrepresentative governance are as readily visible as now-empty river systems that used to be gorged with salmon. Destructive cultural bias is baked into the metrics that states use to measure health and safety, and therefore how it protects people and nature. When formulating clean water regulations that affect what Washington considers a healthy rate of salmon consumption, regulators wildly underestimated the importance of this staple fish in Native people's diets. According to Debra, Native Americans eat six to eight ounces of salmon in one to two days. As a result, the release of toxins into the environment that bioaccumulate in fish flesh means "we're poisoning ourselves," says Debra. "You could go and tell the elders, 'Don't go down and eat the shellfish down there. The refinery's right there.' Or, 'Industry is right there [releasing] pollution.' They're still going to sneak down there at night and dig up their clams and eat them. Because they want to eat their resources."

The abuse of Native American peoples and the exploitation of Mother Earth: like nature from culture and culture from name, these things are inseparable from one another. "Once the instream flow is gone, once that area no longer exists—that time of change [in the spring] . . . my spirit and the name I carry, is gone also," says Debra. "I no longer exist as a person. I no longer exist as a value system, because that name is who I am. The environmental justice, the cultural justice, the justice of being a Native American—it goes away when the instream flow goes away. Because those baby frogs, that time of change, is gone."

This is what Debra was wrestling with when she and I first crossed paths in 2019. I was at the annual meeting of the National Caucus of Environmental Legislators (NCEL), an important partner in our Green Amendment movement. I was there to speak to legislators about the power of Green Amendments. After my presentation, I attended some of the breakout sessions, where legislators were meeting and talking about their efforts. I wandered into one breakout where an amazing woman wearing a beautiful, flower-embroidered outfit stepped to the podium and spoke with the power, passion, and conviction of the rivers, bear, salmon, and Native peoples she was speaking for. It was Debra Lekanoff, who had the year before earned NCEL's Rising Leadership Award because of her strong and proactive stance on environmental issues so early in her career.

As a legislator, Debra was searching for a way to infuse environmental justice into all aspects of state-level policymaking. Washington tribes, like those of other states, are unable to rely on their treaty rights to secure the environmental protections they need as a culture and people.

At the same time, Indigenous populations are too often among the first and worst to suffer the consequences of state environmental failures. The more Debra talked with her colleagues about the interconnectedness and interdependence of life, educating them about Native American belief systems and traditional science, the more people started to perceive how—even though the impacts of wanton pollution, lax regulation, and overharvesting wild salmon populations fall disproportionately on tribal communities—they also create a ripple effect that touches every single person in the state. An increase in salmon hatchery numbers, for instance, would bolster commercial, recreational, and treaty fishing, but releasing too many hatchery fish would unduly strain an already fragile ecosystem. As it is, fish and shellfish growth is often stunted in and around the Skagit Valley due to resource scarcity, and orca whales are sometimes found with empty stomachs. "How do I make these decisions as a policymaker of Washington State?" asks Debra. "How do I make these decisions as a mom, and as someone who the Washington tribes and the Washington citizens have entrusted?"

In February 2021, Debra introduced the Washington Green Amendment for consideration by her legislative colleagues, who would need to pass it before the measure could go to the people of the state for a vote. From the day it began to make its way through the legislature, the amendment has been steadily building a following—in no small part as the result of the grassroots leadership of environmental activists David Kipnis and Monica Aufrecht.[32] Despite the ravages that industry has visited on the ancestral lands of the Swinomish and so many other Washington State tribes, Debra is keeping the faith—and just as important, doing the work. Debra knows the woods, the rivers, and the rhythms of their changing through the seasons, year after year. "Decades from now," Debra says, "the animals will return, habitat will return. Climate change will start to be resolved in that area because the trees will become bigger, taller, and healthier . . . and the waters will cool," says Debra. "Russ Hefner's grandson's grandson will fish . . . on that river and see the backs of salmon again." But Debra also knows it is going to require powerful, proactive action by government and people if we are going to realize her vision of a healthy world—including a society where environmental justice isn't merely a goal we are striving for, but a path of equity and respect that we walk every day.

Representative Debra Lekanoff's words to the people of Washington convey a message that can and should carry us all:

> *The Green Amendment is your right as a Washingtonian. The Green Amendment does not recognize the color of your skin, the color of your eyes. It doesn't recognize if you're a Republican, a Democrat . . . who you love, or what god you worship. The Green Amendment recognizes the very right that you have as a human being to be able to breathe clean air, to be able to drink cool and clean water, to be able to walk through the resources and the quality of life that you deserve to have as a human being. The Green Amendment takes care of your neighbor, it takes care of your industry, it takes care of your economy. The Green Amendment takes care of Washington state as it should . . . [and it] says, "We are going to give to the generations ahead of us instead of stealing their future from them."*

Youth on the Front Lines

For Debra Lekanoff, the generational responsibility she talks about is deeply personal and acutely felt, woven throughout the heritage and culture that shape so much of who she is and how she leads. "I still run through the woods with moss up to my ankles. I still feel the pressure of my salmon. I still hear my grandma singing the Indian songs, my Tlingit songs, as she's cutting fish," says Debra. "I still remember going out and catching candlefish with my dad late at night with a dip net, the smell of eulachons filling my whole community in the springtime. And everybody is so happy." For Debra, and for me, it is not good enough that she and I have beautiful memories of time spent in nature. It is critical that the children of today and tomorrow have that experience and develop those memories as well.

This aspiration reflects a crucial, but too often unheralded and under-appreciated, aspect of the fight for environmental protection: Our movement for environmental rights carries a generational imperative. The success or failure of our nation to take strong, proactive environmental and climate action will be enjoyed, or suffered, by younger generations—including those yet to be born.

Whether or not you happen to be a parent yourself, we all shoulder a responsibility to the children of today and tomorrow, including generations yet to come. Hence the name (which I chose carefully and for this exact reason) Green Amendments For The Generations. In fact, part of what makes our Green Amendment movement unique is that unlike a lot of movements that are either adult-based or student-led, and tend to be segregated by age, ours really does bring adults and youth together to fight for change across generations. Supported by this true partnership, young people are seizing the initiative and leading—including on the front lines—in states like New Jersey, where our momentum is building.

In 2017, my Delaware Riverkeeper Network organization, along with my newly founded Green Amendments movement, teamed up with David Pringle, an experienced organizer, activist, and lobbyist in New Jersey. Dave worked for years with Clean Water Action and would soon undertake a political run that was successful in raising important issues, but didn't ultimately secure a seat in the US Congress. After his foray onto the political scene as a candidate, Dave hung out his own consulting shingle. He believes passionately in the advancements that a Green Amendment could bring for environmental protection and was eager to join our team in helping advance progress in his home state. And I was eager to benefit from Dave's years of experience and relation-ships that had brought many New Jersey environmental initiatives from just another good idea to full fruition.

As Dave and I talked about who needed to be at the table for advancing the New Jersey cause, we brainstormed the best leadership voices—Kim Gaddy of Southward Environmental Alliance, Doug O'Malley of Environment New Jersey, and Eric Benson from Clean Water Action, as well as Ed Lloyd and Janine Bauer (names that might be familiar from the Route 29 Extension battle described in chapter 2) and Bridget Brady and Molly Atz from the Delaware Riverkeeper Network. In short order, Rachel Dawn Davis of Waterspirit would also join our leadership team. We started with a series of talks that were open to anyone who wanted to join, along with training sessions about what a Green Amendment is, how it works, and why it would be important for New Jersey.

Youth leaders Svanfridur Mura and Margaret Berei of the New Jersey Student Sustainability Coalition (NJSSC) heard about our training sessions and decided to reach out to learn more. "I was fifteen, and I was learning about this. It made sense to me," Margaret recalls, describing why she has dedicated so much leadership time to the New Jersey Green Amendment initiative. "I had been a part of other environmental groups . . . and fought for different causes before, but none of them made so much sense to me, and [they] weren't as intuitive."[33]

When I first spoke with Margaret and Svan by phone, in 2020, our New Jersey effort was well underway but needed fresh perspectives to inform our work. During that first conversation, the two of them expressed interest in taking a leadership role and wondered whether that might be possible. I was delighted and all-in.

Soon, Margaret and Svan were advertising upcoming trainings to their NJSSC group, energizing others to learn and join in. "It's really easy to connect with other young people on this issue because it's something they understand. You don't have to spend a lot of time explaining it, and everyone can connect it to something that they really care about," Svan told me. "For instance, yesterday I was on the phone with my friend [who] has just joined our team. He's been to a couple of meetings. And the entire time [we were on the phone], he was making Green Amendment graphics."

This instant gravitational pull of young people—to want to help spread the word using graphics, art, and easy-to-understand social media visuals—is quite telling. It's not just how powerfully this message of environmental rights resonates, but also how natural it is for them, having grown up online, to immediately dive in, get involved with their peers, and make something happen. For instance, a young man named Luki Jacisin attended college with my daughter, Anneke. After graduating from college and spending a few years on a more traditional career path, Luki and his twin brother, Kubi, decided to break away from the status quo and follow their passions: a combination of art and paragliding. Shocked at the lack of color and variety in outdoor gear and equipment, the twins founded a company called Warn the West and started putting their art on myriad items, from helmets to trailers to paraglider wings. Their goal was to bring beauty to the paragliding skies and—thanks to Anneke's enthusiasm—they heard about the Green Amendment movement nearly from its inception. The more they learned, the more they wanted to use their artistic flair to help spread the word and bring attention to our cause. As with Svan and Margaret, not only did the message instantly resonate in a clear and understandable way, but it inspired them to bring their talent to our campaign. To me, this is part of the power of the Green Amendment movement.

New Jersey Senator Andrew Zwicker finds the level of youth engagement striking and impactful. "While I hear too many dismissive of the youth voice or perspective as being naive and ill-informed, many more of us recognize that the youth perspective is not only highly informed, [but also] engaging, compelling, and powerful," he says. "Young people deliver their demands for environmental protection and justice with poise and clarity, but also laced with a worry, a desperation even, of those who will face any and all challenges the climate crisis and environmental degradation has to bring if we don't act now."[34]

Drawn by the youth leadership and opportunities for engagement that Svan and Margaret were introducing, more and more passionate, engaged young people joined our cause in New Jersey. Dave Pringle would act as a mentor for their legislative efforts, helping youth leaders navigate the political process, guiding them in how best to approach legislators, and sharing his decades of knowledge so that our young partners could develop skills that would serve them, and their environmental advocacy, for a lifetime.

Among the young leaders who took notice was Aarush Rompally, a high school student from Parsippany, New Jersey—and policy coordinator of the advocacy group Bye Plastic Bags NJ. "Even moving beyond the environmental ramifications of the Green Amendment, I think that just by providing a platform, it empowers you to be able to speak up," says Aarush. "That is a skill: being able to speak to legislators, and have an opinion, and fight for that opinion—that is something that's applicable to all fields. So I think that in terms of generational justice, the movement is about securing those rights that are human rights. But I also think it's about empowering people to be able to secure those for themselves. And I think that's really beautiful."

Svan, Margaret, Aarush, and others didn't just become advocates for the New Jersey Green Amendment; they are fully engaged and empowered leaders of the movement—organizing webinars for legislators, lobbying at the New Jersey statehouse, creating special video shorts, organizing social media weeks of action, holding letter-to-the-editor writing workshops, offering training for other youth online and in their school classrooms, and even organizing a Green Amendment Art Show and Concert to help spread the word. Together, we're building a Youth Leadership Green Amendment model that is helping us inspire youth engagement in other states.

These students and their inspiring work were fresh in my mind one afternoon in the late spring of 2021 as I walked through my New York woodland with my daughter Anneke. As we walked, I thought about how lucky we were to have this time in nature: to breathe the clean air, to experience the peace that comes from hearing the rustling leaves in the wind and birds chirping above, and to enjoy the excitement of, at any moment, seeing a wild animal or a rare new bloom of a special flower.

I thought of Gina Burton and her beloved son, Kiwanis. I thought of that rising generation of young leaders in New Jersey. And I started to wonder about the future of my children. I sometimes hear them talking with friends about their hopes and their fears. They don't just worry and wonder about where they might go to college, what job they might get, whether they'll have children or meet the partner of their dreams. They also carry a desperate fear. They worry and wonder about the Earth: what will it be like to live on this planet, whether the storms of climate change will overwhelm everything, what species will disappear, and whether they should even consider having children of their own in such a world.

I remembered that study about how children attending public schools in urban areas, like nearby New York City, breathe in neuro-toxicants that are harming their physical, emotional, and educational development. The disparity between the experience of my children on that beautiful day in the woods and the experiences of children in environmental sacrifice zones hit me hard. No child should have to worry that the water they drink at home or school is laden with cancer-causing toxins, or be denied the joy of wandering in healthy nature and all of the fun and beauty it provides.

And I thought about my Green Amendment movement.

Green Amendments are about using the strongest and most powerful legal tool we have in our nation—our state and federal constitutions—and putting them to work for true environmental protection and justice. Green Amendments are about creating an opportunity to address the environmental inequities of the present and future—to ensure that our children and communities have clean water to drink and healthy air to breathe, and that no community is being overwhelmed by environmental degradation just so others can enjoy the many benefits of healthy nature. Green Amendments are also about taking the actions we can take today to ensure a more stable climate for our children in the future.

There is not just room for everyone in our Green Amendment movement, but an acute need for everyone to get involved. Enjoying the forest with my daughter, I thought about the hurdles the movement faces—the challenges, the opposition, the need for more resources—but also about my belief in the power of this pathway for securing transformational change and true environmental and generational justice.

Just when this swirling mix of emotions and thoughts hit its peak during that warm spring walk, my daughter pointed off to the side of the path—where in full, glorious bloom was my mother's favorite native wildflower, the lady slipper orchid. Although we had been lucky to host a patch in our Pennsylvania paradise all those years ago (as I mentioned in chapter 1), it is a rare plant to find growing wild in nature. I had walked this rural New York path for years, and never had I seen even a hint of a lady slipper. To me, this was a message from my mother, from the previous generation: that if you keep walking, and thinking, and looking for the path of preservation, restoration, protection, and change, and if you stay dedicated to that path, you will be rewarded with environmental beauty and victory that can be enjoyed by all.

CHAPTER NINE

YOU'RE NOT EXPENDABLE!

My mother never smoked a day in her life. She always ate a healthy diet. She didn't really exercise, per se, but she was consistently active: gardening, biking (rather than driving), traveling, spending time in nature, and keeping up with her big extended family. As the youngest of thirteen children, with siblings, nieces, nephews, and others, most of them in Holland, family wasn't always easy to keep track of. But her love and vivaciousness were a big part of what knit us all together—and her energy and desire to engage in meaningful ways with the world only seemed to grow as she advanced in years. This only makes it all the more heartbreaking to think of what might've been, and the time we might've had together, had she not been diagnosed with pancreatic cancer in the beginning of 2003, when she was just sixty-five years old.

She had just returned from a trip to South America when she started to feel ill. Over the course of a few weeks, she developed a bit of jaundice, saw a doctor, and was tested for hepatitis in all its various forms, along with the other usual suspects where jaundice was concerned. None of the tests came back positive, and the cause remained a mystery—until she called me one day while I was at home with my daughter, and told me her doctors had finally alighted upon a diagnosis. It was a shock—and not just because of the worrying prognosis. Pancreatic cancer is known to run in families. Yet combing through everything we knew about our family health history, we could not find evidence of even a single relative who had been diagnosed with pancreatic cancer. Her case was singular—a striking anomaly.

Just over half a year after her diagnosis, my mother celebrated her birthday. Then Christmas (also my birthday) came around. And then— the following March—she was gone. A wonderful, vibrant light in my life and in so many others, my anchor in this world from the day she brought me into it, was taken long before her time.

The loss of my mother affected me deeply, and its senselessness—the seeming randomness of pancreatic cancer—still feels somehow unresolved to me. Or at least it did, until my work brought me into contact with some new research into the long-term health effects of pollution, and air pollution in particular. One of the many observed outcomes associated with exposure to air pollution is an increased risk of developing pancreatic cancer, which (like a history of heavy smoking or similar behaviors) might explain its diagnosis in an otherwise healthy patient with no family history or genetic predisposition. When I learned this, I immediately wondered: *could it have been the war?*

My mother had spent her formative years in the Netherlands, growing up with her dozen siblings in the city of Eindhoven. She was nearly three in May 1940, when Germany violated Dutch neutrality and launched a full-scale invasion of the Low Countries. There had been no warning, let alone a formal declaration of war. All across the Netherlands, people just woke up one morning to the rumble of German airplane engines—and in some places, to the whistle of falling bombs overhead. My mother was young at that time. She didn't ever talk with me about the experience of the bombings. But I saw it firsthand after the surgery when they were attempting to excise her cancer. She awoke wide-eyed and in terror, calling out for safety—clearly reliving, just for a few minutes, the time when the bombs were falling. After five days of fighting, the Dutch military capitulated, the Queen fled to Britain, and five long, cruel years of Nazi occupation began.

Now I am left to wonder: Had my mother been exposed to something toxic during that initial German invasion and aerial bombardment? Was she affected by the aftermath of the attack, which had reduced whole city blocks to rubble—and which dispersed countless harmful chemicals, waste, and other potential carcinogens into the air? How long had those contaminants lingered, and what else had transpired during that lengthy, brutal occupation?

At this point, I can only speculate about whether my mom's cancer might have been related to something that happened during the war. It might also have been one of those activities—bicycling instead of driving, for instance—that she thought was keeping her healthy. By riding along the side of the road all those years, had she been breathing car exhaust that (especially before 1970, when the Clean Air Act imposed emissions standards) exposed her to dangerous levels of carcinogens? I won't ever know. But I do know that both war and air pollution take a heavy toll on people's health.

World War II affected my mom in other ways, imparting at least one defining family trait that she passed along—quite potently—to me: an overriding, almost visceral drive to stand up for justice and to defend the defenseless. Watching the darkness of the Third Reich descend over her homeland, my mother also witnessed the power that a single individual can summon from within to do what's right, despite overwhelming odds.

Her father, Ernst Wijsmuller, was the town accountant and a pillar of the community—well and widely respected throughout Eindhoven. Not long after the Nazi occupation began, he learned that the German invaders had begun going door to door, conscripting any young men they encountered, by force, to serve in Hitler's military. Horrified but determined that no child of his would serve the Nazis and become party to their abhorrent abuses, my opa took an enormous risk by ordering his sons to hide before the Nazis came to the door—and then, when he opened it to face them, he was openly defiant. "No," he told them, in effect, according to my mother's account. "You can't have them."

The Germans assured my opa that they would be back in short order, and that his sons had better be there. But when they returned, his sons were still nowhere to be found. So the occupying authorities arrested and incarcerated him—a terrifying prospect. By 1941, deportations were routine: trains full of prisoners were leaving Holland regularly, en route to Germany. By the end of the occupation, some half a million Dutch citizens were transported by force and made to work in German factories.[1] As long as Opa was in custody, there was no telling what would happen.

Of course, he had known all too well that by defying German orders, he had virtually guaranteed that he, too, would be taken away. Still, there was something in him that couldn't abide the idea that his sons might be forced to fight for the Nazis. I remember my mother telling me about his courage with a mix of pride and awe, and I remember the sadness of loss in her voice—exhortation that I should remember this man I'd never had the chance to meet, and that I should live by his example. I knew him only through my mother's eyes, as Opa and as a hero of Eindhoven during the war—a man of prominence who stood up to horrible evil because it was the moral, decent, and right thing to do. But over the years, I've come to understand the love and grief and gratitude with which she spoke about him, because I now speak about my mother the same way.

In the end, my opa was released from jail after only a few days—an unexpected mercy in a brutal and merciless time. He had been saved by his prominence and high regard in the community, my mother explained to me: the occupying authorities feared that news of his arrest and detention risked galvanizing the local populace against them. So they let him go. And when all was said and done, my mother's brothers never did serve under, for, or with the Nazis.

It wasn't until years later that we came to find out my mother's aunt, Geertruida Wijsmuller-Meijer, had been an even more notable figure in standing up to the Nazi regime. To members of our family, she had always been Tante (the Dutch word for "aunt") Truus, or "Tru-Tru." To many others, although her name is not widely known, she was a hero responsible for saving thousands of Jewish people, many of them children, from Nazi brutality.

Even before the occupation, in 1938, Tante Truus met directly with one of the Holocaust's principal architects, Adolf Eichmann, to secure permission to bring six hundred Jewish children to Holland from the Third Reich; both Eichmann and Hitler himself reportedly agreed to her request. Not unlike my opa, Tante Truus had a reputation and local connections that left her in a position of relative strength to stand up for what was right and help others—which she did with remarkable courage and persistence, at times orchestrating the rescue of hundreds of children at once. When the Gestapo arrested and interrogated her in 1941, she took greater care to keep a low profile but did not abandon her lifesaving work. Even as late as 1944, she was scheming and engaging in subterfuge against the Nazis in order to rescue every last child she could reach—at one point diverting fifty captive Jewish orphans from transportation to Auschwitz by passing them off as "Aryan," thereby ensuring their privileged treatment throughout the remainder of the war.[2]

Among the 140,000 Jewish people who lived in Holland as of 1941, only thirty-eight thousand survived until the end of hostilities in 1945.[3] It's at once breathtaking and humbling to think that some share of that total, reputedly somewhere in the thousands, credit their survival to Tante Truus. She lived until 1978 but never much spoke about her heroic actions during the occupation, nor had any biological children of her own—though in a broader sense not only children but entire families, now spanning multiple generations, count themselves today as Truus Wijsmuller's descendants.

My own inheritance from Tante Truus—other than gratitude for the fact that, by some happy accident of my family tree, she happened to be my great-aunt—was both modest and indirect: a family ethos, instilled in my mother by her and by Opa. My mother, in turn, passed it on to me: a contrarian, anti-authoritarian streak that has always driven me, in emulation of these family role models, to fight as hard as I can for what I believe is right, and to continue striving to find that path to secure needed action, protection, and justice—no matter how long it takes or how hard the work.

As the Delaware Riverkeeper, I take on battles for my watershed piece by piece—a development here, a pipeline or dredging project there. Every battle is a fight for the specific communities harmed, but also involves a great effort to secure strong precedent to help set the stage of success for others. As the "Mother" of the Green Amendment movement (a title given me by Gwynne Ann Unruh, a reporter with *The Paper* in New Mexico), I am trying a different approach: creating a transformative constitutional path of change and protection that will strengthen all environmental struggles, across all issues, all communities, and all generations. We know this path is needed because "piece by piece" will never be enough to prevent real people from being harmed by environmental pollution and degradation. Every day, lives are being destroyed and even lost. These are harms that can and should be prevented.

A Veteran's Fight

Iraq looks a lot like New Mexico, in Nicole Olonovich's opinion. And she would know: before serving with the US Air National Guard in Iraq, she spent much of her life in her home state of New Mexico. In point of fact, Nicole's ancestors had lived in New Mexico since prior to statehood, and she returned to her home in Albuquerque after being medically discharged from the military.

Growing up, Nicole had lived all over New Mexico and Arizona. Her family had moved thirteen times by the time she reached the age of thirteen. "Parents are really good at hiding your reality from you—at least my moms were," Nicole recalls. "I didn't know we were poor, even though we lived in trailers and I had free lunch. [For a long time], I didn't know [my moms] were gay."

Nicole's family moved all the time until they finally settled in Albuquerque. "It was the first house we ever lived in that wasn't a trailer." Despite her family's modest means, Nicole was happy—and she excelled in high school, graduating a year early, and as one of the top ten students in her class. "I looked like a Christmas tree graduating. I had my French honor society, regular honor society. I got [a school] leadership award. I was the editor of the literary magazine. I was in mock trial, speech, debate, and a thespian. And I had all the cords, all the ribbons, all of the things. I was super active," Nicole recalls.[4]

Nicole was the first one in her family to go to college—and the only top-performing member of her high school's graduating class to attend an institution outside the state. One day during her freshman year, an envelope bearing her mother's name arrived at her dorm room in Alamosa, Colorado. Perplexed, she opened it—only to discover that her mom had taken out a $5,000 loan to pay for her college housing and was already in default. "I remember breaking down and crying in my dorm room, about the fact that I was going to make my family go poor because I wanted an education," Nicole recalls. "And what's crazy is, I didn't understand the gravity of how poor we already were."

Stunned and in desperation, she began to search for an alternate path. Surely there must be a way to finish her education with assistance, or even for free. "In that regard, the military does really target poor people," says Nicole. "I looked up all the different ways I could go to school for free, and the type that seemed the least invasive was the New Mexico Air National Guard." She had already been making the four-hour trip home every weekend, having found that it was cheaper to eat and do laundry at her parents' house than to do so at school. Now, she'd simply make the same trip for drill weekends.

Nicole knew her family would never approve. So, she decided not to tell them, and instead just came home one weekend, unbeknownst to any relatives, to make her enlistment official. "I remember the rows of people who were signed up . . . their parents and them. And you have to stand in front of this flag and raise your right hand and . . . swear to defend and protect the Constitution," says Nicole. She was there alone, committed to following through on her decision. Nicole put up her hand and swore her oath to the Constitution that day. It wasn't until a month before she was due to leave for basic training that she finally told her mom she'd enlisted—news that was every bit as unwelcome as she'd anticipated.

"Over my dead body!" her mother exclaimed. "Are you crazy? We're not in one war. We're in two." Then she asked if Nicole was doing poorly at college.

"She asked me if I was failing. She asked me if I was serious." Nicole made it clear to her mother that there was nothing anyone could do to alter her decision. She'd already signed on the dotted line. At this point, failing to report for basic training would amount to going AWOL, which bore serious consequences that would follow her for the rest of her life.

Nicole went to basic training, followed by tech school. When presented with a decision about which career field to pursue within the military, she chose Munitions Systems—or AMMO, as it's known to enlistees—because it was one of the few paths that came with extra pay. "I was joining the military for a reason, and the reason was so that I didn't go poor trying to go to college," says Nicole. She chose AMMO for a very particular reason: "You get hostile fire pay, you get separation pay, you get hazardous duty pay."

Just as she had in high school, Nicole excelled in both basic training and on-the-job training, reaching the seventh level—"journeyman"—in short order. "What that means is, even though I don't have rank, I can run a crew. And not only can I run a crew, I can troubleshoot a bomb," Nicole says. Soon, she'd have to put her newfound expertise to work: when her fighter wing was activated, a certain number of Munitions Systems specialists would need to deploy to Iraq. As the newest member of the unit, eager to prove herself, she signed up for one of the open slots—and once again, declined to tell her mother until it was almost time to ship out.

"She threw me a going-away party, and being Hispanic at your going-away party to Iraq—it's like being alive at your own funeral. I left wearing every patron saint, mostly St. Michael. I had rosaries, crosses, watches, all of these things," Nicole says, referring to the patron saint of military personnel. "And if you look at any of the pictures of me in Iraq, I'm wearing them."

Nicole recalls touching down under heavy mortar fire at Balad Air Base, about forty miles northeast of Baghdad and one of the most heavily hit US and coalition targets in the region. It was 2004, and she was just nineteen years old. She recalls grueling twelve-hour shifts with little time off. "You don't get the weekend off, and you can't exit base to go anywhere—you're literally in war," she says. She also remembers the toxic fumes that were part of her daily routine.

One area on base for which Nicole and her unit bore responsibility was known as the "bomb dump," where munitions of all descriptions were stored. In order to protect the ammunition from enemy discovery and fire, the military "decided to put the bomb dump right next to the burn pit . . . . So in theory, it's smart. Because the enemy's not going to assume that your bombs are by the firepit," Nicole explains.

But as part of the AMMO team, Nicole performed her daily work just downwind, breathing in the fumes and toxins from all the waste being burned as the means of disposal. She was also exposed to depleted uranium: "We had to move [it]." The more time Nicole spent at the bomb dump, working those arduous twelve-hour shifts, the more toxic waste she inhaled—thick, putrid smoke that included the foul-smelling by-products from burning huge quantities of Styrofoam plates and plastic silverware from the chow hall, fecal matter from the latrine, old tires, and trash bags containing all manner of garbage and other assorted waste produced by a fully operational Air Force base in an active theater of war. All of it was heaped together, doused with jet fuel, and set ablaze in the open air.

"My nineteen-year-old body had never been exposed to anything like that," says Nicole. Unsurprisingly, she soon began to feel more and more ill. But there was no opportunity to swap duty assignments, so she had no choice but to keep showing up for her shifts.

One day, as she and a fellow airman were riding in a specialized vehicle for transporting ordnance to the flight line, she became uncontrollably sick and vomited all down the side of the vehicle. They stopped to make sure she was all right. Once outside, both of them were alarmed to see that wherever Nicole's vomit had touched the paint job, it appeared to have turned from olive drab to neon green. "And so both me and him are thinking, 'Do you think the acid in my vomit has changed the paint color . . . or am I vomiting what's actually neon green?'" she recalls.

Either way, her fellow airman insisted on taking Nicole immediately to the base's "flight doc" for evaluation. As Nicole described her symptoms to the doctor, he was "not surprised at all. *That* was the scariest thing."

The doctor told her to remain in her quarters for three days. But that very evening, a sergeant (who was, in effect, Nicole's supervisor's supervisor) came banging on her door. "I heard you went to night shift," he said.

Nicole explained that she was sick and supposed to remain in quarters.

But her boss's boss wasn't having it. "I don't know. I'm just following orders, man. Get your clothes on," he said.

So she did—but soon found herself struggling, too sick to work. Her fellow airmen noticed and commented on her condition, even debating whether she was "faking it," until at last someone took her back to the flight doctor. Nicole was sent immediately back to quarters, but even that modest relief was short-lived.

Two days later, Nicole was back at work as usual. But her health only kept getting worse. "I got sicker and sicker and sicker, the more that I'm at the bomb dump. [I've stopped] being able to breathe while I'm [on the job], but the whole time my mind is going, 'Great. You joined the military so that they would pay for school, and here you are getting sick.'" By the end of her forty-five-day rotation in Iraq, Nicole was a shadow of the person she'd been on the night she arrived at Balad Air Base.

"Coming back from Iraq didn't just mess me up internally; it messed me *up*," she says. "I couldn't drive on a highway for over a year because a mortar had gone off while I was driving a two-and-a-half-ton truck." She was perpetually scared—and then she started having terrible breathing problems.

Despite her breathing issues, Nicole continued her military service. "I had learned how to run [while] wheezing. I had learned how to run through everything," she says. "Because you can't be sick. You have to be the epitome of health."

On deployment in South Korea, Nicole volunteered every Wednesday at a local orphanage, teaching children how to read. Not only was she helping the children, but her volunteerism had the added benefit of getting her out of physical training for the day, so she could avoid the physical and emotional burden it would impose on her wounded body. Nicole found other ways to ease the physical toll of her day-to-day service—and to make sure nobody noticed she was struggling to breathe.

"I would work out in the morning so my direct supervisor . . . would see me running up and down these hills in South Korea," Nicole recalls, "and write me off on doing PT the second time of the week because she bore witness to it." For a time, it seemed as though this tenuous situation might be sustainable—that she might actually get away with it, if only by the skin of her teeth.

In 2007, Nicole was assigned to Malmstrom Air Force Base, just outside of Great Falls, Montana. Her prowess at crucial back-of-house logistical work had made her invaluable to the Air National Guard—and her future seemed relatively assured. At first, she says, "I'm at drill, my one weekend a month, two weeks a year. Everything's going [well]. Nobody's figured out that I'm sick. Nothing's wrong." Until a nearby fire—one among many in the rising wave of wildfires that routinely scorch vast swaths of the western United States—started to seriously aggravate her breathing problems. Once again, despite her best efforts to push through her increasingly alarming symptoms and pretend nothing was wrong, she was sent for a medical evaluation. This time, the military physician who reviewed Nicole's test results could not have been more cold-hearted.

"You're no longer expendable," he callously told her. "If we're in war and you have to wear your gas mask, you can't take it off to puff on an inhaler. So you're no longer expendable."

The term "expendable," in this military context, means exactly what it sounds like: "capable of being sacrificed in order to accomplish a military objective."[5] Besides how disturbing it is that military personnel are only valued as long as they can go into war to be "sacrificed," it seemed a particularly odd way to refer to Nicole. She couldn't now be an active participant in war where they would literally need her to be expendable, because they had already expended her—taking away the full and healthy life she should have lived. Nicole herself saw the irony in that very moment: "The moment they told me, 'You're no longer expendable, we're going to out-process you, there's no alternative jobs . . . I even said, 'You guys are the ones who did this to me. There's not an alternative job that I can have?'"

The answer was definitive: No. Everybody needs to be deployable and expendable.

Nicole had gotten her bachelor's degree while in the military so that she could become an officer. She'd sacrificed so much, including her health. She had upset and enraged her family, given up beloved hobbies, changed universities, and foreclosed alternate career options in pursuit of this singular goal. Now, in an instant—and with a callous disregard—it was gone: not just the life she was living, but the future she'd imagined for herself since she was a teenager. It was "like I was a throwaway," she recounts, adding, "like people are throwaways. You expect that in war, but not at home."

Nicole was beyond crushed—she was despondent: "[I]t was that weekend that I wanted to show them that I was expendable."

It was winter, and Nicole was living in Great Falls, just a short distance from the frozen Missouri River. One morning, she waited until after her partner had left for work, wrote goodbye letters to her family, and set off walking, barefoot, toward a nearby bridge. "The craziest thing is, my partner at the time—he had forgotten his bottled ice water. He has never come home when he forgets things, but something made him come home this time," Nicole recalls.

Turning back onto the street, he saw her walking and asked, in confusion and alarm, what she was doing.

"*Just go,*" she replied.

He noticed that she was crying, and that she was barefoot and not wearing a jacket. "*Nikki, stop!*" he said.

But she started walking faster, and then running through the snow.

"I thought if I could get to the bridge, and if I jumped headfirst into the frozen Missouri River, that would show that [military doctor] I'm expendable," she says.

Thankfully, Nicole's partner managed to stop her in time. He got her into his truck and got her to help.

Nicole needed to be near family. She returned home to New Mexico, got a job, and started medications that helped her begin to feel better, if only slightly. She began to wonder whether a lack of oxygen, as a result of her damaged lungs, might've contributed to her suicide attempt. Then one day, while trying to use her military health insurance benefits, she hit a snag—and when she called to figure out why, all they could tell her was, "I'm sorry, your Tri-Care [military health] insurance has been canceled."

When she got home from work that evening, July 8, 2008—a date that's now seared into her memory as "7-8 of '08"—Nicole checked the mail and found an envelope. The letter inside informed her that, without any prior notice, she'd been discharged from the military.

It was an honorable discharge on medical grounds, but it brought all of Nicole's worst fears to life. Her civilian job didn't offer health insurance. How would she get access to the medicines that were finally making a difference? How could she afford treatment without her military income? Her discharge papers had been accompanied by a check that was supposed to be for $5,000, but it was taxed at 40 percent. "And I remember thinking, '*Wow*,'" Nicole says. "My life is worth $3,000 and not so much as a call."

Her mental health again began to spiral. Out of despondence and desperation, exactly a month later, on August 8 ("8-8 of '08")—Nicole remembers it as one of the rainiest days on record in New Mexico—she tried once again to end her life.

"I just couldn't. I had given up my youth. I had given up my personality. Who I was is not who I am right now," she says. She got in her car and drove to the top of a nearby mountain, aimed toward what was sure to be a deadly drop-off, stomped the accelerator—and lost control, spinning out rather than plummeting to her death.

Refusing to accept this as a sign, she went to her car's trunk, where she kept her medications, and took as many as she could stand. The police eventually found her, but rather than rushing Nicole to the hospital, they transferred her to Albuquerque's Metropolitan Detention Center. She soon found herself in front of a judge, who seemed ready to throw the book at her. Nicole just spoke up and said, "I wasn't trying to hurt anybody. I was trying to take my own life. I am a disabled veteran and the military just discharged me . . . and I'm not doing okay."

The proceeding ended with Nicole transferred to Mental Health Court and enrolled in court-mandated therapy. Staring down the long road to mental and physical recovery, Nicole kept fighting doggedly for the resources and assistance to which she was entitled.

Nearly two decades after her forty-five-day rotation in Iraq, Nicole still suffers from a badly burnt esophagus that causes ongoing vocal cord damage, for which she continues to do physical therapy. Nobody's lung capacity is 100 percent, but hers is unusually poor at 70 percent. "So, even on a good breath, I'm fighting it going through my burnt esophageal passage, and I'm fighting for room inside of my lungs," she explains. Nicole also suffers from serious liver and circulatory problems. "My liver is no longer processing my blood; my blood is too thick, and I'm not holding on to iron."

Nicole dreads the constant parade of oncologists, hematologists, and X-ray technicians to which the Veterans Administration (VA) keeps sending her to examine her liver, lungs, and chest—especially since, no matter the outcome of each successive appointment, things never seem to get better. She's still struggling to cut through all the red tape and get the treatments she needs.

"Even though you're sick and your body's blatantly sick, they don't just hear you. Since I've come back from Iraq, it feels like ants are crawling up my legs," Nicole says. "There are things that are wrong with me that they can't understand. And my story is just a little one . . . . There are some people who were deployed that suddenly have breast cancer, [likely from] being deployed and being downwind of burn pits."

All this explains why Nicole has chosen to be a leading champion for a Green Amendment in New Mexico. "I did not just sign up for the United States Air Force. I signed up for the New Mexico Air National Guard. I signed up for my state," she says, "[and] I paid with my literal life, my quality of life, and my health. I paid one of the highest prices to serve New Mexico, and all I'm asking New Mexico to do is give me clean water and clean air and clean enough soil so I can eat foods that aren't going to exacerbate my already dying body."

To address contaminants in the local water supply, Nicole's doctors recommended that she install a reverse osmosis system. Without one, the many contaminants in her drinking water cause physical reactions in her body, including with her medications. This water is not in violation of legal standards, mind you; this water complies with the law. And so in a very real way, when it comes to assessing the quality of New Mexico's environment, Nicole is a canary in a coal mine.

Nicole's body reacts more quickly and acutely to contaminants, but that does not mean others are safe from harm. "I'm so sick," she says, "my doctors are telling me [I] can't go outside." They advise her not to live in northern New Mexico. Why? There's too much methane leaking there, and it affects her ability to breathe. "Rather than addressing the methane that's leaking, they'll tell a veteran like me to just *not* live in northern New Mexico because it will deteriorate my esophagus," she says. "And if you're telling me, a sick person, that the methane leaks are going to make my life worse, what is it doing to a healthy body?"

Nicole is direct about what the rest of us can do to repay her for all that she's sacrificed—and for all that's been taken from her unjustly. "I think well-intentioned people thank my cohort for our service, and just don't know how vital it is for them to put action to those words in the form of environmental justice," Nicole says.

As she's done throughout her life, Nicole is fighting for herself, but also for the rest of us. She is at the forefront of the Green Amendment movement, believing that all people deserve an environment of quality—and taking exception to how lightly state and federal governments sacrifice clean air, safe water, and healthy soil so industry can make more profit. Her dedication to justice for all is backed by experience. "I'm literally living it right now. I'm living the consequence of toxic exposure and continued toxic exposure," says Nicole, who gets an alert on her phone when the VA has determined that the breathing conditions are too bad for her to go outside. "So the VA and the medical professionals are very aware of methane leaks. They're very aware of water contaminants. They're very aware of pollutants in the air"— enough to tell her to be aware, or to accommodate her house to make things palatable or breathable or drinkable—"but they're not doing anything on a bigger scale."

When people tell Nicole, "Thank you for your service," she appreciates the expression of gratitude. But what she needs is for people to demonstrate their appreciation by recognizing and enforcing her right— as a New Mexican, as an American, and as a person—to clean and safe water, air, and soil, and healthy ecosystems and environments. "Don't tell me," Nicole told a crowd of legislators and activists considering their support for a Green Amendment. "Show me."

Fighting for the Falls

Codifying everyone's right to a clean, safe, and healthy environment is a moral and practical imperative. We are a part of nature, and our health, individually and collectively, is inextricably entwined with nature's health. *We* must therefore be good stewards of this world and its delicate ecosystems, for nature's sake—but for our own sake, too. The human element of environmental protection, the generational responsibility we all share, the impacts on people and communities that I see as I travel the country: *this* is what fuels our environmental rights fight.

You may have noticed that among all the stories in this book, not a single one strays from a primary driving element: harm to human health. This thread is woven through every anecdote. It touches every facet of our fight. It allows our Green Amendment movement to span all political, generational, moral, economic, and geographic boundaries.

We are all in this together.

The damaging human consequences of environmental pollution and degradation—from loss of air and water quality, to climate disruption, to the destruction of ecosystems and the loss of species—together represent an egregious systemic failure of our environmental laws and governance. The intensity of these negative impacts makes abstract ideas like "constitutional environmental rights" deeply personal—in turn making the case for Green Amendments self-evident. In other words, it's bad enough that our government and laws allow industry to harm the environment. But when those harms are so widespread, so out of control, and so significant that they rebound on innocent people and destroy human lives, too? It's hard to imagine a more obvious illustration of the wild inadequacy of our current legal framework—and the urgency of getting back to first principles: making the rights of people to a protected environment, versus a right of industry to pollute, our starting point.

Even more impactful than the legal and constitutional arguments for environmental rights is the fact that health impacts have a unique and immediate power to impel people—including entire communities—to focused, relentless action that gets results. Consider Gina Burton and the dozens of Millsboro residents who banded together to hold Mountaire Farms accountable (and beat them). Consider the residents of General Warren Village and their battle to stop development of a still-toxic Bishop Tube site, and to secure government action to hold parties like Johnson Matthey and Whittaker Corporation accountable for cleaning up the toxins still fouling the stream, groundwater, and surrounding environments after more than thirty years of contamination. Whenever bad actors, enabled by government, veer so far from the realm of what's acceptable that they start to harm people's health, it inspires a visceral, personal, and eminently righteous desire to fight back.

This sense—that feel-it-in-your-bones certainty that what happened to Gina's son Kiwanis and to Kate Stauffer's daughter Liz, and what is happening right now to Nicole, should be not just illegal but *unconstitutional*—is what inspires the kind of collective community action that can change our lived reality. This certainty can galvanize the transformational shift in law and governance that will be necessary to protect our health and environment.

In the small community of Hoosick Falls, located thirty miles north of Albany in upstate New York, a sign welcomes people to town: "Village of Hoosick Falls, Home of New York State's Best Drinking Water, 1987." But gazing at a picture of that sign, Hoosick Falls resident Michele Baker can only manage a sardonic laugh.[6]

Michele purchased her home in Hoosick Falls in 1998. Within a few short years, she welcomed her recently widowed mother, Maryann, into the area, and gave birth to her daughter, Mikayla. As of 2017, Michele, Maryann, and Mikayla all had elevated levels of PFOA coursing through their veins. "My child and mother have PFOA in their blood because two of the largest companies on this planet decided to pollute our little town," Michele explains.

To which I add: and our government let them do it.

For decades, unbeknownst to Michele and her fellow residents, two multinational conglomerates—the plastics manufacturer Saint-Gobain, and the consumer and aerospace systems firm Honeywell—had been contaminating Hoosick Falls water. In the course of their operations, these companies had leached perfluorooctanoic acid (PFOA) contaminants into municipal water systems and had pumped it into the air through industrial smokestack emissions.[7] As of 2017, many Hoosick Falls residents contained twelve to fifteen times the national average of

PFOA concentrations in their bloodstreams.[8] They also suffered from increased illnesses, cancer rates, and premature death. Like the communities of Paulsboro, New Jersey; Bucks and Montgomery counties, Pennsylvania; and the farmers of Maine and New Mexico—all highlighted in chapter 5—the people of Hoosick Falls were soon to learn their lives, homes, businesses, and bodies had been invaded by a hidden menace that government should have protected them from but didn't.

When Mikayla was born, she arrived prematurely—a potential side effect of PFOA. Maryann, whose blood had triple-digit parts-per-trillion PFOA concentrations, suffered a stroke—yet another potential result of PFOA exposure that the family laments. During a harrowing eight-day ordeal, Maryann was shuttled away in a helicopter and struggled for her life in an intensive care unit. Ever since these episodes, any time Michele's daughter develops an infection or her mother starts to cough, Michele wonders if they have sprouted a new PFOA-related illness. "Every day you go home, and you hate looking at your house because you know [about the contamination]," she notes wistfully.

Saint-Gobain continued to use PFOA-containing materials in some of its Hoosick Falls operations until sometime in 2014. That same year, news of PFOA contamination in the small village made national headlines, thanks to insurance underwriter Michael Hickey, who was shocked and brokenhearted when his vigorous, healthy father died of kidney cancer. There was nothing in his family's genetic background that predisposed his father to such an illness, so Michael began investigating on the internet. "All I typed in was Teflon and cancer, because that's what was in the [Saint-Gobain] factory that was in Hoosick Falls where my father worked," said Michael.[9] He was convinced that PFOA took his dad's life, and he also believed the contaminant was responsible for a whole series of strange illnesses and premature deaths afflicting his small village.

When Michael discovered the water's toxicity, he immediately notified Hoosick Falls government leaders. Yet they did nothing about it. In fact, the state health department issued a statement in January 2015 alleging that the water test "does not constitute an immediate health hazard," and that "health effects are not expected to occur from normal use of the water."[10] In November 2015, however, Judith Enck, a regional administrator for the EPA, sent a letter to Hoosick Falls mayor, criticizing the village leadership for not protecting its residents from waterborne toxins. The letter recommended that the village provide an alternative source of drinking water for residents, and that they not use the town's water for cooking, not even for steaming vegetables.[11] In a public statement issued on December 17, 2015, the EPA formally warned residents not to drink the water.[12] The following January, Enck held an informational session at a high school and, before a standing-room-only crowd, apologized for the town's situation and reiterated the EPA's message, urging everyone to stop drinking the water *immediately*.[13]

In addition to the health problems they experienced, residents like Michele have taken a severe economic hit from the contamination of their water. Back in 2015, Hoosick Falls had been experiencing a renaissance, with new bike paths, arts and culture centers, and small artisanal businesses sprouting up. As the *Albany Times Union* related, Hoosick Falls was "the kind of place that seems primed to attract families looking for a great place to raise children."[14] So imagine Michele's shock that same year upon learning that her bank wouldn't approve her application to refinance the mortgage on her property, citing nonpotable drinking water in her home. "I have a private well three miles away," she explained to the bank unsuccessfully. "I don't rely on village water."

After news of the contamination broke, a group of concerned mothers (Michele among them) formed an advocacy group to raise awareness and protect the community. In addition to balancing homemaking, caring for their children, and employment, these moms were talking to government officials and other advocacy groups, attending environmental events and government hearings, and organizing meetings at local coffee shops. In time, Hoosick Falls children became involved. One Friday afternoon in February 2016, they convened a press conference at Hoosick Falls High School, expressing their fear and frustration, and taking the governor to task for failing them.

"This is not a selfish request," said one student. "This is a moral imperative. Please just let our voices be heard."[15]

While adults in Hoosick Falls hadn't gotten Governor Andrew Cuomo's attention despite their indefatigable efforts, their angry and visibly scared children sure did. That very day, Governor Cuomo promised to allocate money from the state's Superfund program to filter water for the residents. David Borge, the mayor of Hoosick Falls, praised the children for their work, saying, "Our local students brought this issue to everyone's attention today. I commend each student who participated in today's forum. Their poignant comments demonstrated the toll this crisis has taken on each and every one of us."[16]

Hoosick Falls became part of a clear and growing call to action for many New Yorkers. Something was wrong with the law when it came to environmental protection. Jerry Williams, an attorney with the law firm Williams Cedar, represented a number of Hoosick Falls residents seeking redress for the incredible injury they had suffered because of the actions of Saint-Gobain, Honeywell, and potentially others. He notes that lead filtered into the infamous Flint, Michigan, water supply for the same reason that PFOA leached into Hoosick Falls source: a fundamental "shortcoming of government."[17] And the contamination was so severe, it was not just taking the healthy lives of families in Hoosick Falls at the time; it was threatening the future health and lives of their children.

What illnesses would befall the children, and their children, and their children—all because industry had been allowed to infect the water for profit, and government had helped them get away with it? New Yorkers were looking for solutions.

Right next door, Pennsylvania was seeing victories—victories against a seemingly impenetrable opponent when it came to the environment, human health, and community quality of life. That opponent—the shale gas industry—was just as big as the industry giants Hoosick Falls was facing. And we were winning. So to me, it was clear the environmental laws in place in New York were not strong enough. Pennsylvania had the right idea: a constitutional amendment to protect environmental rights was needed.

New York is one of the states where I work as the Delaware Riverkeeper. My Delaware Riverkeeper Network organization was joining forces with the newly formed Green Amendments For The Generations and with powerful key allies Peter Iwanowicz and Kate Kurera with Environmental Advocates New York (EANY) and Cathy Pedlar with the New York Adirondack Mountain Club, as well as with communities like Hoosick Falls, to bring our Green Amendment concept to New York State. Also stepping up as a leader in the effort was Nicholas A. Robinson, an internationally recognized expert on environmental law, founder of the environmental law programs at Pace University School of Law, and a leader with such a long, distinguished, and prestigious career he has too many accolades to list. (To me, personally, he was a mentor while in law school and, as such, helped launch me on my journey of environmental protection.) New York lawyer Katrina Kuh, a respected professor at the Elisabeth Haub School of Law at Pace University, and Bob Meek, a former public interest lawyer who dedicated his career to always helping others, also became powerful Green Amendment voices within New York legal and grassroots circles. Together, we were catalyzing the movement for an environmental amendment to the state constitution.

Within the halls of the capitol in Albany, Assemblyman Steve Englebright was the first and most stalwart New York legislator who decided he would champion the environmental rights of all New Yorkers. Assemblyman Englebright pulled together a growing group of legislative allies to join him in cosponsoring, advocating for, and voting for the amendment as it advanced through hearings and votes of the New York Legislature. On 2021's National Green Amendment Day—an annual event that on July 13 spreads the message about the power of our movement—just months before New Yorkers voted 3 to 1 to add a Green Amendment to the state's constitutional Bill of Rights, Assemblyman Steve Englebright told me: "Life, liberty and pursuit of happiness is the goal, [but] you don't do that if you have large portions of your population breathing contaminated air or injured from having only contaminated water to drink."[18]

It is clear to me that the kids of Hoosick Falls and their mothers, along with our cadre of New York leaders, had all learned the same important, fundamental life lesson that I had learned growing up from my opa, Tante Truus, and my mother: Every person can make a difference. If you believe in a greater moral truth and value, and you are willing to fight for it, whatever it takes, you can make a difference. The Green Amendment movement is that opportunity for the environment. It is a chance for all of us, everywhere, to make a difference in protecting all environments, all communities, and all people—in this generation and for all the generations to come. Now is our chance to leave a lasting legacy of immense legal and protective power when it comes to truly securing the right of all people to clean water and air, a stable climate, and healthy environments.

Most objectors to constitutional recognition of environmental rights invariably raise the scary specter of lost money and jobs as a basis for their opposition. "Times are hard," they will say.

"We need this new industrial operation or development project in order to increase our tax base, pump money into the local economy, and create jobs," they offer.

"Protecting the environment sounds nice, but it hurts people. If we want jobs around here—if we want a thriving economy—industry needs to be able to invest and build as it sees fit," they will argue.

As we'll explore in the next chapter, such logic is deeply flawed. Not only is environmental protection economically feasible, it actually provides enduring financial benefits to our community, state, regional, and national economies. Opponents of Green Amendments might protest that our society simply can't afford it. The truth is the opposite: we can't afford *not* to put strong, constitutional safeguards in place to protect the environment for ourselves and our posterity.

CHAPTER TEN

CAN WE AFFORD A GREEN AMENDMENT?

In the summer of 2015, my family rented a cabin near Tomannex State Forest, located along the East Branch of the Delaware River in upstate New York. It was both a sad and an exciting time for us. I had recently entrusted my mother's Columbia County forest to its original owner, who promised to safeguard it against fracking, and my family was in search of our new piece of paradise. My then-ten-year-old son, Wim, had developed an interest in fishing, and when he asked during our vacation if he could cast a line into the river, I told him that we hadn't brought our fishing equipment from home. Imagine my surprise when Wim approached his dad and me as we enjoyed a morning cup of coffee on the deck, clutching a mass of knotted-up fishing line and a broken stick. My husband, Dave, a veteran angler, sprang into action. He looked everywhere for a barbless hook for Wim, finally finding one that had been shoved into an old cork dart board. Within an hour, Wim had a fishing rod.

Although the East Branch of the Delaware River is renowned for its fly-fishing, we didn't anticipate a catch that day. Wim had no experience, and his makeshift rod didn't allow the line to go out very far. But Wim stood on the riverbank the entire afternoon as Dave waded again and again through the water to unhook Wim's casts from overhanging tree branches so he could try again. I found a nice place to sit and listen to the water rush and the leaves rustle, marveling as a bald eagle soared overhead and a kingfisher surveyed the landscape for food from his perch on a branch. As evening came and it began to cool off, I ventured down the riverbank to tell the fellows it was time to go. I found them transfixed as Wim's fishing line became taut. After some effort, Wim and Dave reeled in a big, beautiful rainbow trout. Unbelievable!

Wim spent a few moments marveling at the trout's size and beauty. Then we gently released the fish back into the river's flowing waters. On our walk back to the cabin, Wim was flush with excitement. He couldn't believe that with his primitive pole he had caught something so magnificent, and neither could Dave. "This could never have happened at home!" Dave said, smiling in triumph.

My son then looked up at me, puzzled and confused. "We live near the Delaware River, too, Mum," he said. "Why can't we catch fish like this at home?"

"The upper Delaware, where we are now, is a very special place," I explained to Wim. "It's one of the most special in our country." Then I told him this story.

The reason the upper Delaware River has such bountiful, healthy fish is because the water is pure. New York City residents rely on this part of the watershed for their drinking water, referring to it as "the champagne of tap water."[1] As I related to Wim, much of the city's water originates in the rugged and rural Catskill Mountain range, whose towering peaks capture rainfall from coastal storm systems and winter snow. Gravity then transports the water via a system of reservoirs and aqueducts to the metropolis below. The water tastes good because the Catskills' unique geology makes the water crisper and more crystalline than filtered alternatives.[2] Gourmands praise the water's ideal balance of magnesium and calcium, which some credit for the city's world-famous pizza crust and "crispy-on-the-outside, chewy-on-the-inside" bagels.[3] City officials and planners love the water system because it is gravity-fed, allowing residents in one of the world's largest cities to proudly drink unfiltered water from the tap, while keeping costs low.

Yet the ongoing provision of this pure water did not come without some struggle. During the 1980s, small farms dotting the Catskills fell on hard times and began industrializing their operations or selling their land to larger outfits. As water expert Daniel Moss and former DEP commissioner Albert Appleton relate, "Nutrient use increased, erosion accelerated, and pathogen contamination began to grow. Farmers also began selling off the forested portions of their land for environmentally damaging exurban development."[4] These trends intensified as the decade wore on, forcing the city to either yield to the pressures of industrial pollution and install expensive water-filtration systems or protect the watershed and its historically pristine waterways.

Recognizing that agriculture was polluting the watershed and its streams, the city devised a plan to help farmers reduce their pollution inputs while also supporting the efficiency of their farms. Working closely with individual Catskill farmers, city officials funded customized plans for each farm to achieve economic growth while responsibly stewarding the environment. Though the program wasn't mandatory, 93 percent of farmers volunteered to join.[5] Coupled with upgrades to wastewater treatment systems, the program reduced the amount of phosphorus flowing into one of the system's most imperiled reservoirs, the Cannonsville Reservoir, by more than 95 percent! Cannonsville had once turned neon green on account of the high nutrient content, but no longer.[6]

City officials became convinced that with some extra investment, they could maintain and even improve the city's water supply without mechanical filtration. In the early 1990s, the city applied to the federal EPA for a water filtration waiver, based on the purity of the water it provided to residents and a suite of programs designed to protect the watershed long into the future. Such a waiver was necessary because all surface water supplies in the United States must be filtered unless the supplier can demonstrate excellent water cleanliness, robust protections, and the ability to meet strict quality standards. New York was now up for the challenge.

In January 1993, the EPA granted New York City its first filtration waiver. From that time until 2017, New York City invested $1.7 billion in stream restoration projects, stormwater and wastewater management, land acquisition, forest and wetland programs, protective regulations, and economic stimulus initiatives.[7] In December 2017, the city committed to invest an additional $1 billion to continue and expand its elite water protection program. Because of its unique and successful suite of programs, state and federal regulators have continued to renew water filtration waivers for New York City after every legally mandated review. According to David Warne, assistant commissioner of New York City's Watershed Protection Program, this investment in protecting drinking-water quality at its source has saved the city *billions*. A mechanical filtration system would cost approximately $10 billion in up-front construction costs and anywhere from $30 million to $100 million a year to operate.[8]

In addition to allowing New York City to avoid the costs of filtration, the Watershed Protection Program has added economic value throughout the region in myriad ways. Watershed farmers consistently tell Assistant Commissioner Warne, for example, that safeguarding water quality also supports the economic viability of their businesses. For example, a typical plan involves testing crop fields for soil quality to ensure that farmers are not spreading more fertilizer and manure than necessary. This protects water quality by limiting the phosphorus load that could infect tributaries. But it also saves farmers money. The soil tests often reveal that farmers can buy less fertilizer and still produce the same crop growth in their fields. Covered barnyards or manure sheds have also helped farmers manage their herds within controlled structures rather than on muddy hillsides. Such infrastructure has improved the health of young animals like calves, which are prone to infections or disease if their rearing areas are not kept clean during the first few months of their lives.

The New York City Watershed Protection Program also provides reimbursements for home repairs, benefitting residents, the economy, and the environment alike. Failing septic systems, for example, can pose a threat to water quality if they do not properly collect and treat wastewater. Approximately seventy thousand people live in the Catskill Mountains, a part of the watershed that surrounds New York City's unfiltered water supply. Septic systems service most of these homes. Fixing an ailing system can cost homeowners between $15,000 and $20,000. But if you live in the Catskill Delaware watershed and your septic system fails at your home or business, New York City provides funding to repair, rehabilitate, or replace it. Full-time residents receive 100 percent funding, while second-home owners and part-time residents receive a smaller but substantial subsidy.

When a septic system fails, furthermore, the program employs local businesses to fix it. The entire watershed program employs nearly five hundred people in the Catskills and hires local contractors and engineers to fix septic systems or perform other vital tasks like stormwater retrofits and stream restoration projects. These employees and contractors pump their salaries back into the local economy, creating an economic ripple. By 2018, the program had supported the repair or replacement of 5,200 systems treating a combined 1.7 million gallons per day of sewage. As explained to the *New York Times* by Timothy Cox of the Catskill Watershed Corporation, this means "homeowners get a septic system that is working and the city gets 1.7 million gallons of clean water."[9]

For conservationists like me, one of the watershed program's most exciting initiatives is the land acquisition program, designed to prevent adverse impacts to water quality associated with inappropriate development. The protection program surveys lands with high ecological value, proximity to a water feature, or development potential in the watershed. If identified lands fit the criteria and have willing sellers, the program purchases the property or preserves it through a conservation easement. The program also acquires easements on farmlands, helping farmers to keep their lands agriculturally productive while preventing the lands from being subdivided or developed when those farmers retire.

A similar program purchases streamside properties ravaged by flooding, simultaneously allowing homeowners to secure market value for their lands and enabling the city to protect and/or restore floodplains, which benefits water quality and provides downstream flood protection. At the same time, people who have suffered the damages and heartache of flooding can move to higher, safer ground. Between 1997 and about 2017, when the new agreement was signed, the land acquisition program had already secured more than 180,000 acres of land—and it's been growing ever since. When you combine that acreage with the 210,000 acres of state-owned land in the area, as well as other preserved lands, the entire watershed that feeds New York City's drinking water reservoirs is now approximately 40 percent protected![10]

It gets better: the Watershed Protection Program also features an economic development initiative called the Catskill Fund for the Future, which helps stimulate the local economy. Between 1997 and about 2017, this development fund had already provided local businesses with $60 million in loans and grants. This money has helped create a thriving ecotourism industry in the region. People from around the nation and the world now descend on the area to enjoy trout fishing, boating, kayaking, and the many other recreational amenities that a healthy watershed provides. Such tourism boosts local businesses and real estate prices, since visitors often purchase second homes near great fishing and paddling. This tourism couldn't exist—let alone thrive—without clean waters.

No other public water system in the world has come close to rivaling New York's watershed-management program. As Paul Rush, the deputy commissioner who manages New York City's water supply, has noted, "I'm not aware of any other program in the United States or around the globe that is using all of the techniques we're using, on the scale that we're using them." If New York City had installed a filtration system for its water, a large percentage of the tens of millions in annual filtration costs would have gone to purchase the energy and chemicals necessary to treat contaminated water. Instead of lacing the water with these expensive decontaminants, this progressive program has invested in *protecting the environment*, thereby preventing contaminants from getting into the water in the first place.[11]

New York's program also has regulations in place to ensure that future development and activities on privately owned land won't threaten water quality. The regulations make clear the city's expectations for all present and future landowners so they can use their land in a way that does not harm others. But the incentives and financial support are carefully crafted to motivate participation and compliance as much as possible. Overall, the New York City Watershed Protection Program is focused, to the greatest possible extent, on mobilizing the power of economic incentive and partnership to benefit the environment, individual house-holders, small businesses, and the regional economy.

The program's popularity and efficacy have inspired others through-out the country and the world. Government officials from Australia, Canada, Mexico, Colombia, Chile, Singapore, Korea, Great Britain, and India (the country where I was born and to which I feel a great connec-tion) are among those that have visited the watershed to learn how New York protects water quality through agricultural programs, forestry, and its other watershed protection practices.[12] As others learn more about what New York has done, we can hope that one day soon many more cities around the world will be boosting their economies while serving champagne-quality tap water to their residents. Wim thinks this is a good idea, too!

The Costs—and Benefits—of Environmental Constitutionalism

In making the case for Green Amendments across the nation, I would be remiss if I didn't consider a predictable counterargument: it's eco-nomically unsustainable. Public policy analysts routinely suggest that we must choose between a healthy environment and a thriving economy. Ill-advised political leaders similarly pit job creation and economic growth against environmental regulations. Impose too much "green tape," they say, and the cost of business becomes too burdensome. They paint nightmarish scenarios, predicting that factories and stores will close their doors and relocate abroad, where standards are less stringent. Jobs will be lost, they warn, and families will go hungry and lose their homes. The lights will go out from lack of energy as power plants find themselves unable to operate under the burden of regulation. Both national political parties routinely peddle such misinformation. Former president Barack Obama abandoned many of his environmental initiatives, like heightened ozone restrictions, under pressure from politicians and business groups that said they were simply too expensive.[13] His successor, Donald Trump, promised to abandon "unnecessary" environmental regulations and defund environmental protection agencies so that he could get America working again. He and his conservative allies pursued these goals with reckless abandon during his tenure in office.[14]

But as Kerri Evelyn Harris (whom we met in chapter 8) so aptly points out, "There's no part of the Green Amendment that says there shouldn't be [a] way to make money. We're just saying you shouldn't make money and kill people as a result."[15]

Yes, complying with existing regulations—environmental or otherwise—does cost, but it is not an outlay of cash without reward. To the contrary, it is an investment in better economic growth, not to mention ensuring happy, healthy, and quality lives for people. In 2012, the most expensive regulatory year on record, businesses and individual taxpayers did contend with new environmental regulations as well as extra red tape associated with the Affordable Care Act and Dodd-Frank legislation.[16] According to the American Action Forum, a conservative think tank, 2012 cost Americans a grand total of $216 billion in compliance fees and eighty-seven million hours of paperwork. Compliance with new fuel emissions standards and restrictions on mercury emissions from coal- and oil-fired power plants accounted for three-quarters of these costs. That sounds like a lot of money. And it surely is—when you consider only this one side of the balance sheet.

As DC-based economic policy correspondent Jim Tankersley notes, the American Action Forum study considers only the up-front and annualized costs of regulatory compliance. It fails to consider the *economic benefits* that such regulations provide. That's like complaining about all the money you sink into paying for a college education without considering how tremendously an education *pays you back* over time through higher salaries, more career opportunities, and a richer, well-rounded life. If you consider both the costs and the benefits, for most people a higher education makes a great deal of sense, despite high student debt. That's because the economic benefits of a four-year college degree are tremendous.[17]

Likewise, if you think about the benefits of environmental regulation, the overall picture looks entirely different. According to the EPA, 2012's mercury standards cost an annual $10 billion in compliance and implementation. But they delivered between $37 billion and $90 billion in public health savings! Automobile energy compliance costs $150 billion—just a fraction of the $475 billion that consumers are projected to save on gasoline costs alone. Furthermore, someone also had to build and install all the new technology required to meet the new standards. These new standards not only saved lives but supported jobs.

An analogous cost-benefit pattern emerges when we consider discrete pieces of legislation, like the Clean Air Act.[18] The law ensures we reduce dangerous air pollution, including fine particulate matter, sulfur dioxide, oxides of nitrogen, carbon monoxide, suspended particles, and ozone. A 2020 analysis calculated that every year, the Clean Air Act costs taxpayers $120 billion to comply with the law. But in exchange for that investment, we secure significant and wide-ranging benefits—benefits that are valuable, life altering, and add up to fully $3.8 trillion in total returns. Trillions, over billions, every year! What this means is that, as a society, the benefits we receive from the law are up to thirty-two times greater than its costs. More important than the money, the law allows us to avoid the premature death of some 370,000 people annually. In addition, every year, forty-six thousand heart attacks are prevented, missed days at work are reduced by nearly twenty-two million, and missed days at school are down by eight million.[19]

Best of all, these benefits accrue year over year—so every year, more dollars are secured and more lives are saved. In addition, people are living longer, healthier, and more active lives. As neurologist Dr. Alan H. Lockwood, who wrote his book *The Silent Epidemic* on this very topic, asks, "Who among us has an investment that has performed this well?"[20]

Contrary to what some politicians would have you believe, business support for environmental protection is wide-ranging. In 2014, the American Sustainable Business Council conducted a scientific poll of small-business owners across the political spectrum. The poll found that approximately 91 percent of Democratic-affiliated business owners and 78 percent of business owners identifying as Republican favored expanding water safety regulations. Sixty-two percent of all respondents polled believed water regulations were good for business, and 67 percent expressed anxiety that their businesses could be harmed by water pollution.[21]

The quickly accelerating climate crisis is causing increasing harm to business operations—and in so doing, is also driving up support for needed regulatory action by government. According to Deloitte's 2021 poll of business executives, 80 percent are concerned about the impacts of climate change, 27 percent say their business operations are already being affected by its impacts, and 72 percent agree that governments need to take stronger action to protect the environment.[22] In fact, policies, programs, laws, and regulations that address environmental issues—including the climate crisis—are fueling the creation and advancement of a greener economy.

The resulting advancement of industries focused on renewable and alternative energy sources, pollution control and cleanup, energy conservation, and natural resource conservation is growing a US "green economy" that generates $1.3 trillion in sales revenue each year—and is supporting 9.5 million full-time jobs.[23] In addition, businesses are starting to recognize that demonstrating their commitment to environmental protection makes their products and businesses more attractive to customers. According to a 2021 Gallup poll of Americans, 75 percent of adults consider a company's impact on the environment when considering whom to reward with their purchasing power.[24] Clearly, committing to environmental protection is simply good business. And so we have a recirculating benefit: regulations and business decisions that focus on environmental protection provide economic benefits on a community and company scale that are driving more investment and growth in environmental protection.

Clean and healthy environments provide jobs, income, and value on a national scale as well as on a state and local scale. Take coral reef ecosystems, for example, which are recognized as among the most diverse and densely populated environments on Earth, supporting on the order of one million plant and animal species worldwide despite inhabiting just 0.1 percent of the Earth's surface. Coral reefs support income from ecotourism such as snorkeling and diving, provide economic value as the result of the supported recreational and commercial fisheries, supply food for subsistence fishers, offer natural protection from wave erosion, and support living creatures such as seaweeds, sponges, mollusks, soft corals, and sea anemones that contain substances important to the pharmaceutical industry.[25] The Hawaiian islands alone are home to approximately 85 percent of the coral reefs found in the United States, which provide over $360 million of economic benefit every year, with most of this ($304 million) resulting from recreation and ecotourism.[26] And it's not just Hawaii and its coral reefs: every state directly benefits from clean and healthy environments in terms of better health, safer communities, and increased jobs, income, and tax revenues.

Maine's woodlands, wetlands, waterways, fisheries, wildlife, and other natural resources are recognized as contributing $10 billion a year to the state's economy from tourism. When considering the services nature provides, from water purification and erosion and flood protection to water supply and other protective benefits, the economic value grew by $14 billion.[27] Likewise, New Mexico similarly recognizes the tremendous economic value of the many beautiful landscapes and natural resources that make up the "Land of Enchantment." Tourism is New Mexico's second-largest industry, generating $5.7 billion a year of economic value to the state, with the majority of this income being generated by the state's fish, wildlife, and natural ecosystems. Hunting, fishing, and outdoor recreation in New Mexico supports more jobs than farming and forestry combined. Benefits also accrue on a local level. The Festival of the Cranes at the Bosque del Apache National Wildlife Refuge provides Socorro County and local communities with $2.2 million generated in just a six-day period.[28]

There are no two ways about it: regulation that drives environmental protection also drives economic value. In other words, we make money and save money while creating and supporting good-paying jobs.

It's not enough merely to consider how environmental regulations impact the economy. We should also consider what happens from the perspective of the environment. What do industry, mining, energy, and rampant development cost our natural environment? Such natural capital costs, like the pollution of water and the destruction of forests and other carbon-capture landscapes, usually go unpriced in our economies. But when you think about it, that could hardly be more ridiculous. The truth is that clean air, pure water, and healthy wilderness are finite and priceless resources. Further, when natural capital is exploited by business and industry, the cost of their loss or cleanup is externalized, meaning that it is thrust onto others, like local communities and governments. We pay for these costs through our tax dollars, increased health care costs, and the impacts of extreme weather events like flooding and wildfires.

A 2013 study by The Economics of Ecosystems and Biodiversity for Business Coalition set out to determine the natural capital costs of global business, and the results were startling. Global businesses cost the natural environment an astounding $4.7 trillion a year![29] In certain sectors, natural capital costs exceed the revenues generated by business. Natural capital such as water, air, soil, forests, wetlands, wildlife, fish, plants, and even microbes are fundamental to a multitude of businesses and contribute more than $125 trillion to the global economy every year.[30] Absent environmental regulations and other market-based mechanisms that lower the harmful impacts of pollution-based activities, individuals, communities, and governments must shoulder these costs.[31] Politicians and business leaders who complain about regulatory red tape rarely acknowledge natural capital costs like floods, illness, lost recreation, and increased need for drinking-water purification.

Environmental degradation acts as a drain on our health, our economy, and our lives. Requiring industrial operations to curtail pollution will certainly impact the bottom line as they pay the up-front costs of regulatory compliance. But those up-front costs pale in comparison with the *trillions of extra dollars* their pollutants would inflict on the country's health-care system and on taxpayers as we are forced to respond to growing flood damages, wildfires, and more.

If you still doubt the economic harms that result from environmental degradation, despite all of this evidence, consider once again the example of municipal water systems. New York City protected its water, whereas Philadelphia historically did not, and it has paid the price ever since. As Chari Towne documents in her book *A River Again*, the Schuylkill River circa 1799, if not the "champagne of water," was a river of "uncommon purity," according to contemporary accounts.[32] But then the Industrial Revolution intruded, powered by the rise of coal mining. The Schuylkill became contaminated with a witches' brew of waste. Paper mills, sawmills, chemical and gas works, breweries, bleaching and printing operations, textile manufacturers and dye plants, iron furnaces, tanneries, and slaughterhouses all dumped pollution into the river.[33] Sewage waste and cesspool discharges added to the contamination. By 1885, the Schuylkill was so polluted that Philadelphia began to look elsewhere for its water supply.[34] The city continued to use the Schuylkill for drinking water, although not as its primary source. By the 1930s, some considered the Schuylkill the nation's dirtiest river.[35] Eventually authorities worked to cleanse the river, restoring it as a reliable source of drinking water. But that process was extremely time-consuming and costly. Despite the vast funds spent on remediation, the Schuylkill's water would never again have the "uncommon purity" that would allow Philadelphia residents to consume it without filtration.

Quite simply, as New York Assemblyman Englebright said when advocating for passage of the New York Green Amendment: "Our environment is the economy. Our economy suffers if we degrade the environment that we are all a part of and depend upon."[36] Whether you consider the costs of regulation or the costs of degrading the environment, the outcome is the same. It's not a question of whether we can afford laws that protect our environment. It's whether we can afford *not* to have them. Recognizing that environmental protection is good for the economy as well as for the health and vitality of our communities, we simply can't afford *not* to pass Green Amendments at the state and federal levels.

The Value of a River

If we look more closely at the local economic impact of natural resources, the case for enhanced environmental protections becomes even more compelling. Let's consider my Delaware River.[37] From the late sixteenth to the mid-twentieth centuries, residences and industries dumped untold amounts of pollution and waste into the Delaware River system. Those who lived in cities like Philadelphia were subjected to cholera and yellow fever outbreaks as well as sickening smells and unsightly pollution floating on the water. Philadelphia is located hundreds of miles downstream from the Catskills, where New York City sourced its drinking water. By the time water in the Delaware arrived in Philadelphia, development and industry of all kinds had taken their toll.

Weary of living next to a sewer system, nineteenth-century residents began fleeing the area. Those who could afford it retreated to country estates and vacation spots elsewhere during the summers, when waterborne illness was at its worst, and returned to their homes in the city during the winter months only. In time, after extensive cleanup efforts, communities have returned to enjoy life along the river year-round. In recent years, improving water quality along the Delaware River has benefited the real estate market, boosting property values an estimated

8 percent. This yields property value increases of $256 million in just the lower third of the river, the portion known as the Delaware Estuary.

Because of the Delaware's high-quality water and scenic beauty, recreation and ecotourism are vital parts of communities up and down the river. Now that it's clean, visitors flock to the Delaware to enjoy fishing, boating, hiking, bird watching, biking, tubing, swimming, jogging, camping, and wildlife viewing. Fishing, hunting, birding, and wildlife viewing in the Delaware River watershed alone support nearly forty-five thousand jobs and $1.5 billion in wages each year. Paddling in the Delaware River watershed supports another 4,200 jobs and generates nearly $400 million in sales. River recreation in the upper portions of the watershed, including where Wim and Dave caught their prized rainbow trout, is responsible for $27 million annually in economic value.[38] Yardley, New Hope, Lambertville, Stockton, Frenchtown, Milford, Port Jervis, Barryville, Narrowsburg, and Callicoon are among the ecotourism destinations within the Delaware River watershed that visitors enjoy for their local wineries, breweries, nature parks, coffeehouses, museums, restaurants, and interesting shopping.

State and national parks flanking the watershed also add millions in revenue and thousands of jobs. Consider the Delaware Water Gap National Recreation Area, which traverses the Delaware River where it cuts through the Appalachian Mountain range. Every year, approximately five million people visit the region to camp, hike, canoe and kayak, and enjoy the many facets of nature. While in the area, visitors spend over $100 million a year, supporting over 7,500 jobs, providing over $100 million in wages, and making it an important economic driver for communities in the middle portion of the Delaware River system.[39] More important, in my mind, this beautiful recreation area provides wonderful opportunities for adults and kids—families and friend groups alike—to enjoy the beautiful, free-flowing Delaware River (which has no dams anywhere on its main stem), along with its stunning forests, waterfalls, scenic vistas, and living nature. This is just one example of the many public parks that bring economic value based on healthy nature to our region.

Beyond the exciting recreational and educational opportunities it has created, protecting the Delaware River's biodiversity has benefited many other industries, including pharmaceuticals, commercial fishing, agriculture, and craft brewing. In the 1960s, biomedical researchers determined that a horseshoe crab's blood contained special properties that can help us test vaccines, medical devices, implants such as pacemakers, and prosthetic devices to ensure that they are free of bacteria and safe to use. This test, dependent on a special substance in horseshoe crab blood known as limulus amebocyte lysate (LAL), is now standard among pharmaceutical companies, making the Delaware River's horseshoe crab population (the largest spawning population in the world) indispensable to the biomedical industry.[40] As of 2015, LAL industry revenues totaled $50 million, with one gallon of blood alone worth $60,000.[41] In each of the regions in which the industry operates, including the Delaware, it creates jobs and contributes to local economies. Once scientists collect the horseshoe crabs' lifesaving blood, they return the majority to the water *alive*. Harvesting blood does result in some horseshoe crab mortality, and scientists are working to improve their methods, recognizing that these special creatures are more precious alive than dead, both in ecological and in economic terms.

At every opportunity, Dr. Larry Niles and Dr. Amanda Dey—the internationally recognized wildlife biologists and experts on migratory shorebirds introduced in chapter 2—are quick to point out another irreplaceable niche for the horseshoe crabs of Delaware Bay. They constitute the primary food source for migratory shorebirds like red knots, which stop over every spring at the Delaware Bayshore en route from their wintering grounds in South America to their breeding grounds in the Arctic. Thousands of wildlife watchers descend on the Delaware Bay each year to view the spectacle of red knots and other migratory shorebirds feasting on billions of tiny, energy-rich eggs that the horseshoe crabs lay on the bay's beaches. These visitors spend money on equipment, food, accommodations, and more in New Jersey and Delaware each year. The horseshoe crab and migratory bird phenomenon provides upward of $32 million in annual economic benefits to the region.[42] This makes horseshoe crabs a linchpin in the regional ecotourism industry. For me, their value is far beyond the dollars and cents: the horseshoe crabs and migratory birds are a beautiful and essential part of my Delaware River's natural community and personal memories of special times with my daughter, Anneke, and son, Wim.

Horseshoe crabs are hardly the only commercially valuable species to come out of the Delaware. Since the mid-twentieth century, when the river was so polluted that it contained a twenty-mile oxygen-dead zone, the Delaware has rebounded. It now supports local fisheries up and down the Eastern Seaboard, with the river serving as a spawning ground for fish species later harvested elsewhere. There are at least two hundred species of fish known to rely on portions of the river spanning the salty waters of the estuary and bay to the fresh waters of the upper river reaches.[43] The estimated annual economic benefit of recreational fishing in the Delaware Estuary is approximately $52 million a year.[44] Local businesses throughout the watershed sell bait and tackle to anglers and charter sightseeing tours to interested outsiders—they, too, create economic value thanks to a clean Delaware River. After suffering debilitating parasitic diseases, which nearly decimated the entire population, shellfish have also become lucrative again. In the period spanning 2008–2011, the cumulative value of Delaware Bay oysters was an estimated $3.8 million, creating an additional $23 million in the regional economy.[45]

Clean water throughout the river system also sustains the rich soils and irrigation required for basin-based farming. Agriculture has a long history in the Delaware River watershed: Pennsylvania has become famous for its mushrooms and floriculture; New Jersey for its peaches, blueberries, and cranberries; New York for its maple syrup and eggs; and Delaware for its vegetables and strawberries. Thousands of basin farms furnish local restaurants and markets with produce and sustainably raised livestock products. Local shoppers save on transportation costs for food, while decreased food importation in the watershed ultimately reduces the region's carbon footprint.

Clean water from the Delaware River and its tributaries doesn't just provide food and water, but what for many people is another kind of sustenance: craft beer. About a dozen craft beer makers operate within the city limits of Philadelphia alone. Victory Brewing Company touts the great taste and quality of its beer made from the clean water of Brandywine Creek, a major tributary in the Delaware River watershed. Saint Benjamin Brewing Company also boasts of great taste, and its brewing process uses water from Philadelphia's water system (which comes from the Delaware River). Yards Brewing Company, another Philadelphia brewer, gets double value from the Delaware River, using river water for its brewing and its waterfront location as a means of enticing customers.

And then there is the river's historical and cultural value. The Delaware River is the ancestral homeland of the Lenni Lenape people, who used the river for transportation, food, and water. Archaeological remains of Lenape settlements dot the landscape near the Delaware and major tributaries like the Neshaminy Creek. The Lenape Nation remains an important part of our watershed community, contributing their rich culture and river connections.

The Delaware River also figures prominently in the founding of the United States. On December 25, 1776, George Washington crossed the river to surprise his adversaries, scoring an important symbolic victory in the Revolutionary War. Each Christmas, visitors descend on the site in Washington Crossing, Pennsylvania, one of the watershed's most popular tourist destinations.

We should not ignore the significant industrial activity that clean Delaware River water supports. Beginning in the eighteenth century, lumber mills, paper mills, tanneries, stone quarries, cement makers, iron and rubber manufacturers, and later the coal industry set up shop on the Delaware's banks, using the river for transportation and power generation. These industries damaged the river so much that many people turned their backs on the Delaware. Today, many companies (but unfortunately not all of them) are much more appreciative of the values of clean water and recognize their obligation to help protect it.

As this brief overview suggests, the protection of the Delaware River tracks well with the cost-benefit analysis of environmental protections at the local, state, and federal levels. The notion that environmental regulations weigh heavily on business doesn't survive scrutiny in the Delaware River watershed. Besides its immeasurable intrinsic value, the river is an indispensable part of the economy across many sectors. Supporting and advancing environmental protection will continue to enable such value creation going forward. The Delaware River's story is representative of rivers and ecosystems worldwide. As I often say when ending one of my public talks: when we best protect the river, we best protect ourselves.

Answering the Critics

Economic objections to environmental constitutionalism are misguided. As we've seen, safeguarding our natural resources is an excellent economic investment. New York City's water supply system demonstrates how such farsighted, environmentally responsible stewardship of natural resources saves billions in dollars while stimulating the regional economy. My Delaware River also testifies to the manifold benefits that conservation and protection confer. We all deserve to drink pristine champagne-quality tap water and enjoy the many economic amenities that natural resources like the Delaware River provide. But what about you and your community? Although the notion of a Green Amendment may sound good, you might have another objection to raise. Or perhaps you live in a state where environmental constitutionalism seems hopelessly unrealistic. With industry so powerful and public officials at every level so eager to do their bidding, do we really stand a chance at getting our right to a healthy environment recognized in the constitution? How can that possibly happen?

It is possible. For one thing, merely campaigning for a Green Amendment brings significant benefits. When people come to demand their rights to pure water, clean air, a stable climate, and a healthy environment, they change the way they think about the environment, their rights, and whether those whom they are electing to office will help protect or thwart those rights. On the flip side, we surely know that a Green Amendment will never happen if we don't try. The key is to get started and work our way up.

When I first visited New Mexico, a state where oil and gas has immense power, I was told time and again: "This can't happen here." While the oil and gas industry certainly mobilized against us, grassroots activists were dedicated to advancing this powerful protection. Organizations like Indivisible Albuquerque, Interfaith Power and Light, Southwest Native Cultures, and Youth United for Climate Crisis Action (YUCCA) were first to mobilize. But quickly the coalition grew to include over forty-five groups, with OLÉ, Adelante Progressive Caucus, New Mexico Environmental Law Center, Great Old Broads for Wilderness, 350 Santa Fe, and Sierra Club Rio Grande Chapter all joining the movement as key leaders.

Our ranks of champions in state government quickly grew, too. During our first effort in 2021, we had four great sponsors in Senator Antoinette Sedillo Lopez and Representative Joanne Ferrary, supported by Senator Bill Soules and Senator Harold Pope Jr. But as we approached the 2022 legislative session, many more were eager to join in that support, including Senator Carrie Hamblen, Senator Gerald Ortiz y Pino, Senator Bobby Gonzales, Senator Shannon Pinto, Senator Jeff Steinborn, Senator Benny Shendo, Senator Bill Tallman, Senator Nancy Rodriguez, Representative Tara Lujan, Representative Patricia Roybal Caballero, Representative Pamelya Herndon, and recognized leaders in the legislature like Representative Gail Chasey, Senator Liz Stefanics, and Representative Linda Lopez. And by the middle of the 2022 session, twenty-five lawmakers had signed on as cosponsors.

As New Mexico demonstrates, once the call for a Green Amendment begins, the movement will quickly build. But we have to get started.

State Senator Mike Gabbard, our lead Green Amendment champion in Hawaii, beautifully lays it out: "Throughout generations, the 'Āina [the land] has given and given and given, asking nothing in return.

However, our 'Āina, our land, she needs our help—the one who has given to us for all these years needs our help—and she needs it now! So it is time for all of us to step up for the one who has stepped up for us for all of these years."[46]

In the next chapter, we will talk about how Green Amendment movements are getting started in many of our key states. One thing they all have in common is that there was a person (or people) who stepped up and got the ball rolling.

CHAPTER ELEVEN

FIGHTING FOR A
GREEN AMENDMENT

This book has highlighted a select few of the countless environmental stories that are harrowing and outrageous for those living through them—but that also carry serious ramifications for others downwind, downstream, or up the food chain, who may not even be aware they are in danger. These anecdotes are just a sampling of the many environmental assaults and injustices that people are experiencing every day, all across our nation— and that have implications across generations. Whether it's fracking gas companies setting up shop on your local cattle farm, a mega warehouse complex ruining your town, government permitting yet another industrial operation to spew pollution into already-overburdened communities of color, developers cutting forests and causing flooding, legal and illegal pollution contaminating rivers, or chemical spills and industrial contaminants damaging your children's health, these stories are scary—and they are *real*.

Every day, local, state, and federal agencies grant industries permission to pollute, deforest, denigrate, and despoil our natural environment. And we all stand in witness to government officials who are willing to perpetuate a fossil fuel industry that is creating an irreversible climate catastrophe, portending a terrifying future for our children.

Living in the United States, people don't realize that while we recognize and protect speech, property, and gun rights, we don't meaningfully recognize a right to drink clean water, breathe clean air, or live in the stable climate and healthy environments essential to supporting and sustaining healthy lives. Instead, these fundamental human rights are entrusted to a political system with competing demands, where money, power, and connections have primacy over justice and basic human needs, and where partisan gamesmanship is often more important than facts, science, and problem solving. The ramifications of this reality are crystal clear. Rather than constitutionally recognized and protected environmental rights for the people, the law is mostly on the side of the polluters. That means whenever we, as individuals or communities, find ourselves facing a threat to our water, air, climate, or environments, our options to defend ourselves are limited. It is within this legal framework that I undertake my environmental advocacy.

I spend my days working with victims of environmental degradation, helping them organize and take action so they can try to restore sanctity to their homes and reclaim their rights to a healthy environment. When we are just starting out, we all feel the same way: powerless and overwhelmed. Everyone is stunned to learn the reality of environmental rights—that unless you live in one of a very few states, you simply don't have any.

But don't despair, and don't feel powerless. You *can* help protect our environment, now and for future generations. It's time to *fight* for the passage of a Green Amendment in your state, in every state, and eventually at the federal level. It's time for we the people to take our power back—and make clear to government that our rights to a clean and healthy environment are now among the rights they must protect. While continuing to fight as the voice of the Delaware River, I have also founded the Green Amendments For The Generations organization so I can work directly with you to advance this vision for powerful protection and transformational change.

Is Environmental Constitutionalism Undemocratic?

Opponents of constitutional Green Amendments often try to misappropriate the language of democracy as a basis for their criticism, advancing a misplaced or even bad-faith argument that such amendments are somehow undemocratic. Antagonists insist there are drawbacks to any approach to activism that meaningfully includes the court system, asserting that we should rely only on the legislative branches of our state and federal governments. Using the courts to challenge environmentally harmful action on constitutional grounds is fundamentally undemocratic, they contend.[1] According to their argument, in a free and democratic society like the United States, we elect legislators to enact our collective will. So when we appeal to constitutions for our rights, we empower the (largely unelected) judiciary to interpret the constitutionality of individual policies (for example, allowing PFAS drinking water contamination) and pieces of legislation (such as Act 13)—a process known as judicial review. Why should we create vast new opportunities, these antagonists complain, for a handful of unelected judges to invalidate legislation created by the representatives of millions of voters?

The answers are simple, clear, and very democratic. In the United States, judicial review is a fundamental underpinning of our democracy. We have three indispensable branches of government—legislative, executive, and judicial. Each is empowered to act as a check on the others when necessary, the judicial included. For the judiciary to play a role in advancing good governance is unremarkable in a democracy such as the United States. Throughout American history, the judiciary has exercised appropriate influence on our nation's policies and protections. Courts have legalized gay marriage and instituted affirmative action policies. Perhaps the most famous and far-reaching instance of judicial review occurred in the foundational civil rights case *Brown v. Board of Education of Topeka* (1954). With the stroke of a pen, nine federal judges invalidated, on constitutional grounds, more than a century of state and federal legislation that had provided for the segregation of Black and white Americans. As the court argued, segregationist policies promulgated under the doctrine of "separate but equal" violated the equal protection clause of the US Constitution's Fourteenth Amendment. As a result of this decision, the entire country was desegregated over a period of years. Both liberals and conservatives today applaud the outcome of the *Brown* decision and other decisions like it, because in the final analysis they are about equitably protecting the rights of all people here in the United States. As Vice President Kamala Harris has recognized, the Supreme Court "is often the last refuge for equal justice when our constitutional rights are being violated."[2] That was certainly the outcome in *Brown v. Board*.

In general, and over the course of history, the courts have maintained a strong record of upholding democratic rights. Of course, they do sometimes get it wrong—even catastrophically so. But when language is embedded in the US Constitution, and when strong rights advocates stay engaged, eventually we drive the path whereby the courts correct course. The unambiguous language in the Green Amendments that are advancing and passing provides a clarity that makes it hard even for activist judges to overtly undermine environmental rights.

As I talked about in the first few chapters, the 1970s marked the full flowering of global environmentalism and the broader rights-based revolution that would sweep our nation and much of the world. During this time, most of the world's constitutions came into existence or were significantly modified in order to grant rights to previously overlooked groups of people, like Indigenous communities, and previously overlooked entities, like the environment. But the mere existence of constitutional rights doesn't guarantee that people can exercise them.

Critically, it was the *combination* of constitutional empowerment backed by court enforcement that ultimately granted environmental rights to the people of Pennsylvania. If the judiciary lacks the power of review, then the people can be left without a remedy. The inimitable Cass Sunstein, professor of jurisprudence at the University of Chicago, put it well: "Without judicial review, constitutions tend to be worth little more than the paper on which they are written. They become mere words, or public relations documents, rather than instruments which confer genuine rights."[3] While it has taken time, the courts have played a critical role in securing recognition of many of our constitutional rights. Without judicial review, the courts wouldn't have struck down segregation, and both the civil rights and environmental movements would be significantly worse off today. In Pennsylvania (where the state supreme court justices are in fact democratically elected), we never would have gotten our Act 13 decision and had our environmental rights recognized and restored.

As we've observed throughout this book, large business interests like shale gas and chemical conglomerates exercise disproportionate influence in our democratic institutions. In 2014, researchers at Princeton and Northwestern universities released a well-known study comparing all the laws passed between 1981 and 2002 and voter preferences on each policy decision. As researchers found, the policies overwhelmingly *didn't* reflect the will of the people, but rather the preferences of special interest groups. As the study notes, policies "tend to tilt towards the wishes of corporations and business and professional associations," and especially diverge from the will of non-elite Americans.[4] This finding holds especially true in relation to the environment. Despite current legislative and executive threats to environmental regulation and policy, Americans want enhanced protection. In 2016, nearly 75 percent of Americans responding to a Pew Research Center poll said that the US "should do whatever it takes to protect the environment."[5]

We can no longer rely on legislatures and regulatory agencies, all too often beholden to special interests, to protect the environment. Given these circumstances, turning to the courts as a final arbiter—as our forebears have so often and legitimately done, and as the authors of our federal constitution originally envisioned—can help reinforce, actualize, and reinvigorate the will of the people.

Of course, whatever your view of the courts, constitutional provisions securing our environmental rights are, in the first instance, a result of the will of the people carried out through a democratic process. In our Green Amendment movement, starting at the state level, the people are the ones casting the final votes for whether or not to amend the constitution. In this sense, environmental constitutionalism is quite firmly in accord with our democratic traditions. In fact, when given the opportunity to cast their ballots, the people have overwhelmingly voted for constitutional environmental rights—whether it's 80 percent of the people in Pennsylvania (in 1971) or 70 percent in New York (in 2021).

As members of a democracy, we all deserve to have our voices heard. Rather than obscuring or thwarting the will of the people, environmental constitutionalism actually allows for its clear expression. With Green Amendments in place, the majority who care about the environment will finally be able to make themselves heard, overwhelming the powerful industrial interests that have shaped and distorted environmental public policy in recent decades. Democracy will reign, our natural environments will be protected, and our communities will grow and prosper.

People Taking Their Power Back

Some of the most powerful Green Amendment movements that are advancing right now began with a single person like you, or a community organization like yours. Mike Neas, a retired general contractor and New Mexico resident, was the first person from New Mexico to call and urge me to visit the state to advocate for a Green Amendment. He had heard me on the radio show *The Thom Hartmann Program* and reached out almost immediately. On that first phone call, in the winter of 2019, Mike sounded hesitant but determined. As we spoke, I could tell he had immediately grasped how powerful a Green Amendment could be for environmental protection. And after that first conversation, he started to connect me with others in New Mexico who were working on environmental or social justice issues. Sometimes he sent the person an introductory email; at other times he just offered me a name or even an organization's name, leaving it to me to get in touch. Slowly but surely, important relationships began to develop.

There was Terry Sloan, a well-regarded Native American leader, director of the NGO Southwest Native Cultures, and an active advocate in New Mexico and at the United Nations; Nicole Olonovich, who shared her story about serving in the Air National Guard in chapter 9; Robert Cordingly with 350 Santa Fe; Luis Guerrero, the legislative and political organizer with the Rio Grande Chapter of the Sierra Club in New Mexico; and Artemisio Romero y Carver an artist, poet, and youth environmental justice leader with the organization Youth United for Climate Crisis Action (YUCCA). From there, we began to connect with legislative leaders.

Senator Antoinette Sedillo Lopez was a new state legislator who was already emerging as an unwavering environmental champion. When she and I first met for coffee, she was interested and inquisitive but a bit skeptical. Over time, we continued to talk. She read the first edition of this book, and from there she has quickly risen to the top as a national Green Amendment champion. As a former law professor, Antoinette is able to take on the false arguments we so often hear with a clarity that is important in a state where her political opposition is well-supplied with talking points from the oil and gas industry.

Soon after Representative Joanne Ferrary learned of the Green Amendment at one of my National Caucus of Environmental Legislators (NCEL) talks, she wanted to sign on as its champion in the New Mexico House. Joanne is just about the nicest person you could hope to meet, as is her husband, Rich. But no one should mistake her kindness for weakness: Joanne is proving a formidable advocate for the Green Amendment. One day, she was outside the legislative chamber, questioning someone in political leadership about the Green Amendment and their lack of support. They were responding to Joanne's challenge with all kinds of hypotheticals and legalese—excuses, really, for why they were not supporting the amendment. "I'd had enough," Joanne recalled as she was telling me about the encounter. "And so I just blurted out, 'So we support your bills in a tough spot, but you can't support ours?'"[6] Walking away from the encounter, Joanne mused to herself: "One-way streets never circle back."

Together, these two women—along with a growing grassroots movement in New Mexico—have inspired more leaders in the legislature and at the grassroots level to see this as a top environmental priority for the state. New Mexico is now at the forefront of our Green Amendment movement. But it all began with that first phone call from Mike Neas.

As you may recall from chapter 7, Maine's story started quite similarly. Michelle Henkin picked up the phone and called me after reading the first edition of this book; we talked, we planned, and then we met and got to work. Now, Maine is also at the forefront of the Green Amendment movement. In Maryland, the first phone call came from Rabbi Nina Beth Cardin; the next day we were meeting with a legislator she thought would be interested in advancing the idea. In Colorado, it was environmental lawyer, author, and former teacher Wendy Kerner.

In your state, it might just be you.

In New Jersey and New York, our Green Amendment effort started differently. As you read about in chapters 8 and 9, in these states a collaboration of environmental organizations joined forces to organize and advance the call for constitutional change, and in due time other organizations, individuals, and youth would join as key leaders. Sometimes leadership has started with visionary legislators who heard the Green Amendment message and wanted to pursue it in their state. The most powerful vehicle for helping reach those legislators has been our partnership with the National Caucus of Environmental Legislators, an organization dedicated to helping state legislators advance groundbreaking environmental protections.

Early on, I had been introduced to NCEL's conservation senior advisor, Ruth Musgrave—a longtime environmental leader who, I was told, might be interested in the Green Amendment concept. It turned out we would soon be crossing paths in an airport as each of us was traveling for work: I was on my way to Massachusetts to give a Green Amendment talk, and she was returning from a meeting of her own. So we met up for a light meal during overlapping layovers. Ruth was quick to express interest in the effort and wanted to explore a potential partnership with NCEL. Naturally, I jumped at the chance! Ruth introduced me to the NCEL leadership, and our partnership quickly blossomed.

As a result, I have had the opportunity to present at a number of in-person and online NCEL events for legislators about Green Amendments. After each of these meetings, new leaders in new states have joined the movement: Senator Mike Gabbard of Hawaii, Senator Juan Mendez of Arizona, Representative Evan Hansen of West Virginia, and Representative Chuck Isenhart of Iowa, to name just a few. Once it's clear that a Green Amendment is going to be introduced in a state, it's essential that grassroots leaders and activists come forth as well—after all, the amendment will ultimately pass only if the people of the state authentically believe in and support it.

Determining who takes on that leadership role in a given state generally occurs organically. While in Hawaii the movement began with Senator Gabbard, the community engagement and connections really started to progress after local activists Ted Bohlen and Sherry Pollack were inspired to pick up the leadership mantle at the grassroots level. In Iowa, Representative Isenhart has been introducing us to grassroots organizations in his state so we can start to develop the partnerships and broad-based community engagement necessary for success. Meanwhile, in Washington, our grassroots progress began to take off after environmental activist David Kipnis and Monica Aufrecht with 350 Washington Civic Action Team asked the question, "Who is taking the lead for the grassroots in the state?" To which I immediately responded: "No one yet. But maybe you?"

Thus far, every state has had a different Green Amendment origin story, but common to each successful effort is that they are advancing in partnership with my Green Amendments For The Generations organization. By working in partnership, we can all benefit from the learning and experience that each state and its people bring to this effort—and we can also ensure that we are building upon a growing foundation of knowledge rather than having to reinvent the wheel in each state (and potentially doing something harmful to the movement as a whole).

One of the most powerful benefits of partnership is ensuring that the language stays on track and secures all the rights that come from meeting the true definition of a Green Amendment. It is easy for the text, and therefore the impact, of an amendment to get derailed by a few seemingly innocuous but impactful tweaks. For example, the first challenge to the language often brought forth by the opposition is: Why does the language have to be in the constitution?

"Constitutional law is just different. In terms of the hierarchy of our laws, constitutional law comes out at the top. And so when the Supreme Court [says], 'There's something about the statute that is not constitutional,' that's a really big deal," explains Professor John Dernbach, an authority on the subject if ever there was one. "And the nonlegal impact of a constitutional amendment is that constitutional values, tend to . . . get an extra bump in terms of public opinion, because they're stated in a constitution."[7]

Up next, we often hear: Why the bill of rights? Won't it work better or just as well with some other placement in the constitution? But that argument is also fundamentally flawed. Very simply: if you want environmental rights to have the most powerful protection available, as other fundamental human, civil, and political rights do, it needs to be codified alongside them in the constitution's bill of rights. And drawing in part on my own experience and expertise, and in part on the unrivaled dedication, experience, and knowledge base of a large and growing network of advocates, lawyers, and experts, I can help you make that case.

Working in partnership also allows us all to grow from language modifications that strengthen the values of a Green Amendment. When we first start to work in a state, I share all of the most powerful language options based on my experience. Because it's not simply about re-proposing what's been adopted in Pennsylvania, Montana, or New York. Each of these three states employs different language and approaches. Each amendment is stronger in some respects but weaker in others; and in each there is something missing that could make it even better.

In your state—which (now that you've made it to the final chapter) will no doubt be next to join our fight—it's crucial that we advance the strongest legal approach, and the language that best suits the personality and priorities of your state. In my experience, as we work state by state to accomplish that goal, we often find new pathways and language that proves helpful to other states. As you read in chapter 3, the idea of protecting the cultural values linked with the environment was first proposed in New Mexico, as a way of respecting sacred sites and environmental beliefs important to Native Americans. In Hawaii, adding the term "native" before the phrase "flora, fauna and ecosystems" was an important advancement to ensure that constitutional protection could not be afforded to harmful invasive species. In Maryland, highlighting human health values in the constitutional language emerged as a priority. These helpful modifications are now part of the language we offer for consideration in other states where analogous ideas might resonate.

Working as partners allows me to help you anticipate and defend against the attacks we know will come. I've heard pretty much all of them, but whenever we encounter a new one, it adds to the body of knowledge from which we can all benefit—as long as we stay connected and keep working together. The claim that a Green Amendment will result in a massive onslaught of frivolous lawsuits is a red herring. It has not proven to be remotely true in Pennsylvania or Montana, and it's also prevented by ethical obligations that bind all attorneys. From a different perspective, New York Assemblymember Phara Souffrant Forrest stated during floor debate of the proposed New York Green Amendment: "We fight for speech, we fight for guns; this bill says that you have the right to fight for clean space, period. As a legislator, I don't concern myself too much about potential . . . torts or legal cases. [A]s a legislator, my job is to defend rights for people."[8]

When people suggest that a Green Amendment is merely an aspirational goal with no legal strength, I can help you bring forth myriad powerful examples to demonstrate the substantive and procedural values of Green Amendment protections. And when opponents claim that passing a Green Amendment will bankrupt the state as a result of monetary damage claims for environmental rights violations, I can help you rebut that spurious argument. Green Amendments are not about money damages for environmental pollution. They're about securing fundamental change in the government's decision-making and actions that cause harm. I can also share with you the powerful responses of other thoughtful Green Amendment champions from other states. For instance, when faced with the question "How can we afford a New Mexico Green Amendment? Won't it cost our state if we are found to have violated somebody's constitutional rights?" New Mexico Senator Harold Pope Jr. responded, "We can't replace this planet, our land, our water, and we can't replace our people. People are worried about the cost, the cost to the state. But no harm, no cost. Cost is the wrong focus—we can't afford the harm."[9]

While all of the states you have read about in this book have either passed state Green Amendments or begun to advance proposals, each is progressing at a different pace. In some states the movement is growing quickly, as in Maine and New Mexico. In other states, the amendment is going to take more time to push across the finish line—but having a proposal gives something for engaged legislators and community leaders to point to, and to rally around. As Hawaii's Ted Bohlen said in response to disappointment when their 2022 proposal didn't secure enough votes yet for passage: "As you all know, major changes take time to pass! Women's suffrage took seventy years. Civil rights and voting rights for African Americans took even longer. For climate, it is frightening because we don't have the time to wait . . . . I've been trying to get cesspools upgraded in Hawaii for ten years now. Sausage-making ain't pretty, but we are privileged to have a vision of a better world and the abilities to help make it happen. So let's keep fighting for that!"[10]

A Strategy for Success

Like Green Amendment language and leadership, our strategy for success will also be unique to your state. Understanding the process of constitutional change will help us craft the best strategic path forward. While some states have a pathway through a constitutional convention, which opens the door to overhauling every aspect of your state's constitution—and as a result, is not a path that most states are eager to pursue—other states allow modification through a petition and ballot initiative driven by the people. Across the states where we've engaged so far, we are consistently finding that the most effective paths are those that start with legislation and end with a vote of the people. In this legislative context, there is no official role for state governors; they can use their bully pulpit for or against an issue, but cannot exercise veto power. Once the requisite number of legislators vote in support, the amendment goes to the people to decide. This path also allows us to find legislative champions who understand and embrace the imperatives of Green Amendment language and placement—and who are eager to work in lockstep with our grassroots leaders, so we can be assured of the advancement of a meaningful and protective amendment with all the essential elements.

Whatever the path, amending a state constitution is never easy. But once the protection is secured, it is most likely to remain in perpetuity, regardless of future opposition or lobbying efforts.

Also important is understanding what your state constitution already has to say about the environment, so we can be prepared to explain why and how a Green Amendment could make a meaningful difference. As we explored in chapter 3, language that protects fishing, hunting, and navigation instead of *all* shared natural resources, or that describes environmental rights only as important policy or to be defined solely by the legislature, falls well short of the strength and vigor of a Green Amendment. But the differences between what exists and what we are advocating for may not be immediately apparent on its face—so we need to invest significant time and effort in educating around this point. If you live in a state with a preexisting but inadequate provision, our messaging will need to convince the public that while environmental language may exist in your constitution, it does not rise to the necessary level of protection—and a change is needed.

Not Just Any Language Will Do

Green Amendments are not composed of just any language, placed anywhere in the constitution that talks about the environment or environmental rights. They comprise the elements needed to place environmental rights legally on par with other civil, human, and political rights. A Green Amendment protects all people, regardless of race, ethnicity, or socioeconomic status. In addition, it creates a duty that binds all government entities and officials, subject to the constitution, to respect and protect enumerated environmental rights; this duty is not limited to the legislature. Importantly, Green Amendments provide protection even in cases when there is no specific law that speaks to a given issue of environmental concern. Consider the situation with PFAS, in which gaps in the law enabled the devastating consequences of widespread contamination. Green Amendments provide generational protection, increase the potency of environmental laws that are already on the books, and stand as strong foundations for new protections whenever they are needed.

Before we get any further into how we work together to make all this happen, I want to assure everyone reading this book: you have all the knowledge you need to fight for a constitutional Green Amendment in your state (and ultimately at the federal level, when the time is right). You know that, as a person, you need clean air and water, healthy environments, and a stable climate. You know in your heart that these are rights that belong to you by virtue of the fact that you are a person here on Earth. You know it is fundamentally and morally wrong for industry, developers, or politicians to compromise or destroy these needs that are basic to all life in order to advance their own personal, political, or profit-making goals. You know it is wrong for some communities to have their water and air contaminated, and to be forced to live in paved environmental sacrifice zones, so that others can enjoy clean water, healthy air, and beautiful environments. You know it is fundamentally offensive for us to live our lives today in a way that is causing a climate catastrophe that will force our children, our grandchildren, and future generations to live in a scary and unsafe world.

If you know all this, then you know everything you'll need in order to be a leading voice in support of the movement for constitutional Green Amendments. But for those who'd like to understand even more, let's dig a little deeper.

The term "Green Amendment" was coined and defined in 2017 in the first edition of this book, *The Green Amendment: Securing Our Right to a Healthy Environment*. Certain criteria are required for a constitutional provision to rise to the level of a Green Amendment capable of securing all the powerful protections I've written about. First and foremost, to achieve the highest level of constitutional protection, an environmental rights provision must exist in the state constitution's bill of rights (or "declaration of rights," in some states). This is where we find fundamental rights like speech, gun, and property rights, and it reflects the primacy of the liberties in question, ensuring they are to be used as a guide for all laws passed and all official actions taken. This placement also makes clear that the people's environmental rights are not to be subjugated to the interests of others, such as industry or property owners. It also brings certain governmental obligations, such as the need for a demonstrated, compelling state interest whenever and wherever an infringement may occur.

The amendment must also contain an affirmative statement that these are the rights of the people, and it must recognize and protect specific environmental rights that are fundamental to human life, health, and community. (By now, you know the ones I mean: clean water and air, a stable climate, and healthy environments.) Recognizing and protecting the rights of people to the natural, human health, scenic, recreational, and/or Indigenous cultural values of the environment can help ensure that a Green Amendment respects and protects the environment in a well-rounded way, including by addressing benefits and values of the natural environment that may be of particular importance to a state and its diverse communities. While such language will inevitably be attacked as being "too broad," rest assured: broad terms are characteristic of all fundamental rights—and it would be inappropriate to treat the environment differently. As with those other fundamental rights we all hold dear, broad terminology is valuable for ensuring the amendment provides overarching guidance, strong and sweeping protections, and viability throughout time.

Crucially, the amendment must apply to all levels of government: town, county, and state. And it must be legally self-executing—meaning that it has legal and enforceable strength in its own right and is not limited to only those environmental protections defined by legislation or regulation. For example, while Pennsylvania's bill of rights says, "The people have a right to clean air, pure water, and to the preservation of the natural, scenic, historic and esthetic values of the environment," the General Provisions section of Florida's constitution says, "It shall be the policy of the state to conserve and protect its natural resources and scenic beauty." Florida's choice of language and placement has relegated environmental protection to a policy statement—which, at its core, is no more binding than simple advice. By contrast, but just as problematically, article 11, section 9 of Hawaii's constitution states that "each person has the right to a clean and healthful environment," but only "as defined by laws"—thereby handing the power to the state legislature rather than the people. In both instances, the legal outcome is starkly different from Pennsylvania's language, which confers the status of an enforceable, definitive right of the people.

Finally, environmental amendments are further strengthened if they include language that designates the state as a trustee of all natural resources, which the government has a duty to protect and maintain for the benefit of all the people, including future generations. Having the state described as a "trustee" is ideal because such language invokes the rigorous duties that trustees shoulder in other legal contexts. Bill of rights placement, along with ensuring the rights extend to all people, provides enforceable environmental justice protections. But the strength and clarity of the equitable protection obligation (regardless of race, ethnicity, or socioeconomic status) is vastly improved when trustee language is included. In addition, extending the responsibilities of the designated trustee to both present and future generations sets a high bar for environmental protection. Other states will benefit from emulating such an explicit declaration of our intergenerational obligation to preserve and protect a healthy environment.

What is clear from the history of other fundamental rights, and from our environmental rights victory in Pennsylvania, is that an emphatic and explicit statement of constitutional rights and protections is essential. This is the only way to take the power away from unthinking, uncaring, or unscrupulous politicians or judges—and to make sure that whenever there is a decision to be made or a case to be decided, the environmental rights of the people are incontrovertible and clearly established.

All these legal technicalities and considerations are admittedly complex and daunting. This is precisely why I launched my Green Amendments For The Generations organization: to provide education, resources, training, and support that can help make it happen in your state—and so that once a Green Amendment has been secured, we can work together to ensure it is fully and fairly enforced. And once we've reached that key tipping point of awareness, support, and activism on the state level, we'll be well on our way to the support we need to secure a federal Green Amendment.

But make no mistake, the people of your state will need to take the leading roles to achieve success. Green Amendments For The Generations will be just one member of your state's leadership team. If you are interested in beginning the process in your state, please take a look at our website, www.ForTheGenerations.org, and get in touch. Send me an email or give me a call, and let's start our partnership! If there's already an effort underway in your state, we'll be delighted to loop you in. We also have specific websites for every state that has joined the forefront of the movement—so just type in your state's abbreviation (such as NM for New Mexico, HI for Hawaii, or NJ for New Jersey) followed by GreenAmendment.org (for example, www.NMGreen Amendment.org), and you'll find your state's website. Through Green Amendments For The Generations, we're working to turn the daunting process of altering a state constitution into something achievable.

By working together, we will generate the groundswell of support, community by community, necessary to achieve our goals of a Green Amendment in every state and ultimately in the US Constitution. Together, we can make this happen—we just need to get it started!

Generating the Groundswell

Creating a groundswell for environmental constitutionalism may not prove as hard as it seems—because we've reached a moment of environmental reckoning. When he was first advancing the language that ultimately became article 1, section 27, Pennsylvania Representative Franklin Kury said that "population and technology have run amok through our environment and natural resources. If we are to save our natural environment we must therefore give it the same Constitutional protection we give to our political environment."[11] This statement is as true today for our nation as it was in 1971 for Pennsylvania. And today's cause is even more urgent. There is, finally, emerging recognition of the devastating consequences of a history of environmental racism. At the same time, as a planet, we are confronting an existential threat in the form of a quickly advancing climate crisis that requires immediate and dramatic action. Green Amendments will be a crucial part of our efforts to avert disaster for ourselves and future generations.

Our Green Amendment movement must bring together support from all quarters if we are to achieve our goals of constitutional environmental rights nationwide.

Experienced guidance and engagement from environmental activists, lobbyists, and environmental justice leaders—those who already know the ropes when it comes to successful grassroots organizing and environmental activism—will bring knowledge of the best organizing and communications tactics for your state and community. They will also bring credibility and preexisting relationships that will encourage open-hearted and wide-ranging consideration of the Green Amendment approach. Experienced leaders who understand the problems and pitfalls of environmental protection that Green Amendments can help us address and overcome will also ensure that our messaging and outreach address the right points of concern for those who may be curious but skeptical, or who wonder why investing time and resources into the Green Amendment movement versus other areas of work is worth their time and consideration.

As I had hoped, experienced activists are seeing the transformational strength that Green Amendments can bring to environmental protection and justice work. As a result, our movement is uplifting the hearts and minds of longtime activists who have faced a lifetime of small victories but also big defeats. These words from one such activist speak volumes: "I felt humbled just thinking about how powerful this [movement] is, how it can change the course of this democracy and the environment for the better. Things have been so degraded. My heart breaks again and again, but this is a game changer and offers real hope for the future and for our children."

In addition to passionate and committed activists, we also need those who join the movement because of their personal life experiences. I've often witnessed how environmental catastrophes have inspired newcomers to assume the mantle of leadership, and how these newcomers can bring an unparalleled level of credibility to the message. There is nothing more powerful than a message delivered by the tearful, angry, or joyful voice of an impacted person. Quite simply, there is no justifiable legal, political, or moral counter to, for example, Kate and Larry Stauffer's call for cleanup of the Bishop Tube site after hearing them recount their daughter's repeated struggles with multiple brain tumors, likely because of her exposures to toxins.

We also need youth voices who are undeterred by those who will say it can't be done—and who have a message *only they* can deliver. A few years ago, my then-fifteen-year-old daughter, Anneke, struck a poignant chord when speaking about the burdens her generation will bear due to the environmental catastrophe engulfing this world. She was facing a senior member of US Congress as part of a group of environmental activists speaking against congressional support for fracking. He was obviously hostile to their anti-fracking message. I saw her spine stiffen—so slight that only a mother would notice. When it was her turn to speak, Anneke said simply, directly, and eloquently:

> *My generation is the one that will suffer the consequences of the decisions you are making today. We are going to have to clean up the mess you are creating for us all. We are going to have to suffer the devastating environmental harm. We are the ones that are going to miss out on the benefits and beauty of healthy nature. So I am here to ask you to change, and to make decisions that protect our Earth for the benefit of us all.*

Anneke's statement speaks to the fundamental injustice facing contemporary youth. They've done the least to contribute to the environmental harms now in motion, but they will pay the highest price as inheritors of despoiled lands, toxic water supplies, and a destabilized climate system. Youth leaders have an irreplaceable standing in the Green Amendment movement; we need their frank and direct call for meaningful protection from government leaders.

As we have demonstrated in the chapters up until now, there are many facets to the arguments supporting passage of constitutional Green Amendments, including how pollution and degradation harm human health and the economy, why current technologies are inflicting irreparable harm under the current system of law, and how our current political framework that values dealmaking over environmental protection is benefited by having constitutional guidance. As a result, successful Green Amendment initiatives will seek and embrace participation of professionals from all walks of life. Scientists, technical experts, business professionals, doctors and other health professionals, and former government agency staffers, justices, and legislators each bring a body of knowledge, experience, and expertise that can help make the case for how and why a Green Amendment is of value.

Artists, too, play an important role in the Green Amendment

movement, lending their incredible talent for capturing and communicating the essence of our message in a painting, performance, poem, or song. Ashley Flowers created an emotionally impactful call to action in a singular painting focused on the ramifications of environmental racism and the benefits of a Green Amendment: a stirring rendering of a beautiful Black woman surrounded by vibrant, colorful flowers but also by industry, with toxic smoke swirling into her nostrils. (If you're intrigued, you can find Ashley's art on our www.ForTheGenerations.org website shop.)

I distinctly recall sensing the power of art during an environmental hearing over fracking, held by the Delaware River Basin Commission. Expert after expert delivered three-minute speeches at the podium about the importance of protecting clean water and instituting a fracking ban. These people were armed with powerful facts, figures, and citations from scientific journals, and they even delivered gripping personal stories of how a fracking operation or pipeline cut through their property and personally harmed them. All this data was vitally important, but you could see the DRBC commissioners in the front of the room biding their time, completely unengaged. Until a young woman approached the microphone and, in a nervous and shaky voice, began to sing. She sang about the Earth, about the beauty of the environment, about the important role the environment plays in all our lives, and about how important it is to protect the environment from fracking. Everyone was enthralled, and after she finished, the auditorium fell into a stunned silence. Such is the power of art.

Art can help advance environmental activism, and it doesn't have to be in the public space. One night, I was sitting alone at my computer, working on comments to advance a New Mexico Green Amendment, and it was a particularly daunting moment: a hearing the day before had not gone well, and we needed an extra boost of some kind to fend off the opposition and inspire our allies. That's when an email came in from Green Amendments supporter Michael Hollander. It was a poem written by Michael and his friend David LaMotte—an original take on the well-known verse "First They Came," by the German pastor Martin Niemöller. Their poem helped me to dig deep and find the words I was searching for.

First They Came

First they came for the insects
the moths, the bees, and butterflies,
for the myriad winged ones
the flies, mosquitos, and gnats
whose buzz and bite and sting
went unmourned, and then
they came for the spiders
with their silky billowing webs
the ants and beetles and all
other creeping things.

Who spoke for them?

Then they came for the frogs, the lizards,
toads and snakes, their croak and hiss
lost in the discord of the day.
They came for the birds and bats
their hungry chicks gone silent
in mouldering nests.

Who spoke? Who spoke for them?

The silence of field and forest
was deafening to those with ears to hear
but we could not hear and did not speak.

The fish and beaver, buffalo and cattle,
pigs and horses, grasses, beans, and corn
all began to die. Flowers withered,
leaves fell, the forests burned and burned,
and when the fire came for us,
finally, we opened our mouths,
and there was no one there
to hear our cry.

Complementing these grassroots voices—the experienced, the youthful, and those inspired by life's challenges to act—with the voices of bold legislative leaders who are committed to advancing legacy Green Amendment protections is proving to be a successful multilevel strategy.

But let's not forget, while we need leaders willing to be out front who can galvanize millions of diverse individuals to join the Green Amendment movement, we can't do any of this without those who are working behind the scenes to provide critical support. We need social media powerhouses who have an incredible way of using the online medium to inspire even casual observers who cross paths with us online to join our Green Amendment movement. We need dedicated people who are willing to disseminate flyers, organize events, make infographics exposing environmental harms, and write letters to the editor. We need people who are eager to walk their neighborhoods putting door hangers on every door, or to share our message and our social media presence with everyone around them. And we also need way, *way* behind-the-scenes supporters like my husband, Dave, who cares so deeply about the work and its impact that he will do whatever it takes without recognition—from helping me find an Airbnb to use as a home base when I'm working in a state for a prolonged period, to setting up and breaking down tables at a speaking event. Whether whistleblower or workaday, everyone is vital.

As we do this work, don't be fooled into thinking this is a partisan issue—that one political party or perspective will be with you, and everyone else against. That is not the case. As Kerri Evelyn Harris so eloquently put it: "This idea of freedom is universal to Americans. There is no American that doesn't feel like you're infringing on their freedom if you slowly kill their bodies, if you start to take away their children's health as well, their children's opportunities."[12]

Ultimately, we will need people from all walks of life, all ages, all ethnicities, all levels of wealth, all colors of skin and every political affiliation, from the most liberal to the most conservative. And we very much need you, too. As this book has demonstrated, it matters little whether a person's ultimate concern is the environment, jobs, education, the economy, family values, recreation, property rights, health, or public safety. A clean and healthy environment is in everyone's best interest.

When I'm not advocating on behalf of Green Amendments or the river I love, or helping a community mobilize, I go with my family to our special New York forest. I try to take these trips as often as I can, and I know that Dave, Wim, and Anneke enjoy them too. We walk amid the trees, kayak the nearby Delaware River, and sit and enjoy the peace and silence. But as much as we love to immerse ourselves in these natural places, I feel the constant threat of intrusion from development, industry, and pollution. I know that our rights to a clean, safe, and healthy environment are not well protected. It is time to change that. We *must* change that—for our own sake, and to protect the generations still to come.

I'm tired of having government laud the importance of industry and belittle kids, communities, and the harmed.

I love to hear the sound of a gentle rain, a light wind (or even a strong one), the frogs as they mate and the birds as they chirp, kids playing in nature, and friends and family enjoying time together outdoors. I love to hear nature sing.

And I worry. I worry about the day our forests will go silent, or the weather will become deafeningly and deathly out of control.

But I also believe. I believe in the power of constitutional Green Amendments. I have seen them at work, in the courtroom but also in the hearing room, in legislative meetings, and in our communities. I have witnessed their ability to inspire and empower people to rise up in defense of themselves, their loved ones, and their environment.

Imagine what it could be like if, stepping up to speak to a legislator or government-agency decision maker about the next threat facing your environment, you and your neighbors are able to open with these words:

We the people of our state have a right to a clean, safe, and healthy environment, including pure water, clean air, stable climate, and healthy native ecosystems and environments.

These are rights that belong to present and future generations.

And you the government may take no action that would infringe upon these rights.

More than that, as trustee, you are constitutionally obligated to conserve, protect, and maintain our state's natural resources for the benefit of all the people, regardless of race, ethnicity, wealth, or generation.

I believe in the power of Green Amendments, and I believe in the power of you and I working together to get them passed—and to put them powerfully to work.

I hope the next call I get is from you.

NOTES

Chapter 1: My Green Amendment Epiphany

1 Mary Ellen Cassidy, "Here They Come Again! The Impacts of Oil and Gas Truck Traffic," FracTracker Alliance, September 11, 2014, https://www.fractracker.org/2014/09/truck-counts.

2 Christopher Bateman, "A Colossal Fracking Mess," *Vanity Fair*, June 2010, http://www.vanityfair.com/news/2010/06/fracking-in-pennsylvania-201006.

3 If a ban is not pursued correctly or successfully, moreover, municipalities are at risk. As a result, the ability of a Pennsylvania town to ban fracking still hangs in the balance, with communities seeking other options until their right to enact a ban is legally vetted and decided. Jordan Yeager, personal correspondence with author, June 20, 2017.

4 Pa. Envtl. Def. Found. v. Commonwealth, 161 A.3d 911, 940 (Pa. 2017).

Chapter 2: Living in the Sacrifice Zone

1 Special Report: The Smokestack Effect, *USA Today*, accessed 2017, http://content.usatoday.com/news/nation/environment/smokestack/school/86422; Lynne Peeples, "Keystone XL Risks Harm to Houston Community: 'This Is Obviously Environmental Racism,'" *Huffington Post*, updated December 6, 2017, http://www.huffingtonpost.com/2013/03/27/keystone-xl-pipeline-houston-air-pollution_n_2964853.html; Dave Mann, "Separate but Toxic," *Texas Observer*, March 23, 2007, https://www.texasobserver.org/2451-separate-but-toxic-the-houston-environmental-magnet-school-thats-an-environmental-catastrophe/.

2 Javier Sierra, "A Toxic Bone," Sierra Club, accessed 2017, http://vault.sierraclub.org/ecocentro/ingles/bone.asp.

3 Sierra, "A Toxic Bone."

4 Sierra, "A Toxic Bone."

5 For example, Roy Scranton, assistant professor of English at the University of Notre Dame and author of the environmental bestseller *Learning to Die in the Anthropocene* (2015), calls Manchester "one of the most polluted neighborhoods in the United States." Scranton, "When the Next Hurricane Hits Texas," *New York Times*, October 7, 2016, http://www.nytimes.com/2016/10/09/opinion/sunday/when-the-hurricane-hits-texas.html?_r=0.

6 According to a University of Texas School of Public Health study that widely shocked the country. See the summary "Disease Clusters in Texas," National Disease Clusters Alliance

/National Resource Defense Council, March 2011, https://www.nrdc.org/sites/default/files /texas_diseaseclusters.pdf; Cindy Horswell, "Study: Children Living Near Houston Ship Channel Have Greater Cancer Risk," *Houston Chronicle*, January 18, 2007, http://www .chron.com/news/houston-texas/article/Study-Children-living-near-Houston-Ship -Channel-1544789.php; and the study's executive summary, "Preliminary Epidemiologic Investigation of the Relationship Between the Presence of Ambient Hazardous Air Pollutants (HAPs) and Cancer Incidence in Harris County," City of Houston official website, Health and Human Services, https://www.houstontx.gov/health/hazardous.pdf.

7   Mann, "Separate but Toxic."

8   Mann, "Separate but Toxic." See also Eric Kayne, "Fighting for Clean Air in the Shadow of Oil Refineries," Earth Justice, accessed 2017, http://earthjustice.org/slideshow/fighting-for -clean-air-in-the-shadow-of-oil-refineries. Resident Yudith Nieto, for example, developed stomach pains after eating contaminated fruit.

9   Dianna Wray, "Benzene Leaks from Pipelines Have Been Quietly Adding to the Ship Channel Toxic Mix," *Houston Press*, May 10, 2016, http://www.houstonpress.com/news /benzene-leaks-from-pipelines-have-been-quietly-adding-to-the-ship-channel-toxic -mix-8389333.

10   Loren Elliott, "These Houston Residents Dream of Moving to Where the Air Is Clear," *Reuters*, January 3, 2020, https://www.reuters.com/article/us-usa-pollution-houston -widerimage/these-houston-residents-dream-of-moving-to-where-the-air-is-clear -idUSKBN1Z215B.

11   Jessica Roake, "Think Globally, Act Locally: Steve Lerner, 'Sacrifice Zones,' at Politics and Prose," *Washington Post*, September 22, 2010, https://www.washingtonpost.com/express /wp/2010/09/23/steve-lerner-book-sacrifice-zones/.

12   Dave Pruett, "We're All in the Sacrifice Zone Now," *Huffington Post*, May 3, 2016, http://www .huffingtonpost.com/dave-pruett/were-all-in-the-sacrifice-zone-now_b_9823482.html.

13   "Deepwater Horizon–BP Gulf of Mexico Oil Spill," United States Environmental Protection Agency, accessed 2017, https://www.epa.gov/enforcement/deepwater-horizon -bp-gulf-mexico-oil-spill.

14   Joan Meiners, "Ten Years Later, BP Oil Spill Continues to Harm Wildlife—Especially Dolphins," *National Geographic*, April 17, 2020, https://www.nationalgeographic.com /animals/article/how-is-wildlife-doing-now--ten-years-after-the-deepwater-horizon.

15   Merlin Hearn, "Water Benefits Health: 20 Water Pollution Facts for the US and throughout the World," Water Benefits Health, accessed 2017, http://www.water benefitshealth.com/water-pollution-facts.html.

16   Water Resources, "Water Quality in the Nation's Streams and Rivers—Current Conditions and Long-Term Trends," United States Geological Survey, March 2, 2019, https://www .usgs.gov/mission-areas/water-resources/science/water-quality-nation-s-streams-and-rivers -current-conditions?qt-science_center_objects=0#qt-science_center_objects; "The National Rivers and Streams Assessment 2008/2009," United States Environmental Protection Agency, accessed 2022, https://www.epa.gov/sites/default/files/2016-03/documents/fact _sheet_draft_variation_march_2016_revision.pdf; Hearn, "Water Benefits Health."

17   "Chromium in Drinking Water," United States Environmental Protection Agency, accessed 2022, https://www.epa.gov/sdwa/chromium-drinking-water.

18   Bill Walker, "'Erin Brockovich' Carcinogen in Tap Water of More Than 200 Million Americans," September 20, 2016, http://www.ewg.org/research/chromium-six-found-in-us -tap-water.

19   American Lung Association, *State of the Air 2021*, https://www.lung.org/getmedia
      /17c6cb6c-8a38-42a7-a3b0-6744011da370/sota-2021.pdf.

20   Emily Underwood, "The Polluted Brain," *Science*, January 26, 2017, http://www.sciencemag
      .org/news/2017/01/brain-pollution-evidence-builds-dirty-air-causes-alzheimer-s-dementia;
      International Agency for Research on Cancer, "IARC: Outdoor air pollution a leading
      environmental cause of cancer deaths," World Health Organization press release no. 221,
      October 17, 2013, http://www.iarc.fr/en/media-centre/pr/2013/pdfs/pr221_E.pdf.

21   Tyler Cowen, "Air Pollution Kills Far More People Than Covid Ever Will," *Bloomberg
      Opinion*, March 10, 2021, https://www.bloomberg.com/opinion/articles/2021-03-10/air
      -pollution-kills-far-more-people-than-covid-ever-will.

22   "International Decade for Action 'Water for Life 2005–2015," United Nations Department
      of Economic and Social Affairs (UNDESA), accessed 2017, http://www.un.org/water
      forlifedecade/quality.shtml.

23   Underwood, "The Polluted Brain."

24   "U of T Researchers Part of Study Linking Dementia to Living Near Major Traffic,"
      University of Toronto News, January 6, 2017, https://www.utoronto.ca/news/u-t-researchers
      -part-study-linking-dementia-living-near-major-traffic.

25   "Key Findings: Trends in the Prevalence of Developmental Disabilities in US Children,
      1997–2008," Centers for Disease Control and Prevention, accessed 2017, https://www.cdc
      .gov/ncbddd/developmentaldisabilities/features/birthdefects-dd-keyfindings.html.

26   Currently, the Centers for Disease Control and Prevention suggests one in every forty-four
      American children have autism, with many more boys than girls diagnosed. The reasons
      for the increase are, of course, complex. "Autism Spectrum Disorder: Data & Statistics,"
      Centers for Disease Control and Prevention, accessed 2017, http://www.cdc.gov/ncbddd
      /autism/data.html; Jessica Wright, "The Real Reasons Autism Rates Are Up in the US,"
      Scientific American, March 3, 2017, https://www.scientificamerican.com/article/the-real
      -reasons-autism-rates-are-up-in-the-u-s/.

27   "Attention-Deficit/Hyperactivity Disorder (ADHD): Data and Statistics About ADHD,"
      Centers for Disease Control and Prevention, accessed 2017, http://www.cdc.gov/ncbddd
      /adhd/data.html; Lisa Rapaport, "More than One in 10 US Kids Have ADHD as
      Diagnosis Rates Surge," *Reuters*, December 8, 2015, http://www.reuters.com/article
      /us-health-adhd-diagnosis-surge-idUSKBN0TR2SJ20151208.

28   "America's Children and the Environment (ACE): Health—Respiratory Diseases," United
      States Environmental Protection Agency, accessed 2022, https://www.epa.gov/americas
      childrenenvironment/ace-health-respiratory-diseases.

29   "Air Pollution Linked with Increased Risk of Autism in Children," Harvard T.H. Chan
      School of Public Health, accessed April 18, 2022, https://www.hsph.harvard.edu/news
      /hsph-in-the-news/air-pollution-linked-with-increased-risk-of-autism-in-children/.

30   The National Resource on ADHD, "About ADHD—Overview," CHADD, accessed 2017,
      http://www.chadd.org/Understanding-ADHD/About-ADHD.aspx.

31   Molini M. Patel and Rachel L. Miller, "Air Pollution and Childhood Asthma: Recent
      Advances and Future Directions," National Institutes of Health, accessed 2017, https
      ://www.ncbi.nlm.nih.gov/pmc/articles/PMC2740858/pdf/nihms121748.pdf.

32   Jef Akst, "Study Looks for Effects of Fetal Exposure to Air Pollution," *The Scientist*, August
      1, 2021, https://www.the-scientist.com/notebook/study-looks-for-effects-of-fetal-exposure
      -to-air-pollution-68991; Frederica P. Perera et al., "Prenatal Airborne Polycyclic Aromatic

Hydrocarbon Exposure and Child IQ at Age 5 Years," *National Library of Medicine*, July 20, 2009, https://www.ncbi.nlm.nih.gov/pmc/articles/PMC2864932/.

33 Marie Pedersen et al., "Ambient Air Pollution and Low Birthweight: A European Cohort Study," *The Lancet: Respiratory Medicine* 1, no. 9, November 2013, 695–704, https://www.sciencedirect.com/science/article/abs/pii/S2213260013701929; Children's Hospital of Philadelphia, "Low Birthweight," accessed April 22, 2022, https://www.chop.edu/conditions-diseases/low-birthweight.

34 Lisa W. Foderaro, "Group Petitions to Save a Prehistoric Fish from Modern Construction," *New York Times*, July 21, 2015, http://www.nytimes.com/2015/07/22/nyregion/group-petitions-to-save-a-prehistoric-fish-from-modern-construction.html?_r=0.

35 Dewayne Fox, PhD (associate professor at Delaware State University), interview with author, June 29, 2017.

36 Daniel Kelly, "Universities Team Up to Track Atlantic Sturgeon and Prevent Accidental Bycatch," *Environmental Monitor*, May 22, 2013, https://www.fondriest.com/news/track-atlantic-sturgeon-and-prevent-accidental-bycatch.htm#:~:text=In%20one%20of%20the%20efforts,avoid%20accidentally%20catching%20the%20creature.

37 "Species Directory, Atlantic Sturgeon," National Oceanic and Atmospheric Administration Fisheries, https://www.fisheries.noaa.gov/species/atlantic-sturgeon.

38 "Sturgeon More Critically Endangered Than Any Other Group of Species," International Union for Conservation of Nature, March 18, 2010, https://www.iucn.org/content/sturgeon-more-critically-endangered-any-other-group-species.

39 Atlantic sturgeon were nearly the exclusive source of caviar in the Delaware River. John Nathan Cobb, *The Sturgeon Fishery of Delaware River and Bay* (Washington, DC: Government Printing Office, 1900); John A. Ryder, *The Sturgeons and Sturgeon Industries of the Eastern Coast of the United States: With an Account of Experiments Bearing upon Sturgeon Culture* (Washington, DC: Government Printing Office, 1890).

40 Juliet Eilperin, "Atlantic Sturgeon Listed as Endangered Species," *Washington Post*, February 1, 2012, https://www.washingtonpost.com/national/health-science/atlantic-sturgeon-listed-as-endangered-species/2012/02/01/gIQARbAmiQ_story.html.

41 Erik Silldorff, PhD (aquatic ecologist), interview with author, May 2, 2017.

42 Fox, interview, June 30, 2017.

43 Ted Williams, "Atlantic Sturgeon: An Ancient Fish Struggles against the Flow," February 12, 2015, *Yale Environmental 360*, https://e360.yale.edu/features/atlantic_sturgeon_an_ancient_fish_struggles_against_the_flow.

44 Williams, "Atlantic Sturgeon." When it comes to nuclear energy, I agree with Naomi Klein's assessment: "About 12 percent of the world's power is currently supplied by nuclear energy, much of it coming from reactors that are old and obsolete." Governments, she suggests, should impose moratoria on existing construction, retire unsafe facilities, and phase them out as renewable energies improve. Naomi Klein, *This Changes Everything: Capitalism vs. The Climate* (New York: Simon & Shuster, 2014), 137–38.

45 A. M. Stoklosa et al., *A Review of Dissolved Oxygen Requirements for Key Sensitive Species in the Delaware Estuary: Final Report Submitted to the Delaware River Basin Commission*, The Patrick Center for Environmental Research, Academy of Natural Sciences of Drexel University, November 2018, https://www.nj.gov/drbc/library/documents/Review_DOreq_KeySensSpecies_DelEstuary_ANStoDRBCnov2018.pdf.

46 Jon Hurdle, "Oxygen Levels in Delaware River Met Standards, Commission Says," *NJ*

Spotlight News, October 6, 2021, https://www.njspotlightnews.org/2021/10/delaware-river
-basin-commission-rejects-environmentalist-claims-low-oxygen-levels/.

47   Mallory Malesky, "Minimum Oxygen Concentration for Human Breathing," *Sciencing* by
Leaf Group, March 10, 2018, https://sciencing.com/minimum-oxygen-concentration
-human-breathing-15546.html.

48   Silldorff, interview, May 2, 2017.

49   US Department of Transportation Maritime Administration, "US Department of
Transportation Announces a New Marine Highway and Six Marine Highway Designations,"
press release, August 19, 2021, https://www.maritime.dot.gov/newsroom/press-releases
/us-department-transportation-announces-new-marine-highway-and-six-marine; Center for
Biological Diversity v. United States Maritime Administration, 4:21-cv-00132, October 12,
2021, https://s3-us-west-2.amazonaws.com/s3-wagtail.biolgicaldiversity.org/documents
/MARAD-complaint.pdf.

50   Jared Margolis, interview with author, November 2021.

51   "Forest Habitat: Overview," World Wildlife Fund, accessed 2017, https://www.world
wildlife.org/habitats/forest-habitat.

52   "Deforestation Explained," *National Geographic*, accessed 2017, http://www.national
geographic.com/environment/global-warming/deforestation/.

53   "Land Cover," United States Environmental Protection Agency, Exhibit 3, accessed 2017,
https://cfpub.epa.gov/roe/indicator.cfm?i=49#3.

54   "Deforestation Explained," *National Geographic*; Emily Adams, "Eco-Economy Indicators:
Forest Cover," Earth Policy Institute, August 31, 2012, http://www.earth-policy.org
/indicators/C56/forests_2012.

55   "Forest Habitat: Overview," World Wildlife Fund.

56   "How Do Wetlands Functions and Why Are They Valuable?" United States Environmental
Protection Agency, accessed 2017, https://www.epa.gov/wetlands/what-are-wetland-functions.

57   R. E. A. Almond, M. Grooten, and T. Petersen, eds., *Living Planet Report 2020—Bending
the Curve of Biodiversity Loss*, World Wildlife Fund, 2020, https://f.hubspotusercontent20
.net/hubfs/4783129/LPR/PDFs/ENGLISH-FULL.pdf.

58   Craig Cox, "Going, Going, Gone!" Environmental Working Group, July 23, 2013, http
://www.ewg.org/research/going-going-gone.

59   "68% Average Decline in Species Population Sizes Since 1970, Says New WWF Report,"
World Wildlife Fund, September 9, 2020, https://www.worldwildlife.org/press-releases/68
-average-decline-in-species-population-sizes-since-1970-says-new-wwf-report; Almond et
al., eds., *Living Planet Report 2020*.

60   "68% Average Decline," World Wildlife Fund.

61   Almond et al., *Living Planet Report 2020*.

62   Rob Jordan, "Stanford Researcher Declares That the Sixth Mass Extinction Is Here,"
Stanford News, June 19, 2015, http://news.stanford.edu/2015/06/19/mass-extinction
-ehrlich-061915/.

63   The idea was popularized by Scranton's *Learning to Die in the Anthropocene*.

64   Jordan, "Stanford Researcher Declares."

65   Janine Bauer, personal correspondence with author, June 11, 2017. I rely on Janine for the
background on this story about South Trenton's Jersey Shore.

66   "Trucking," New Jersey Department of Transportation, accessed 2017, http://www.state.nj
.us/transportation/freight/trucking/faq.shtm.

67   "Urbanization," United Nations Population Fund, accessed 2017, http://www.unfpa.org
/urbanization; United Nations, Department of Economic and Social Affairs, Population
Division, *Population 2030 Demographic Challenges and Opportunities for Sustainable
Development Planning*, 2015, https://www.un.org/en/development/desa/population
/publications/pdf/trends/Population2030.pdf.

68   Mathias Basner et al., "Auditory and Non-auditory Effects of Noise on Health," *The Lancet*
383, no. 9925 (October 30, 2013): 1325–1332, https://www.thelancet.com/journals/lancet/
article/PIIS0140-6736(13)61613-X/fulltext.

69   World Health Organization, *Burden of Disease from Environmental Noise: Quantification of
Healthy Life Years Lost in Europe*, 2011, https://apps.who.int/iris/handle/10665
/326424; Ron Chepesiuk, "Missing the Dark: Health Effects of Light Pollution,"
Environmental Health Perspectives 117, no. 1 (January 2009): A20–27, https://www.ncbi
.nlm.nih.gov/pmc/articles/PMC2627884/.

70   A. Huss et al., "Aircraft Noise, Air Pollution, and Mortality from Myocardial Infarction,"
Epidemiology 21, no. 6 (2010): 829–36, https://journals.lww.com/epidem/Fulltext/2010
/11000/Aircraft_Noise,_Air_Pollution,_and_Mortality_From.13.aspx.

71   Basner et al., "Auditory and Non-auditory Effects."

72   Richard Louv (author), interview by Dan Rodricks, *National Public Radio*, March 18, 2014,
http://wypr.org/post/adults-and-nature-deficit-disorder.

73   Louv, interview by Dan Rodricks.

74   John Abraham, "Global Warming Continues; 2016 Will Be the Hottest Year Ever
Recorded," *Guardian*, October 21, 2016, https://www.theguardian.com/environment
/climate-consensus-97-per-cent/2016/oct/21/global-warming-continues-2016-will-be-the
-hottest-year-ever-recorded.

75   "Top 10 Warmest Years on Record," Climate Central, January 15, 2020, https://www
.climatecentral.org/gallery/graphics/top-10-warmest-years-on-record.

76   Tom Di Liberto, "Astounding Heat Obliterates All-Time Records across the Pacific
Northwest and Western Canada in June 2021," National Oceanic and Atmospheric
Administration (NOAA), June 30, 2021, https://www.climate.gov/news-features/event
-tracker/astounding-heat-obliterates-all-time-records-across-pacific-northwest.

77   Klein, *This Changes Everything*, 1.

78   Jon Hurdle, "DNREC Says New Report of Big Decline in Rare Shorebird Is Only a
'Snapshot,'" *Delaware Public Media*, June 18, 2021, https://www.delawarepublic.org/science
-health-tech/2021-06-18/dnrec-says-new-report-of-big-decline-in-rare-shorebird-is-only
-a-snapshot.

79   Hurdle, "DNREC Says New Report."

80   For reference to this literature, see Richard Louv's *Last Child in the Woods* (New York:
Workman Publishing Group, 2005).

81   George Monbiot, "If Children Lose Contact with Nature They Won't Fight for It,"
Guardian, November 19, 2012, https://www.theguardian.com/commentisfree/2012/nov/19
/children-lose-contact-with-nature.

82   Monbiot, "If Children Lose Contact with Nature."

83   Monbiot, "If Children Lose Contact with Nature."

84 Samantha Friedman et al., "Understanding Changes to Children's Connection to Nature during the COVID-19 Pandemic and Implications for Child Well-being," *People and Nature*, British Ecological Society, April 14, 2021, https://besjournals.onlinelibrary.wiley .com/doi/full/10.1002/pan3.10270.

85 Susan Carroll, "Texas High Court Rejects City Air Pollution Rules," *Houston Chronicle*, April 29, 2016, http://www.houstonchronicle.com/news/houston-texas/houston/article /Texas-high-court-rejects-city-air-pollution-rules-7384795.php.

86 Juan A. Lozano, "Texas Court Blocks Houston From Using Tougher Clean-Air Laws," *Associated Press*, April 30, 2016, https://apnews.com/article /b6caf6fe274045a68cb74b0962d7e84a.

87 Lozano, "Texas Court Blocks Houston."

Chapter 3: The Right to a Healthy Environment

1 David James Duncan, "The War for Norman's River," *Sierra*, May/June 1998, https://vault .sierraclub.org/sierra/199805/blackfoot.asp.

2 Duncan, "The War for Norman's River."

3 David James Duncan, *My Story as Told by Water: Confessions, Druidic Rants, Reflections, Bird-Watchings, Fish-Stalkings, Visions, Songs and Prayers Refracting Light, from Living Rivers, in the Age of the Industrial Dark* (San Francisco: Sierra Club Books, 2001), 137.

4 Duncan, *My Story as Told by Water*, 137–138; Jeffrey St. Clair and Alexander Cockburn, "The Senator, The Gold Mine and The Sundance Kid," *Washington Post*, December 17, 1995, https://www.washingtonpost.com/archive/opinions/1995/12/17/the-senator-the-gold -mine-and-the-sundance-kid/74ffa134-c2e3-4ce2-ace2-48d97228dab2/.

5 Duncan, "The War for Norman's River"; Duncan, *My Story as Told by Water*, 138.

6 Duncan, "The War for Norman's River," 138.

7 Duncan, "The War for Norman's River," 139.

8 Duncan, "The War for Norman's River."

9 Katy Spence, "Montana's Right to a Clean & Healthful Environment," Montana Environmental Information Center (blog), April 29, 2012, http://meic.org/issues /constitution-of-montana-and-mepa/clean-healthful-environment/.

10 Spence, "Montana's Right."

11 "America's Sewage System and the Price of Optimism," *Time*, August 1, 1969, http ://content.time.com/time/magazine/article/0,9171,901182,00.html.

12 Barton H. Thompson Jr., "Constitutionalizing the Environment: The History and Future of Montana's Environmental Provisions," *Montana Law Review* 64 (2003): 160, https ://scholarworks.umt.edu/cgi/viewcontent.cgi?article=2290&context=mlr.

13 Thompson, "Constitutionalizing the Environment," 157–158.

14 Sanders-Reed ex rel. Sanders-Reed v. Martinez, 350 P.3d 1221 (2015).

15 Maya van Rossum, Antoinette Sedillo Lopez (New Mexico state senator), and Joanne Ferrary (New Mexico state representative), "NM Water & Natural Resources Interim Committee Considers Proposed Constitutional New Mexico Green Amendment," press release, September 8, 2021.

16 Franklin Kury (former Pennsylvania state senator), interview with author, September 26, 2019.

17 Kury, interview.

18   Commonwealth v. Nat'l Gettysburg Battlefield Tower, 454 Pa. 193; 311 A.2d 588 (PA Supreme Court, Oct 3, 1973).

19   *Nat'l Gettysburg Battlefield Tower*, 454 Pa. 193.

20   *Nat'l Gettysburg Battlefield Tower*, 454 Pa. 193.

21   Thompson, "Constitutionalizing the Environment," 171–72. See also Cape-France Enterprises v. Estate of Peed, 29 P.3d 1011 (Mont. 2001).

22   Thompson, "Constitutionalizing the Environment," 172.

23   Park County Environmental Council & Greater Yellowstone Coalition v. MT DEQ & Lucky Minerals Inc. 2020 MT 303, (Dec. 8, 2020).

24   Pa. Environmental Defense Found. v. Commonwealth 161 A.3d 911 (Pa. 2017).

25   Pa. Environmental Defense Found. v. Commonwealth, 255 A.3d 289 (Pa. 2021).

26   Green Amendments For The Generations, "Marple Township Board Member on the Constitutional Duty to Uphold Article 1 Section 27," December 16, 2020, YouTube video, https://www.youtube.com/watch?v=1SeHlhb_zaM.

27   Adrienne Marofsky, "County Will Acquire 213-Acre Property at Don Guanella Site in Marple Township," Delaware County, Pennsylvania (website), press release, June 15, 2021, https://www.delcopa.gov/publicrelations/releases/2021/largestcountyownedpark.html.

28   Jim May (environmental attorney and professor), interview with author, February 7, 2021.

29   David R. Boyd, *The Environmental Rights Revolution* (Vancouver: University of British Columbia Press, 2012), 68.

30   According to Portugal's Article 52 (Right to petition and right to popular action), "Everyone shall be granted the right of actio popularis, to include the right to apply for the appropriate compensation for an aggrieved party or parties, in such cases and under such terms as the law may determine, either personally or via associations that purport to defend the interests in question. The said right shall particularly be exercised to: a) Promote the prevention, cessation, or judicial prosecution of offenses against public health, consumer rights, the quality of life or the preservation of the environment and the cultural heritage." Boyd, *The Environmental Rights Revolution*, 71.

31   Boyd, *The Environmental Rights Revolution*, 70.

32   May, interview with author.

33   John Dernbach (environmental attorney and professor), interview with author, February 27, 2022.

34   Mark Buckley and Austin Rempel, "Economic Benefits of Installing a Closed-Cycle Cooling System at Salem Nuclear Generating Station," *ECONorthwest,* September 2015, https://www.delawareriverkeeper.org/sites/default/files/DRN%20Expert%20EcoNW%20 Final%20Report%20re%20Salem%20NGS%2009%2017%2015%20reduced_Part1.pdf.

35   Jordan Yeager (environmental attorney), interview with author, October 4, 2016.

36   Mike Goens, "Other States Show How, and How Not, to Reform Constitution," *Tuscaloosa News*, November 18, 2001, https://www.tuscaloosanews.com/story/news/2001/11/19/other -states-show-how-and-how-not-to-reform-constitution/27814700007/.

37   Yeager, interview with author.

38   Afua Dapaah (student and concerned Delaware resident), email exchange with author, May 2022.

Chapter 4: Fracking Away Our Future

1   "Terry Greenwood: Pennsylvania Farmer; Location: Daisytown, Washington County, PA," *Shalefield Stories: A Project of Friends of the Harmed*, https://pennenvironment.org/sites /environment/files/reports/ShalefieldStoriesnp_1_0.pdf.

2   Briget Shields (founder of Friends of the Harmed), interview with author, January 18, 2017.

3   Iris Marie Bloom, "Gas Drilling Impacts: PA Farmer Terry Greenwood's Cows Gave Birth to Zero Calves This Year, After Ten Dead Calves in 2008," *Protecting Our Waters*, November 4, 2011, https://protectingourwaters.wordpress.com/2011/11/04/gas-drilling-impacts-pa -farmer-terry-greenwoods-cows-gave-birth-to-zero-calves-this-year-after-ten-dead-calves -in-2008/; "Terry Greenwood: Pennsylvania Farmer."

4   Kirsi Jansa, "Gas Rush Stories: A Cattle Farmer," Vimeo, https://vimeo.com/74660630.

5   Bloom, "Gas Drilling Impacts."

6   Bloom, "Gas Drilling Impacts."

7   Jansa, "Gas Rush Stories."

8   Jansa, "Gas Rush Stories."

9   Bloom, "Gas Drilling Impacts."

10 Jansa, "Gas Rush Stories"; "Terry Greenwood: Pennsylvania Farmer."

11 Bloom, "Gas Drilling Impacts."

12 The first instance of multi-stage slickwater fracturing of horizontal wells was in 2002, and the first time this occurred in the Marcellus Shale was in 2003. The technologies making this possible, however, were "perfected" in the late 1990s. Cornell University professor Dr. Anthony Ingraffea elaborates on this timeline and other features of slickwater hydraulic fracturing in a late 2010 lecture at Luzerne County Community College in Nanticoke, Pennsylvania. Dr. Anthony Ingraffea, "Facts on Fracking," June 15, 2011, YouTube video, https://www.youtube.com/watch?v=mSWmXpEkEPg. See 21:29 for this timeline.

13 For a schematic overview of the process, see "Fracking: Is Exploration a Danger to Earth or Much-Needed Boost to Energy?" *CNN*, August 16, 2013, http://edition.cnn.com/2013 /08/16/business/fracking-shale-gas-process-infographic/index.html.

14 Delaware River Basin Commission, *Comment and Response Document: Proposed Amendments to the Administrative Manual and Special Regulations Regarding High Volume Hydraulic Fracturing Activities; Additional Clarifying Amendments*, February 25, 2021, https://www .state.nj.us/drbc/library/documents/CRD_HVHFrulemaking.pdf.

15 Steven Habicht, Lars Hanson, and Paul Faeth, "The Potential Environmental Impact from Fracking in the Delaware River Basin," *CNA Analysis & Solutions*, August 2015, iv, https ://www.cna.org/CNA_files/PDF/IRM-2015-U-011300-Final.pdf.

16 Jenny Lisak (Pennsylvania resident and activist), interview with author, December 12, 2016.

17 Itai Vardi, "Pennsylvania Lawmaker Advancing Pro-Fracking Legislation Profits from Leasing His Land to Drillers," *DeSmog*, May 9, 2018, https://www.desmog.com/2018/05 /09/pennsylvania-senator-gene-yaw-pro-fracking-legislation-profits-leasing-drillers/.

18 Conservation Voters of PA, "View Gas Industry Donations to Candidates," Marcellus Money, http://marcellusmoney.org/candidate.

19 Conservation Voters of PA, "View Gas Industry Donations to Candidates."

20 Rachel Morgan, "Revolving Door: Report Shows Link between Governor's Office and Gas Industry," *The Times*, March 4, 2013, https://www.timesonline.com/story/news/2013/03/05 /revolving-door-report-shows-link/18463895007/.

21 Kristina Marusic, "Fractured: Harmful Chemicals and Unknowns Haunt Pennsylvanians Surrounded by Fracking," *Environmental Health News*, March 1, 2021, https://www.ehn.org /fractured-harmful-chemicals-fracking-2650428324.html.

22 Marusic, "Fractured."

23 Jake Hays and Seth B. C. Shonkoff, "Toward an Understanding of the Environmental and Public Health Impacts of Unconventional Natural Gas Development: A Categorical Assessment of the Peer-Reviewed Scientific Literature, 2009–2015," *PLOS One*, April 20, 2016, http://journals.plos.org/plosone/article?id=10.1371/journal.pone.0154164.

24 Concerned Health Professionals of New York and Physicians for Social Responsibility, *Compendium of Scientific, Medical, and Media Findings Demonstrating Risks and Harms of Fracking (Unconventional Gas and Oil Extraction)*, 7th ed., December 2020, https://www.psr .org/wp-content/uploads/2020/12/fracking-science-compendium-7.pdf.

25 Alan Neuhauser, "Respiratory, Skin Problems Soar Near Gas Wells, Study Says," *US News and World Report*, September 10, 2014, http://www.usnews.com/news/articles/2014/09/10 /respiratory-skin-problems-soar-near-gas-wells-study-says.

26 Concerned Health Professionals, *Compendium of Scientific, Medical, and Media Findings*, 7th ed.

27 Alan Neuhauser, "Toxic Chemicals, Carcinogens Skyrocket Near Fracking Sites," *US News and World Report*, October 30, 2014, http://www.usnews.com/news/articles/2014/10/30 /toxic-chemicals-and-carcinogens-skyrocket-near-fracking-sites-study-says.

28 Neuhauser, "Toxic Chemicals."

29 David Templeton and Don Hopey, "Are the 27 Cases of Ewing's Sarcoma Near Pittsburgh a Cluster?," *Pittsburgh Post-Gazette*, May 14, 2019, https://newsinteractive.post-gazette .com/ewing-sarcoma-cancer-cluster-pittsburgh-washington-westmoreland/.

30 Concerned Health Professionals, *Compendium*, 7th ed., 36, 195, 198.

31 Christopher Busby and Joseph J. Mangano, "There's a World Going on Underground— Infant Mortality and Fracking in Pennsylvania," *Journal of Environmental Protection* 8, no. 4 (April 2017), https://www.scirp.org/journal/paperinformation. aspx?paperid=75575&PageSpeed=noscript.

32 "Water Facts—Worldwide Water Supply," Bureau of Reclamation, accessed 2022, https ://www.usbr.gov/mp/arwec/water-facts-ww-water-sup.html.

33 Elizabeth Ridlington, Kim Norman, and Rachel Richardson, "Fracking by the Numbers: The Damage to Our Water, Land and Climate from a Decade of Dirty Drilling," Environment America Research & Policy Center, April 2016, https://environmentamerica .org/sites/environment/files/reports/Fracking%20by%20the%20Numbers%20vUS.pdf.

34 Delaware River Basin Commission, *Comment and Response Document*.

35 Concerned Health Professionals, *Compendium*, 7th ed., 74–75.

36 Rick Jervis, "Oklahoma Earthquake Reignites Concerns That Fracking Wells May Be the Cause," *USA Today*, November 7, 2016, https://www.usatoday.com/story/news/2016/11/07 /oklahoma-earthquake-fracking-well/93447830/.

37 Andrew Dewson, "A Disaster Waiting to Happen in Oklahoma? The Link between Fracking and Earthquakes Is Causing Alarm in an Oil-Rich Town," *Independent*, April 6, 2015, http://www.independent.co.uk/news/world/americas/a-disaster-waiting-to-happen -in-oklahoma-the-link-between-fracking-and-earthquakes-is-causing-alarm-10158524 .html; "Explainer: Earthquakes," *National Public Radio* (StateImpact), https://stateimpact .npr.org/oklahoma/tag/earthquakes/; "Oklahoma Has Had a Surge of Earthquakes Since

2009—Are They Due to Fracking?," United States Geological Survey, https://www.usgs.gov
/faqs/oklahoma-has-had-surge-earthquakes-2009-are-they-due-fracking. From 2014-
2017 Oklahoma led the forty-eight contiguous United States in earthquakes. As William
Ellsworth, professor of geophysics at Stanford, notes, Alaska registers the most tremors
overall (Jervis, "Oklahoma Earthquake Reignites Concerns").

38 Henry Fountain, "In Canada, a Direct Link between Fracking and Earthquakes," *New York
Times*, November 17, 2016, https://www.nytimes.com/2016/11/18/science/fracking-earth
quakes-alberta-canada.html?_r=0. Elsewhere, in regions like Ohio and western
Pennsylvania, increased seismicity is due to fracking itself (Michael Rubinkam, "DEP Ties
Fracking to Western Pa. Earthquakes" *Times Leader*, February 17, 2017, http://timesleader
.com/news/635744/dep-ties-fracking-to-western-pa-earthquakes).

39 Jervis, "Oklahoma Earthquake Reignites Concerns."

40 Anna Kuchment, "Even If Injection of Fracking Wastewater Stops, Quakes Won't: Salty
Fluid Sinks and Puts Pressure on Rock, Potentially Triggering Faults in Oklahoma for Years
to Come," *Scientific American*, September 9, 2019, https://www.scientificamerican.com
/article/even-if-injection-of-fracking-wastewater-stops-quakes-wont/.

41 Dewson, "A Disaster Waiting to Happen."

42 Dewson, "A Disaster Waiting to Happen."

43 Tim Fitzsimons, "Magnitude 4.1 Earthquake Rattles Oklahoma, Also Felt in Texas and
Kansas," *NBC News*, May 25, 2021, https://www.nbcnews.com/news/us-news/magnitude
-4-1-earthquake-rattles-oklahoma-also-felt-texas-nebraska-n1268553.

44 Concerned Health Professionals of New York and Physicians for Social Responsibility,
*Compendium of Scientific, Medical, and Media Findings Demonstrating Risks and Harms of
Fracking (Unconventional Gas and Oil Extraction)*, 4th ed., November 17, 2016, 18, http://
concernedhealthny.org/wp-content/uploads/2016/12/COMPENDIUM-4.0_FINAL_11
_16_16Corrected.pdf.

45 Concerned Health Professionals, *Compendium*, 4th ed., 22.

46 Concerned Health Professionals, *Compendium*, 4th ed., 23.

47 Joe Romm, "Methane Leaks Erase Climate Benefits of Fracked Gas, Countless Studies
Find," *Think Progress*, February 17, 2016, https://thinkprogress.org/methane-leaks-erase
-climate-benefit-of-fracked-gas-countless-studies-find-8b060b2b395d#.ijt2yr683.

48 Alan Buis and Carol Rasmussen, "NASA-Led Study Solves a Methane Puzzle," National
Aeronautics and Space Administration, January 2, 2018, https://www.nasa.gov/feature/jpl
/nasa-led-study-solves-a-methane-puzzle.

49 Concerned Health Professionals, *Compendium*, 4th ed., 209; 7th ed., 7.

50 Neuhauser, "Toxic Chemicals."

51 "Vermont First State to Ban Fracking," *CNN*, May 17, 2012, http://www.cnn.com/2012
/05/17/us/vermont-fracking/index.html.

52 Jon Hurdle, "With Governor's Signature, Maryland Becomes Third State to Ban Fracking,"
National Public Radio (StateImpact), April 4, 2017, https://stateimpact.npr.org
/pennsylvania/2017/04/04/with-governors-signature-maryland-becomes-third-state-to
-ban-fracking/.

53 Concerned Health Professionals, *Compendium*, 4th ed., 4–5; "Scottish Government
Confirms 'No Fracking' Policy," *BBC News*, October 3, 2019, https://www.bbc.com/news
/uk-scotland-scotland-politics-49924749.

54   DTE Staff, "Ireland Becomes the Fourth EU Country to Ban Fracking," *Down To Earth*, July 11, 2018, https://www.downtoearth.org.in/news/energy/ireland-becomes-the-fourth -eu-country-to-ban-fracking-61091; David Sánchez and Frida Kieninger, "Spanish Climate Law: Another Nail in the Coffin for Fracking in Europe," Food & Water Action Europe, May 5, 2021, https://www.foodandwatereurope.org/blogs/spanish-climate-law-another -nail-in-the-coffin-for-fracking-in-europe/. While some assert that Germany has banned fracking, the so-called ban is time bound and not yet complete, and there is still debate about how long-lived it will be. Therefore, I have chosen not to list it. For more on the situation in Germany, see "Fracking in Germany: Truly Banned, Allowed a Little, or Even Soon Back in Vogue?," *Energy Transition*, July 1, 2020, https://energytransition.org/2020/07/fracking-in -germany-truly-banned-allowed-a-little-or-even-soon-back-in-vogue/.

55   Priyanka Shrestha, "Ireland Plans to Ban Fracked Gas Imports and Stop LNG Terminal Developments," *Energy Live News*, May 24, 2021, https://www.energylivenews.com/2021 /05/24/ireland-plans-to-ban-fracked-gas-imports-and-stop-lng-terminal-developments/; Barry Roche, "Plans to Import Fracked Gas through Cork Shelved," *Irish Times*, January 18, 2021, https://www.irishtimes.com/news/ireland/irish-news/plans-to-import-fracked-gas -through-cork-shelved-1.4461032.

56   Aleem Maqbool, "The Texas Town That Banned Fracking (and Lost)," *BBC News*, June 16, 2015, http://www.bbc.com/news/world-us-canada-33140732.

57   Maqbool, "The Texas Town That Banned Fracking."

58   Bruce Finley, "Colorado Supreme Court Rules State Law Trumps Local Bans on Fracking," *Denver Post*, updated June 23, 2016, http://www.denverpost. com/2016/05/02/colorado -supreme-court-rules-state-law-trumps-local-bans-on-fracking/.

59   Concerned Health Professionals, *Compendium*, 4th ed., 6.

60   Brian Coppola (former Robinson Township supervisor), interview with author, October 4, 2016.

61   Dave Ball (Peters Township councilman), interview with author, October 25, 2016.

62   Eli Watkins and Joyce Tseng, "Trump's Policies and How They'll Change America—in Charts," *CNN*, March 15, 2017, http://www.cnn.com/2017/03/14/politics/donald-trump -policy-numbers-impact/; Morgan Winsor, Connor Burton, Phillip Mena, James Hill, and Julia Jacobo, "Dakota Access Pipeline Protest Site Cleared After Police in Riot Gear Enter Main Camp," *ABC News*, February 23, 2017, http://abcnews.go.com/US/police-riot-gear -enter-main-protest-camp-dakota/story?id=45684166.

63   House Committee on Oversight and Reform, "Subcommittee Releases Preliminary Findings Showing FERC Pipeline Approval Process Skewed Against Landowners," April 28, 2020, https://oversight.house.gov/news/press-releases/subcommittee-releases -preliminary-findings-showing-ferc-pipeline-approval.

64   Marcy de Luna, "U.S. Liquefied Natural Gas Exports Rise 16%, to New Record," *Reuters*, April 1, 2022, https://www.reuters.com/business/energy/us-liquefied-natural-gas-exports -rise-16-new-record-2022-04-01/#:~:text=U.S.%20LNG%20exports%20to%20all,of%20 7.25%20MT%20in%20January.

65   Zachary D. Weller, Steven P. Hamburg, and Joseph C. von Fischer, "A National Estimate of Methane Leakage from Pipeline Mains in Natural Gas Local Distribution Systems," *Environmental Science & Technology*, Vol. 54 No. 14, June 10, 2020, https://pubs.acs.org /doi/10.1021/acs.est.0c00437.

66   Spencer Phillips, PhD, Sonia Wang, and Cara Bottorff, "Economic Costs of the PennEast

Pipeline: Effects on Economic Services, Property Value, and the Social Cost of Carbon in Pennsylvania and New Jersey," *Key-Log Economics*, January 2017, http://www.keylog economics.com/uploads/1/1/9/5/119575398/penneast_technicalreport_201702.pdf. The Delaware Riverkeeper commissioned this study.

67   Alycia and Mark Egan, interview with author, March 22, 2017.

68   Phillips et al., "Economic Costs of the PennEast Pipeline," 24–31.

69   Karen Feridun (founder of Berks Gas Truth), interview with author, October 25, 2016.

70   For up-to-date data about pipeline incidents, see the Pipeline and Hazardous Materials Safety Administration website, www.phmsa.dot.gov. These figures are taken from "Significant Incidents," https://portal.phmsa.dot.gov/analytics/saw.dll?Portalpages&Portal Path=%2Fshared%2FPDM%20Public%20Website%2F_portal%2FSC%20Incident%20 Trend&Page=Significant.

71   See, e.g., "Are Old Pipelines Really More Dangerous?" Pipeline Safety Trust, spring 2015, http://pstrust.org/wp-content/uploads/2013/03/Incidents-by-age-of-pipes-PST -spring2015-newsletter-excerpt.pdf; Jon Hurdle, "New York State Denies Permit to Constitution Pipeline, Halting Construction," *National Public Radio* (StateImpact), April 22, 2016, https://stateimpact.npr.org/pennsylvania/2016/04/22/new-york-state-denies -permit-to-constitution-pipeline-halting-construction/.

72   Office of Attorney General Josh Shapiro, "AG Shapiro Charges Mariner East Developer with Environmental Crimes," October 5, 2021, https://www.attorneygeneral.gov/taking -action/ag-shapiro-charges-mariner-east-developer-with-environmental-crimes/; David E. Hess, "Attorney General Shapiro's Statement Announcing 48 Environmental Criminal Charges Against The Mariner East Pipeline In 11 Counties," *PA Environment Digest Blog*, October 5, 2021, http://paenvironmentdaily.blogspot.com/2021/10/attorney-general -shapiros-statement.html.

73   Shapiro, "AG Shapiro Charges Mariner"; Hess, "Attorney General Shapiro's Statement."

74   Pennsylvania Department of Environmental Protection, "Sunoco Pennsylvania Pipeline Project/Mariner East II," June 2016, https://www.chescoplanning.org/pic/PDF/Sunoco Mariner062616.pdf.

75   "OBIT: Daisytown Farmer Terry Greenwood, Whose Well Water Was Polluted by Dominion Energy, Dead at 66," *Marcellus Monitor: Investigative Journalism from the Shale Fields of Pennsylvania*, June 10, 2014, https://marcellusmonitor.wordpress.com/2014/06/10 /obit-daisytown-farmer-terry-greenwood-whose-well-water-was-polluted-by-dominion -energy-dead-at-66/.

Chapter 5: Wasted

1   For background on PFOA and DuPont, I rely on Nathaniel Rich, "The Lawyer Who Became DuPont's Worst Nightmare," *New York Times Magazine*, January 6, 2016, https ://www.nytimes.com/2016/01/10/magazine/the-lawyer-who-became-duponts-worst -nightmare.html?_r=0, and Sharon Lerner's The Teflon Toxin series, especially "The Teflon Toxin, Part 1," *The Intercept*, August 11, 2015, https://theintercept.com/2015/08/11/dupont -chemistry-deception/.

2   Lerner, "The Teflon Toxin, Part 1."

3   "C8 Science Panel Final Quarterly Newsletter," *C8 Science Panel*, November 2012, http ://www.c8sciencepanel.org/newsletter10.html; Paula I. Johnson et al., "The Navigation Guide—Evidence-Based Medicine Meets Environmental Health: Systematic Review of

Human Evidence for PFOA Effects on Fetal Growth," *Environmental Health Perspectives* 122 (2014).

4   Rich, "The Lawyer Who Became DuPont's Worst Nightmare."

5   "Fact Sheet: 2010/2015 PFOA Stewardship Program," United States Environmental Protection Agency, https://www.epa.gov/assessing-and-managing -chemicals-under-tsca/fact-sheet-20102015-pfoa-stewardship-program.

6   Molly Wood et al., "The Two-Decade Legal Battle with DuPont over a Toxic Chemical," *Marketplace*, October 15, 2019, https://www.marketplace.org/2019/10/15/the-two-decade -legal-battle-with-dupont-over-a-toxic-chemical/.

7   Lerner, "The Teflon Toxin, Part 1."

8   For PFOA's infiltration into the Delaware River Basin, along with other general studies and facts in this section, I rely on Tracy Carluccio (deputy director of the Delaware Riverkeeper Network), interview with author, January 17, 2017.

9   Angelo Fichera, "Paulsboro Strikes Deal to Address Water Contamination," *Philadelphia Inquirer*, December 18, 2014, https://www.inquirer.com/philly/blogs/gloucester_county /Paulsboro-strikes-deal-to-address-water-contamination.html.

10   Delaware Riverkeeper Network, "Perfluorooctanoic acid," https://www.delawareriverkeeper .org/ongoing-issues/perfluorooctanoic-acid.

11   Tracy Carluccio (deputy director of the Delaware Riverkeeper Network), interview with author, December 22, 2021.

12   Kirsten Stade, "EPA's PFAS Action Plan A Dud," Public Employees for Environmental Responsibility, press release, October 18, 2021, https://peer.org/epas-pfas-action-plan-a -dud/.

13   Anna Reade, "EPA Finds Replacements for Toxic 'Teflon' Chemicals Toxic," National Resources Defense Council, November 15, 2018, https://www.nrdc.org/experts/anna-reade /epa-finds-replacements-toxic-teflon-chemicals-are-also#:~:text=GenX%20and%20 PFBS%20are%20being,in%20exposed%20people%20and%20wildlife; Ryan Felton, "Solvay Workers Found to Have Unregulated PFAS in Their Blood, Documents Show," *Consumer Reports*, November 25, 2020, https://www.consumerreports.org/toxic-chemicals-substances /solvay-workers-found-to-have-unregulated-pfas-in-their-blood-documents-show -a8773475486/#:~:text=Solvay%20Workers%20Found%20to%20Have%20Unregulated %20PFAS%20in%20Their%20Blood%2C%20Documents%20Show&text=Little%2D known%20chemicals%20used%20by,documents%20obtained%20by%20Consumer%20 Reports.

14   "Highlights from the Clean Air Act 40th Anniversary," United States Environmental Protection Agency, accessed March 30, 2017, https://www.epa.gov/clean-air-act-overview /highlights-clean-air-act-40th-anniversary.

15   "Highlights from the Clean Air Act." Some of these figures are projections, as the precise data were yet to be confirmed.

16   Allison MacMunn, "More Than 4 in 10 Americans Breathe Unhealthy Air, People of Color 3 Times as Likely to Live in Most Polluted Places," American Lung Association, press release, April 21, 2021, https://www.lung.org/media/press-releases/sota-2021.

17   "State of the Air: Key Findings," American Lung Association, 2021, https://www.lung.org /research/sota/key-findings.

18   "National Summary of State Information," United States Environmental Protection Agency, 2017, https://ofmpub.epa.gov/waters10/attains_nation_cy.control#total_assessed_waters.

19   For a more detailed look at EPA findings, see "Fish Tissue Data Collected by EPA Partners," United States Environmental Protection Agency, accessed 2022, https://www.epa .gov/fish-tech/fish-tissue-data-collected-epa-partners.

20   Mark E. Brigham, "Mercury," United States Geological Survey, March 1, 2019, https ://www.usgs.gov/mission-areas/water-resources/science/mercury?field_pub_type_target _id=All&field_release_date_value=&items_per_page=6&src=QHA253&qt-science_center _objects=2&tltagv_gid=129&page=2.

21   Kacy Manahan (attorney for Delaware Riverkeeper Network), email communication with author, December 28, 2021.

22   "Traditional Fishing," Save Bristol Bay, accessed 2022, https://www.savebristolbay.org /tribal-support.

23   "Commonwealth of Pennsylvania Public Health Advisory: 2017 Fish Consumption," Pennsylvania Fish and Boat, accessed 2017, https://files.dep.state.pa.us/Water/Drinking%20 Water%20and%20Facility%20Regulation/WaterQualityPortalFiles/FishConsumption /FishAdvisory/FishConsAdvTables-2021_Update.pdf.

24   "Fish Advisories Data," Washington State Department of Health, accessed 2022, https ://doh.wa.gov/data-statistical-reports/washington-tracking-network-wtn/fish-advisories.

25   "2020 Missouri Fish Advisory," Missouri Department of Health and Senior Services, accessed 2022, https://health.mo.gov/living/environment/fishadvisory/pdf/fishadvisory.pdf.

26   Lawrence Hajna and Caryn Shinske, "New Jersey Updates Fish Consumption Advisories for Lower Delaware River Watershed, Expands Testing to Include PFAS," New Jersey Department of Environmental Protection, press release, July 19, 2018, https://www.nj.gov /dep/newsrel/2018/18_0063.htm.

27   New Jersey Department of Environmental Protection and New Jersey Department of Health, *Fish Smart, Eat Smart: A Guide to Health Advisories for Eating Fish and Crabs Caught in New Jersey Waters*, 2021, https://www.nj.gov/dep/dsr/fish-advisories.pdf.

28   Frank Kummer, "Pa. Warns Not to Eat Fish from Neshaminy Creek Due to 'Concerning' Levels of PFOS Contamination," *Philadelphia Inquirer*, October 13, 2021, https://www .inquirer.com/science/climate/neshaminy-creek-pennsylvania-tyler-state-park-pfos-pfas -fish-contamination-20211013.html.

29   Ann Faulds et al., "Patterns of Sport-fish Consumption at Six Pennsylvania Sites Along the Tidal Portion of the Delaware River with Special Emphasis on Shore Anglers," Pennsylvania Coastal Zone Management Program Technical Report, March 31, 2004, 4–5; "Revised Human Health Water Quality Criteria for Total PCBs for the Protection of Human Health from Carcinogenic Effects," Delaware River Basin Commission, July 2013.

30   For information on the Paulsboro vinyl chloride spill, I rely on Trisha Sheehan (Holistic Moms Network), interview with author, January 6, 2017, and Mark Cuker (environmental attorney), interview with author, March 22, 2017.

31   Kristen D. Jackson et al., "Trends in Allergic Conditions among Children: United States, 1997–2011," *National Center for Health Statistics Data Brief*, no. 121, May 2013, https ://www.cdc.gov/nchs/data/databriefs/db121.pdf.

32   "Vinyl Chloride," National Cancer Institute, accessed July 13, 2017, https://www.cancer.gov /about-cancer/causes-prevention/risk/substances/vinyl-chloride.

33   National Transportation Safety Board, "Conrail Freight Train Derailment with Vinyl Chloride Release: Accident Report," November 30, 2012, http://www.ntsb.gov /investigations/AccidentReports/Reports/RAR1401.pdf.

34   David Matthau, "Fighting to Prevent NJ Chemical Disaster," *New Jersey 101.5*, February 28, 2014, http://nj1015.com/fighting-to-prevent-nj-chemical-disasters-audio/.

35   Tara Nurin, "First Responders Share Blame for Problems at Paulsboro Toxic Spill, NTSB Says," *NJ Spotlight News*, July 30, 2014, http://www.njspotlight.com/stories/14/07/29 /first-responders-at-fault-for-some-problems-at-paulsboro-toxic-spill-ntsb-says/; Rebecca Forand, "First Responders Sue Conrail for Paulsboro Train Derailment Chemical Exposure," August 7, 2013, *NJ.com*, http://www.nj.com/gloucester-county/index. ssf/2013/08/first_responders_sue_conrail_for_paulsboro_train_derailment_chemical _exposure.html.

36   Matthau, "Fighting to Prevent NJ Chemical Disaster."

37   Jane Kay and Cheryl Katz, "Pollution, Poverty, and People of Color: Living with Industry," *Scientific American*, June 4, 2012, https://www.scientificamerican.com/article/pollution -poverty-people-color-living-industry/.

38   Sharon Lerner, "The Teflon Toxin, Part 6," *The Intercept*, December 16, 2015, https://the intercept.com/2015/12/16/toxic-firefighting-foam-has-contaminated-u-s-drinking-water -with-pfcs/.

39   Kyle Bagenstose, "Chemical Taint from Firefighting Foam Being Investigated at Military Bases Across US," *The Intelligencer*, May 1, 2016, https://www.theintell.com/story /news/2016/05/01/chemical-taint-from-firefighting-foam/16786383007/.

40   For this section on the military and foam exercises, I rely on Tracy Carluccio (deputy director of the Delaware Riverkeeper Network), interview with author, January 17, 2017.

41   For this section, I rely on Tom Roeder and Jakob Rodgers, "Toxic Legacy: Air Force Studies Dating Back Decades Show Danger of Foam That Contaminated Colorado Springs–Area Water," *Gazette*, updated July 31, 2020, http://gazette.com/toxic-legacy-air-force-studies -dating-back-decades-show-danger-of-foam-that-contaminated-local-water /article/1588446.

42   Roeder and Rodgers, "Toxic Legacy."

43   Roeder and Rodgers, "Toxic Legacy."

44   Kyle Bagenstose, "Dangers of Firefighting Foam Discussed in 2001, Document Shows," *The Intelligencer*, June 9, 2017, https://www.theintell.com/story/news/2017/06/09/dangers -firefighting-foam-discussed-in/16787301007/.

45   Roeder and Rodgers, "Toxic Legacy."

46   "Firefighting Foam Chemicals: DOD Is Investigating PFAS and Responding to Contamination, but Should Report More Cost Information," United States Government Accountability Office, June 22, 2021, https://www.gao.gov/products/gao-21-421.

47   Kyle Bagenstose, "Ivyland Woman Sues Navy After Finding High PFOA Blood Level," *The Intelligencer*, January 12, 2017, http://www.theintell.com/news/ horsham-pfos/ivyland -woman-sues-navy-after-finding-high-pfoa-blood-level/article_83b1fada-d8e8-11e6-b2c4 -7f62537e561a.html; Hannah Rappleye et al., "A 'Forever Chemical' Contaminates Drinking Water Near Military Bases," *NBC News*, December 16, 2019, https://www .nbcnews.com/health/cancer/forever-chemical-poisons-drinking-water-near-military -bases-n1101736; Lerner, "The Teflon Toxin, Part 6."

48   Kacy Manahan, email communication.

49   Government of Canada, "Per- and polyfluoroalkyl substances (PFAS)," https://www.canada .ca/en/health-canada/services/chemical-substances/other-chemical-substances-interest /per-polyfluoroalkyl-substances.html; Safer Chemicals, Healthy Families, "Final NDAA Will

End Military Use of Toxic PFAS Firefighting Foam; Congress Must Act in 2020 to Hold Polluters Accountable and Clean up PFAS," press release, December 17, 2019, https ://saferchemicals.org/2019/12/17/final-ndaa-will-end-military-use-of-toxic-pfas-firefighting -foam-congress-must-act-in-2020-to-hold-polluters-accountable-and-clean-up-pfas/; Lerner, "The Teflon Toxin, Part 6."

50   Virginia Streva, "Former Bucks County Congressman Mike Fitzpatrick, 56, Dies Following Cancer Battle," *PhillyVoice*, January 6, 2020, https://www.phillyvoice.com/mike-fitzpatrick -congressman-death-cancer-battle-bucks-county/; Justine McDaniel et al., "Mike Fitzpatrick, a Former Republican Congressman from the Philadelphia Suburbs, Has Died at 56," *Philadelphia Inquirer*, January 6, 2020, https://www.inquirer.com/obituaries/mike -fitzpatrick-dead-20200106.html.

51   John Kindschuh et al., "State-by-State Regulation of PFAS Substances in Drinking Water," *JDSupra*, June 4, 2022, https://www.jdsupra.com/legalnews/pfas-update-state-by-state -regulation-4639985/.

52   Sharon Anglin Treat, "With a Second Farm Shuttered Due to Massive PFAS Contamination, Maine Legislators Weigh Easing Access to the Courts," Institute for Agriculture and Trade Policy, July 30, 2020, https://www.iatp.org/blog/202007/second -farm-shuttered-due-massive-pfas-contamination-maine-legislators-weigh-easing.

53   Kaley Green, "Clovis Dairy Farmer Says He Lost Millions in Revenue due to PFAS Contamination," *MyHighPlains.com*, March 5, 2021, https://www.myhighplains.com /news/local-news/clovis-dairy-farmer-says-he-lost-millions-in-revenue-due-to-pfas -contamination/#:~:text=CLOVIS%2C%20N.M.%20(KAMR%2FKCIT,millions%20 of%20dollars%20in%20revenue; Amy Linn, "Groundwater Contamination Devastates a New Mexico Dairy—and Threatens Public Health," *NM Political Report*, February 19, 2019, https://nmpoliticalreport.com/2019/02/19/groundwater-contamination-devastates-a-new -mexico-dairy-and-threatens-public-health/.

54   Linn, "Groundwater Contamination Devastates a New Mexico Dairy."

55   Dennis Hoey, "Maine Issues 'Do Not Eat' Advisory for Deer Harvested Near PFAS-Contaminated Fields in Fairfield Area," *Press Herald*, November 23, 2021, https://www .pressherald.com/2021/11/23/maine-issues-do-not-eat-order-for-deer-harvested-near -pfas-contaminated-fields/#:~:text=November%2024%2C%202021-,Maine%20issues%20 'do%20not%20eat'%20advisory%20for%20deer%20harvested%20near,that%20pose%2 0potential%20health%20risks.

56   "Mapping the PFAS Contamination Crisis: New Data Show 2,854 Sites in 50 States and Two Territories," Environmental Working Group, October 4, 2021, https://www.ewg.org /interactive-maps/pfas_contamination/.

57   Rich, "The Lawyer Who Became DuPont's Worst Nightmare."

58   Lerner, "The Teflon Toxin, Part 3."

59   Information about drinking water regulation in this paragraph provided by Brady Dennis, "In U.S. Drinking Water, Many Chemicals Are Regulated—but Many Aren't," *Washington Post*, June 10, 2016, https://www.washingtonpost.com/national/health-science/in-us -drinking-water-many-chemicals-are-regulated--but-many-arent/2016/06/09/e48683bc -21b9-11e6-aa84-42391ba52c91_story.html?utm_term=.f028880ffe64.

60   Andrea Rimer et al., "EPA Declines to Set Drinking Water Limits for Perchlorate," *Environmental Law and Policy Monitor*, June 18, 2020, https://www.environmental lawandpolicy.com/2020/06/epa-declines-to-set-drinking-water-limits-for-perchlorate/.

61   Kacy Manahan, email communication.

62   For the full text of the executive order, see https://www.governor.pa.gov/newsroom
     /executive-order-2018-08-perfluoroalkyl-and-polyfluoroalkyl-substances-pfas-action-team.

Chapter 6: The Paving of America

1   Kate and Larry Stauffer, personal correspondence with author, March 13, 2022.

2   Anne Pickering, "Bishop Tube Facility Started in 1951, Now Abandoned," *Daily Local
    News*, updated June 2, 2007, http://www.dailylocal.com/article/DL/20070602
    /TMP01/306029998; Gilbert Associates Inc. Engineers and Consultants, *Engineering
    Report Bishop Tube Company*, accessed April 22, 2022, https://files.dep.state.pa.us
    /RegionalResources/SERO/SEROPortalFiles/Community%20Info/Bishop%20
    Tube/2021%20Administrative%20Record/Part%20I%20Initial%20Investigation%20
    Site%20Discovery/1973.4.9%20Gilbert%20Rpt.pdf.

3   Ralph Vartabedian, "How Environmentalists Lost the Battle Over TCE," *Los Angeles Times*,
    March 29, 2006, https://www.latimes.com/archives/la-xpm-2006-mar-29-na-toxic
    29-story.html.

4   Vartabedian, "How Environmentalists Lost."

5   Vartabedian, "How Environmentalists Lost."

6   Vartabedian, "How Environmentalists Lost."

7   United State Environmental Protection Agency, "Trichloroethylene (TCE) TEACH
    Chemical Summary," https://archive.epa.gov/region5/teach/web/pdf/tce_summary.pdf;
    Pickering, "Bishop Tube"; Philip L. Comella and Craig B. Simonsen, "EPA Classifies
    Trichloroethylene (TCE) as Human Carcinogen," *Workplace Safety and Environmental Law
    Alert Blog*, September 29, 2011, http://www.environmentalsafetyupdate.com
    /environmental-compliance/epa-classifies-trichloroethylene-tce-as-human-carcinogen/.

8   Pickering, "Bishop Tube."

9   David Worst, conversation with author, 2017.

10 For this story, I rely on Paula Warren's presentation at a public meeting in East Whiteland
    Township, Pennsylvania, June 7, 2017, and on conversations throughout the spring of 2017.

11 "ToxFAQs for Trichloroethylene (TCE)," Agency for Toxic Substances and Disease
    Registry, accessed July 14, 2017, https://wwwn.cdc.gov/TSP/ToxFAQs/ToxFAQsDetails.
    aspx?faqid=172&toxid=30; "Trichloroethylene Toxicity: What Are the Physiological Effects
    of Trichloroethylene?," Agency for Toxic Substances and Disease Registry, accessed July 14,
    2017, https://www.atsdr.cdc.gov/csem/trichloroethylene/physiological_effects.html.

12 For this section, I am indebted to Liz, Kate, and Larry Stauffer, interview with author, April
    10, 2017.

13 For the prospective purchase agreement between the Pennsylvania Department of
    Environmental Protection and Constitution Drive Partners (a unit of O'Neill Properties),
    see Jon Hurdle, "Chesco Residents Urge Officials to Reject Development Plan for
    Contaminated Site," *National Public Radio* (StateImpact), April 25, 2017, https://state
    impact.npr.org/pennsylvania/2017/04/25/chesco-residents-urge-officials-to-reject
    -development-plan-for-contaminated-site/; Michaelle Bond, "On Toxic Site Abandoned
    for Decades, Developer Sees Townhouses Sprouting in Chesco," *Philadelphia Inquirer*, April
    10, 2017, http://www.philly.com/philly/news/pennsylvania/toxic-brownfield-development
    -East-Whiteland-ONeill-DEP-Bishop-Tube-Malvern.html.

14   Amanda Mahnke, "Planning Commission Discusses Sports Fields at Bishop Tube, Uptown Worthington Rentals," *Malvern Patch*, May 27, 2011, https://patch.com/pennsylvania /malvern/planning-commission-discusses-sports-fields-at-bishop6ec8bd9e8d.

15   Tom Myers, "Technical Memorandum: Review of Bishop Tube Superfund Site and an Assessment of the Site's Proposed Residential Development," prepared for the Delaware Riverkeeper Network, March 23, 2017, http://www.delawareriverkeeper.org/sites/default /files/DRN%20to%20PADEP%20 3.27.17_1.pdf.

16   Mark Freed, email communication with author, December 29, 2021.

17   T. W. Crowther et al., "Mapping Tree Density at a Global Scale," *Nature* 525 (September 2015): 201, http://www.nature.com/doifinder/10.1038/nature14967.

18   Ashley Kirk, "Deforestation: Where Is the World Losing the Most Trees?" *Telegraph*, March 23, 2016, http://www.telegraph.co.uk/news/2016/03/23/deforestation-where-is-the-world -losing-the-most-trees/; Nell Greenfieldboyce, "Tree Counter Is Astonished by How Many Trees There Are," *National Public Radio* (All Things Considered), September 2, 2015, http ://www.npr.org/sections/goatsandsoda/2015/09/02/436919052/tree-counter-is-astonished -by-how-many-trees-there-are.

19   Charles Q. Choi, "The Lost Forests of America," *Live Science*, April 23, 2009, http://www .livescience.com/7725-lost-forests-america.html.

20   "Wetlands: A Global Disappearing Act," The Ramsar Convention Secretariat, http://www .ramsar.org/sites/default/files/documents/library/factsheet3_global_disappearing_act_0.pdf.

21   "Wetlands Disappearing Three Times Faster than Forests," United Nations Framework Convention on Climate Change (UNFCCC), October 1, 2018, https://unfccc.int/news /wetlands-disappearing-three-times-faster-than-forests.

22   T. E. Dahl, "Wetlands: Losses in the United States 1780s to 1980s," United States Department of the Interior, Fish, and Wildlife Service, Washington D.C., 1990, https ://www.fws.gov/wetlands/Documents/Wetlands-Losses-in-the-United-States-1780s-to -1980s.pdf.

23   "Wetlands: A Global Disappearing Act," The Ramsar Convention Secretariat.

24   See definition at https://www.iucn.org/resources/issues-briefs/peatlands-and-climate -change.

25   "Wetlands Disappearing," UNFCCC.

26   Sophie Gallagher, "Humans Have Destroyed 10% of the World's Wilderness in 20 Years," *Huffington Post*, September 9, 2016, https://www.huffingtonpost.co.uk/entry/wilderness -destruction-twenty-years_uk_57d2bea5e4b0d45ff871dc99.

27   James E. M. Watson et al., "Catastrophic Declines in Wilderness Areas Undermine Global Environment Targets," *Current Biology* 26, no. 21 (2016): 2929–2934, https://www.science direct.com/science/article/pii/S0960982216309939.

28   Gallagher, "Humans Have Destroyed."

29   You can learn more about Apple Pond Farm and schedule a visit to this special place at http://www.applepondfarm.com/about-us.

30   Dick Riseling (owner, Apple Pond Farm), conversation with author, May 13, 2017.

31   Derek Thompson, "What in the World Is Causing the Retail Meltdown of 2017?" *Atlantic*, April 10, 2017, https://www.theatlantic.com/business/archive/2017/04/retail -meltdown-of-2017/522384/.

32   Thompson, "What in the World Is Causing the Retail Meltdown of 2017?"

33   Ethan Rothstein, "Even Developers Agree the US Has Way Too Much Retail Space," *Forbes*, April 5, 2017, https://www.forbes.com/sites/bisnow/2017/04/05/even-developers-agree-the-u-s-has-way-too-much-retail-space/3/#36f7d11136f7.

34   Lauren Coleman-Lochner and Jordyn Holman, "Malls Are Moving Away from Shopping to Fill the Wasteland of Vacant Retail Space," *Philadelphia Inquirer*, December 18, 2021, https://www.inquirer.com/real-estate/commercial/malls-retail-vacancies-apartments-casino-20211218.html.

35   Lauren Thomas, "25% of U.S. malls are expected to shut within 5 years. Giving them a new life won't be easy," *CNBC*, August 27, 2020, https://www.cnbc.com/2020/08/27/25percent-of-us-malls-are-set-to-shut-within-5-years-what-comes-next.html; Coleman-Lochner and Holman, "Malls Are Moving Away"; Lisa Fickenscher, "Midtown Has Highest Retail Vacancy Rate in NYC: Report," *New York Post*, October 7, 2021, https://nypost.com/2021/10/07/midtown-has-highest-retail-vacancy-rate-in-nyc-report/.

36   Fickenscher, "Midtown Has Highest Retail Vacancy Rate."

37   For this background on Hamilton Township, I am indebted to George van Amelsfort, interview with author, March 28, 2017. See also Delaware Riverkeeper Network, "New Jersey Stormwater Management Implementation: A Case Study of Hamilton Township, Mercer County," May 2010, http://www.delawareriverkeeper.org/sites/default/files/resources/Reports/Hamilton_Twp_ NJ_SWM_Implementation_Report.pdf.

38   Van Amelsfort, interview with author.

39   Brandon Holveck, "Online Shopping, Highways and Nearby Big Cities Leading to a Boom in Warehouses in Delaware," *Delaware News Journal*, August 31, 2021, https://www.delawareonline.com/story/money/business/2021/08/31/what-makes-delaware-attractive-warehouse-seekers/5376870001/.

40   John Best, "6 million-square-foot warehouse and manufacturing complex pitched for 585 acres in Warren County," lehighvalleylive.com, April 16, 2019, https://www.lehighvalleylive.com/news/2019/04/developer-discusses-potential-6-million-square-foot-development-on-585-acres-in-warren-county.html.

41   Faith Zerbe, email communications with author, January 2022.

42   Kaveh Waddell, "When Amazon Expands, These Communities Pay the Price," *Consumer Reports*, December 9, 2021, https://www.consumerreports.org/corporate-accountability/when-amazon-expands-these-communities-pay-the-price-a2554249208/.

43   Waddell, "When Amazon Expands."

44   Waddell, "When Amazon Expands."

45   Fred Stine (action coordinator for the Delaware Riverkeeper Network), conversation with author, May 6 and 10, 2017.

Chapter 7: Confronting the Climate Crisis

1   "The Elbe River and Its Basin," Internationale Kommission zum Schutz der Elbe, September 2016, https://www.ikse-mkol.org/fileadmin/media/user_upload/E/06_Publikationen/08_IKSE_Flyer/2016_ICPER-Flyer_The_Elbe_River_Basin.pdf.

2   Camila Domonoske, "Drought in Central Europe Reveals Cautionary 'Hunger Stones' in Czech River," *National Public Radio*, August 24, 2018, https://www.npr.org/2018/08/24/641331544/drought-in-central-europe-reveals-cautionary-hunger-stones-in-czech-river.

3   R. Brázdil et al., "Droughts in the Czech Lands, 1090–2012 AD," *Climate of the Past* 9, no. 4 (May 8, 2013): 1985–2002, https://doi.org/10.5194/cp-9-1985-2013.

4   Domonoske, "Drought in Central Europe."

5   Krisztina Fenyo and Krisztina Than, "Water levels in Danube Recede to Record Lows, Hindering Shipping in Hungary," *Reuters*, August 22, 2018, https://www.reuters.com /article/us-europe-weather-hungary-shipping/water-levels-in-danube-recede-to-record -lows-hindering-shipping-in-hungary-idUSKCN1L71DH.

6   Domonoske, "Drought in Central Europe."

7   Ilona Amos, "COP26: Climate Change Will See 320 Million People Worldwide Facing Starvation This Decade, Report Warns," *The Scotsman*, November 8, 2021, https://www .scotsman.com/news/environment/cop26-climate-change-will-see-320-million-people -worldwide-facing-starvation-this-decade-report-warns-3449974; Raymond Zhong, "2021 Was Earth's Fifth-Hottest Year, Scientists Say," *New York Times*, January 10, 2022, https ://www.nytimes.com/2022/01/10/climate/2021-hottest-year.html?smid=tw-share.

8   Nadja Popovich and Winston Choi-Schagrin, "Hidden Toll of the Northwest Heat Wave: Hundreds of Extra Deaths," *New York Times*, August 11, 2021, https://www.nytimes.com /interactive/2021/08/11/climate/deaths-pacific-northwest-heat-wave.html.

9   "Climate Change Indicators: Wildfires," United States Environmental Protection Agency, last updated April 2021, https://www.epa.gov/climate-indicators/climate-change -indicators-wildfires.

10   "Wildfires and Climate Change," Center for Climate and Energy Solutions, accessed December 2021, https://www.c2es.org/content/wildfires-and-climate-change/.

11   "New Mexico: State Profile and Energy Estimates," United States Energy Information Administration, last updated March 18, 2021, https://www.eia.gov/state/?sid=NM.

12   Oil Change International, Earthworks, and Center for International Environmental Law, "Community Impacts," Permian Climate Bomb, accessed December 2021, https://www .permianclimatebomb.org/chapter-5.

13   Oil Change International, Earthworks, and Center for International Environmental Law, "Climate Bomb," Permian Climate Bomb, accessed December 2021, https://www.permian climatebomb.org/chapter-2.

14   Olga Popova and Gary Long, "Drilling and Completion Improvements Support Permian Basin Hydrocarbon Production," United States Energy Information Administration, October 19, 2021, https://www.eia.gov/todayinenergy/detail.php?id=50016.

15   Oil Change International Team, "Full Report: The Permian Climate Bomb Series," Oil Change International, December 15, 2021, https://priceofoil.org/2021/12/15/permian -climate-bomb/; Nick Cunningham, "Activists Call For Action On The Permian 'Climate Bomb,'" *The Fuse*, October 29, 2019, https://energyfuse.org/activists-call-for-action-on -the-permian-climate-bomb/; Center for International Environmental Law, "New Report: Permian Fracking Boom Will Bust the Climate and Intensify Environmental Injustice," press release, October 19, 2021, https://www.ciel.org/news/new-report-permian-fracking-boom-will-bust-the-climate-and-intensify-environmental-injustice/.

16   Oil Change International, Earthworks, and Center for International Environmental Law, "Regulatory Failure," Permian Climate Bomb, accessed December 2021, https://www .permianclimatebomb.org/chapter-6.

17   "The Paris Agreement," United Nations Framework on Climate Change, accessed December 2021, https://unfccc.int/process-and-meetings/the-paris-agreement/the-paris -agreement.

18   Jeff Brady and Joe Hernandez, "U.S. Greenhouse Gas Emissions Jumped in 2021, a Threat

to Climate Goals," *National Public Radio*, January 10, 2022, https://www.npr.org/2022/01/10/1071835575/u-s-greenhouse-gas-emissions-2021-climate.

19   UN Environment Programme, *Emissions Gap Report 2019*, November 26, 2019, https://wedocs.unep.org/bitstream/handle/20.500.11822/30797/EGR2019.pdf?sequence=1&isAllowed=y.

20   Mary Greene and Keene Kelderman, "Port Arthur, Texas: The End of the Line for an Economic Myth," Environmental Integrity Project, August 2017, https://environmentalintegrity.org/wp-content/uploads/2017/02/Port-Arthur-Report.pdf.

21   John Beard Jr. (founder of Port Arthur Community Action Network), interview with author, October 29, 2021.

22   Rebecca Harrington, "Flash Floods Send Texans into 'Survival Mode' as Harvey Hits Port Arthur with 26 Inches of Rain In One Day," *Business Insider*, August 30, 2017, https://www.businessinsider.com/harvey-port-arthur-26-inches-rain-flash-floods-residents-survival-mode-2017-8.

23   Holly Yan, Nicole Chavez, and Ray Sanchez, "Harvey Aftermath: Death Toll Rises; So Do the Floodwaters," *CNN*, August 31, 2017, https://www.cnn.com/2017/08/30/us/harvey-texas-louisiana/index.html.

24   Rebecca Harrington, "Flash Floods Send Texans into 'Survival Mode.'"

25   Yan et al., "Harvey Aftermath."

26   For this section, I rely on Tony Ingraffea, interview with author, February 27, 2017.

27   Gayathri Vaidyanathan, "How Bad of a Greenhouse Gas Is Methane?" *Scientific American*, December 22, 2015, https://www.scientificamerican.com/article/how-bad-of-a-greenhouse-gas-is-methane/; European Environment Information and Observation Network, "Trends in Atmospheric Concentrations of CO2 (ppm), CH4 (ppb) and N2O (ppb), between 1800 and 2017," European Environment Agency, December 5, 2019, https://www.eea.europa.eu/data-and-maps/daviz/atmospheric-concentration-of-carbon-dioxide-5#tab-chart_5_filters=%7B%22rowFilters%22%3A%7B%7D%3B%22columnFilters%22%3A%7B%22pre_config_polutant%22%3A%5B%22CH4%20(ppb)%22%5D%7D%7D.

28   R. W. Howarth, R. Santoro, and A. Ingraffea, "Methane and the Greenhouse-Gas Footprint of Natural Gas from Shale Formations," *Climatic Change* 106 (2011), http://www.eeb.cornell.edu/howarth/Howarth%20et%20al%20202011.pdf; Stacey Shackford, "Natural Gas from Fracking Could Be 'Dirtier' than Coal, Cornell Professors Find," *Cornell Chronicle*, April 11, 2011, https://news.cornell.edu/stories/2011/04/fracking-leaks-may-make-gas-dirtier-coal.

29   Bill O'Boyle, "Nacero to build $6B natural gas to gasoline plant in Luzerne County," *Times Leader*, October 29, 2021, https://www.timesleader.com/news/1520944/nacero-to-build-6b-natural-gas-to-gasoline-plant-in-luzerne-county.

30   Nacero, "Products," accessed May 1, 2022, https://nacero.co/products.

31   Nacero, "Nacero Announces First U.S. Manufacturing Facility," press release, October 22, 2021, https://nacero.co/press-releases/nacero-announces-first-us-manufacturing-facility.

32   O'Boyle, "Nacero to Build"; Office of State Senator Marty Flynn, "Nacero to Build $6 Billion Manufacturing Facility in Luzerne County," October 29, 2021, https://www.senatorflynn.com/nacero-to-build-6-billion-manufacturing-facility-in-luzerne-county/.

33   Alex Bomstein (staff attorney with the Clean Air Council), interview with author, January 6, 2022.

34   For the details of this story, I rely on Karen Feridun (founding member of Pennsylvanians

Against Fracking, and founder of Berks Gas Truth), interviews with author, November 26, 2021 and January 6, 2022.

35   Taylor Goebel, "Texas Fuel Company to Build $6 Billion Plant in Eastern Pennsylvania," *The Center Square*, November 2, 2021, https://www.thecentersquare.com/pennsylvania/texas -fuel-company-to-build-6-billion-plant-in-eastern-pennsylvania/article_bb37cf70-3c2f-11 ec-bd38-4b1f4adf8e1b.html; Ad Crable, "Natural Gas to Gasoline: A $6 Billion Proposal in PA," *Bay Journal*, January 10, 2022, https://www.bayjournal.com/news/natural-gas-to-gas oline-a-6-billion-proposal-in-pa/article_5ca806d6-724f-11ec-9370-8bcb3e9dae64.html.

36   Taylor Kubota, "Stanford Study Casts Doubt on Carbon Capture," *Stanford News*, October 25, 2019, https://news.stanford.edu/2019/10/25/study-casts-doubt-carbon-capture/.

37   Paul Brown, "Carbon Capture and Storage Won't Work, Critics Say," *Climate News Network*, January 19, 2021, https://www.eco-business.com/news/carbon-capture-and -storage-wont-work-critics-say/.

38   Taylor Kubota, "Stanford Study Casts Doubt."

39   Bomstein, interview.

40   Richard Bennett, "Testimony of Senator Richard Bennett before the Joint Standing Committee on Environment and Natural Resources," (LD 489), 130th Legislature Senate of Maine, March 8, 2021, https://legislature.maine.gov/testimony/resources /ENR20210308Bennett132596835080132919.pdf.

41   Kate Cough, "Staggering $1.5 Billion Lithium Deposit Discovered near Newry," *Bangor Daily News*, October 24, 2021, https://bangordailynews.com/2021/10/24/news/central -maine/staggering-1-5-billion-lithium-deposit-discovered-near-newry/.

42   Dwight Bradley and Brian W. Jaskula, "Lithium—For Harnessing Renewable Energy," United States Geological Survey, April 2014, https://pubs.usgs.gov/fs/2014/3035/pdf /fs2014-3035.pdf.

43   R. Moore, J. S. Gunn, and A. Troy, "Valuing Maine's Nature. Manomet Center for Conservation Sciences," *Natural Capital Initiative Report 2012-01*, May 2012, https ://www.manomet.org/wp-content/uploads/old-files/Manomet_ValuingMainesNature _May2012.pdf.

44   Dennis Hoey, "Maine Issues 'Do Not Eat' Advisory for Deer Harvested near PFAS-Contaminated Fields in Fairfield Area," *Portland Press Herald*, November 23, 2021, https ://www.pressherald.com/2021/11/23/maine-issues-do-not-eat-order-for-deer-harvested -near-pfas-contaminated-fields/.

45   Cough, "Staggering $1.5 Billion Lithium Deposit."

46   "IPCC Report: 'Code Red' for Human Driven Global Heating, Warns UN Chief," *United Nations News*, August 9, 2021, https://news.un.org/en/story/2021/08/1097362.

47   "Climate Change and Health," World Health Organization, October 30, 2021, https ://www.who.int/news-room/fact-sheets/detail/climate-change-and-health.

48   Maine Senate Democrats, "Advocates Share Praise, Support for Pine Tree Amendment Sponsored by Sen. Maxmin," March 8, 2021, http://www.mainesenate.org/advocates-share -praise-support-for-pine-tree-amendment-sponsored-by-sen-maxmin/.

Chapter 8: Ending Environmental Racism

1   Maddy Lauria, "Settlement Ends Neighbors' Battle with Poultry Farm as They Look to Future with Clean Water," *News Journal*, February 20, 2020, https://www.jcdelaw.com /files/2020/02/private-settlement.pdf.

2   For the details of Gina's story throughout this chapter, I rely on Gina Burton (Millsboro resident), interview with author, December 6, 2021.

3   "Mountaire Farms Reaches Settlement in Lawsuit," *WattPoultry*, March 2, 2020, https ://www.wattagnet.com/articles/39782-mountaire-farms-reaches-settlement-in -lawsuit?v=preview.

4   For the facts surrounding this story, I am indebted to Maria Payan (senior regional representative, Socially Responsible Agriculture Project), interview with author, November 12, 2022.

5   Maddy Lauria, "Lawyers Threaten Federal Lawsuit To Hold Delaware Chicken Plant Accountable for Pollution," *News Journal*, March 28, 2018, https://www.delawareonline .com/story/news/local/2018/03/28/lawyers-threaten-federal-lawsuit-hold-delaware -chicken-plant-accountable-pollution/447524002/.

6   Lauria, "Lawyers Threaten Federal Lawsuit."

7   Nicole Galan, "What Is Blue Baby Syndrome?" *Medical News Today*, May 29, 2018, https ://www.medicalnewstoday.com/articles/321955.

8   Gina Burton, email communication with author, March 15, 2022.

9   "State Sampling Sussex Wells after Poultry Plant Found Polluting Groundwater," *Delaware Public Media*, December 1, 2017, https://www.delawarepublic.org/science -health-tech/2017-12-01/state-sampling-sussex-wells-after-poultry-plant-found- polluting-groundwater; "DNREC Updates Information on Nitrate Levels Found in Water at Private Residences Near Mountaire Farms' Millsboro Poultry Plant," press release, Delaware Department of Natural Resources and Environmental Control Division of Water, November 30, 2017, https://news.delaware.gov/2017/11/30/dnrec-updates-information -nitrate-levels-found-water-private-residences-near-mountaire-farms-millsboro-poultry -plant/; Maddy Lauria, "Mountaire Farms: Tainted Neighborhood Wells Not Our Fault," *The News Journal*, January 17, 2018, https://www.delawareonline.com/story/news /local/2018/01/17/mountaire-farms-legacy-pollutants-not-its-recent-spills-cause-tainted -wells/1038753001/.

10 Bridget Read, "Delaware Democratic Senate Hopeful Kerri Evelyn Harris Is a Queer Woman of Color Who Wants Politicians With 'Diversity of Experience,'" *Vogue*, August 29, 2018, https://www.vogue.com/article/kerri-harris-delaware-democratic-senate-diversity-of -experience.

11 Kerri Evelyn Harris (community organizer and politician), interview with author, November 12, 2021.

12 Lauria, "Settlement Ends Neighbors' Battle."

13 Melissa Steele, "80 Neighbors Sue Mountaire in New Suit," *Cape Gazette*, July 2, 2018, https://www.capegazette.com/article/second-lawsuit-filed-against-mountaire/160453.

14 Ryan Mavity, "Mountaire Agrees to Settlement in Class-Action Suit," *Cape Gazette*, January 29, 2021, https://www.capegazette.com/article/mountaire-agrees-settlement-class-action -suit/214784.

15 Jessica Kutz, "Will a Wildlife Refuge Benefit a Heavily Polluted Albuquerque Neighborhood?," *Guardian*, April 14, 2021, https://www.theguardian.com/ environment/2021/apr/14/albuquerque-new-mexico-green-spaces-mountain-view.

16 For the facts surrounding this story, I am indebted to Eric Jantz (senior staff attorney for New Mexico Environmental Law Center), interview with author, December 7, 2021.

17   "Air Quality," City of Albuquerque, accessed April 15, 2022, https://www.cabq.gov/air
     quality/regulation-development.

18   Janiece Jonsin, "Mountain View Is City's Industrial Sacrifice Zone," New Mexico
     Environmental Law Center, June 28, 2021, https://nmelc.org/2021/06/28/mountain-view
     -is-citys-sacrifice-zone/?fbclid=IwAR3q_8A9wpY_fah2nt0RNhF-s1cRGMMfBDfB7t
     mZd6VF3ZARxatOoSdo-1E; Jessica Kutz, "Can a Wildlife Refuge Help a Community's
     Fight for Environmental Justice?" *High Country News*, April 9, 2021, https://www.hcn.org
     /issues/53.5/south-wildlife-can-a-wildlife-refuge-help-a-communitys-fight-for
     -environmental-justice.

19   "South Valley Neighborhood Appeals City's Air Permit for Proposed Asphalt Plant," press
     release, New Mexico Environmental Law Center, December 1, 2020, https://nmelc.org
     /wp-content/uploads/2020/12/PR-NMTS-12.1.20-final-2.pdf.

20   Marcus Stern, Savanna Strott, and David Leffler, "Small Plant, Big Polluter," *The Texas
     Observer*, November 2, 2021, https://www.texasobserver.org/small-plant-big-polluter/.

21   "Sulfur Dioxide," Canadian Centre for Occupational Health and Safety, https://www.ccohs
     .ca/oshanswers/chemicals/chem_profiles/sulfurdi.html.

22   Stern et al., "Small Plant, Big Polluter."

23   Ranjani Chakraborty, "One Reason Why Coronavirus Is Hitting Black Americans the
     Hardest," *Vox*, video, 9:02, May 22, 2020, https://www.vox.com/videos/2020/5/22/21267365
     /coronavirus-black-americans-pollution-deaths.

24   Ihab Mikati et al., "Disparities in Distribution of Particulate Matter Emission Sources
     by Race and Poverty Status," *American Journal of Public Health* 108, no. 4 (April 1, 2018):
     480–85, https://ajph.aphapublications.org/doi/full/10.2105/AJPH.2017.304297; "Particle
     Pollution," American Lung Association, accessed April 15, 2022, https://www.lung.org
     /clean-air/outdoors/what-makes-air-unhealthy/particle-pollution.

25   "Populations at Risk," American Lung Association, accessed March 20, 2022, https://www
     .lung.org/research/sota/key-findings/people-at-risk; Robert D. Bullard et al., *Toxic Wastes
     and Race at Twenty 1987-2007*, United Church of Christ Justice & Witness Ministries,
     March 2007, https://www.nrdc.org/sites/default/files/toxic-wastes-and-race-at-twenty
     -1987-2007.pdf.

26   Sara E. Grineski and Timothy W. Collins, "Geographic and Social Disparities in Exposure
     to Air Neurotoxicants at US Public Schools," *Environmental Research* 161 (February 2018),
     https://www.ncbi.nlm.nih.gov/pmc/articles/PMC5760180/.

27   Oliver Milman, "Air Pollution: Black, Hispanic and Poor Students Most at Risk From
     Toxins—Study," *Guardian*, February 1, 2018, https://www.theguardian.com
     /education/2018/feb/01/schools-across-the-us-exposed-to-air-pollution-hildren-are
     -facing-risks.

28   Much of this chapter is informed by the experiences of Debra Lekanoff (New Mexico state
     representative), interview with author, January 6, 2022.

29   "Biography," Washington State House Democrats, https://housedemocrats.wa.gov/lekanoff
     /biography/.

30   "Hatchery Facilities," Washington Department of Fish and Wildlife, accessed April 15,
     2022, https://wdfw.wa.gov/fishing/management/hatcheries/facilities?county=All.

31   "Skagit County Commissioners Announce Plan to Create Skagit County Salmon Heritage
     Program," Skagit County Planning and Development Services, https://skagitcounty.net
     /Departments/planningandpermit/salmonheritage.htm.

32   "Lekanoff Introduces the Washington Green Amendment," Washington State House
      Democrats, February 9, 2021, https://housedemocrats.wa.gov/lekanoff/2021/02/09
      /lekanoff-introduces-the-washington-green-amendment/.

33   Svanfridur Mura, Margaret Berei, Aarush Rompally, and Dave Pringle (activists), group
      interview with author, December 23, 2021.

34   Andrew Zwicker (New Jersey senator), email communication with author, April 26, 2022.

Chapter 9: You're Not Expendable!

1   "Holland's Occupation during WWII," Holland (website), https://www.holland.com
      /global/tourism/holland-stories/liberation-route/hollands-occupation-during-wwii.htm.

2   Renee Ghert-Zand, "Truus Wijsmuller Saved Thousands of Jews in WWII. Why Has No
      One Heard of Her?," *Times of Israel*, October 25, 2017, https://www.timesofisrael.com/truus
      -wijsmuller-saved-1000s-of-jews-in-wwii-so-why-has-no-one-heard-of-her/.

3   "Holland's Occupation during WWII."

4   For the details of Nicole's story throughout this chapter, I rely on Nicole Olonovich (veteran
      of the Iraq War), interview with author, November 30, 2021.

5   *Dictionary.com*, s.v. "Expendable," Dictionary (website), accessed 2022, https://www
      .dictionary.com/browse/expendable.

6   For the details of this story, I rely on Michele Baker (New York Water Project founder and
      tireless advocate), interview with author, April 27, 2017.

7   Frank O'Laughlin, "Saint-Gobain Smokestacks Emitting PFOA, Test Results Show,"
      WMUR Manchester, July 22, 2016, https://www.wmur.com/article/saint-gobain-smokestacks
      -emitting-pfoa-test-results-show/5213272; Brendan J. Lyons and Casey Seiler, "The Story
      Behind the Hoosick Falls PFOA Water Crisis," *Times Union*, July 21, 2021, https://www
      .timesunion.com/projects/2021/hoosick-falls-pfoa-timeline/.

8   Tracy Frish, "Small Towns in New York and Vermont Share a Water Contamination Crisis,
      But Not an Official Response," *In These Times*, September 5, 2017, https://inthesetimes
      .com/article/industrial-pollution-pfoa-drinking-water-contamination-epa-saint-gobain;
      Jesse McKinley, "After Months of Anger in Hoosick Falls, Hearings on Tainted Water
      Begin," *New York Times*, August 30, 2016, https://www.nytimes.com/2016/08/31/nyregion
      /hoosick-falls-tainted-water-hearings.html?_r=0.

9   McKinley, "After Months of Anger in Hoosick Falls."

10   "Filtering Water Fears in Hoosick Falls Demands an Independent Probe," *New York Daily
      News*, July 5, 2016, http://www.nydailynews.com/opinion/filtering-water-fears-hoosick
      -falls-independent-probe-article-1.2696368.

11   WRGB Staff, "Hoosick Falls Residents React to New EPA Documents," *WRGB Albany*,
      June 2, 2016, https://cbs6albany.com/news/local/hoosick-falls-residents-react-to-new-epa
      -documents.

12   "EPA Statement on Hoosick Falls Water Contamination," Village of Hoosick Falls,
      December 17, 2015, http://www.villageofhoosickfalls.com/Media/PDF/EPAStatement
      HoosickFallsWaterContamination.pdf.

13   Dan Turkel, "Officials Took Months to Warn Residents of a Tiny New York Village of an
      Impending Disaster in Their Water Supply," *Business Insider*, March 5, 2016, http://www
      .businessinsider.com/delay-in-warning-hoosick-falls-residents-not-to-drink-water-2016-3.

14   Scott Waldman, "Hoosick Falls Confronts Poisoned Wells and an Uncertain Future,"
      Politico, March 23, 2016, http://www.politico.com/states/new-york/albany/story/2016/03
      /hoosick-falls-confronts-poisoned-wells-and-an-uncertain-future-032864.

15   Scott Waldman, "Hoosick Falls Students Press Cuomo for New Water System," *Politico*,
      February 12, 2016, https://www.politico.com/states/new-york/albany/story/2016/02
      /hoosick-falls-students-press-cuomo-for-new-water-system-031244?_amp=true.

16   Courtney Ward, "Cuomo Announces $10M Plan for Alternate Water Supply in Hoosick
      Falls," *News10 Albany*, February 12, 2016, https://www.news10.com/news/cuomo
      -announces-10m-plan-for-alternate-water-supply-in-hoosick-falls/.

17   Jerry Williams (toxic tort attorney), interview with author, March 10, 2017.

18   Green Amendments For The Generations, "New York Legislator Spotlight: Asm.
      Englebright," July 13, 2021, YouTube Video, https://www.youtube.com/watch
      ?v=ZYyjVfM4GdY.

Chapter 10: Can We Afford a Green Amendment?

1   For this discussion, I am indebted to David Warne (assistant commissioner, NYCDEP
      Bureau of Water Supply), Adam Bosch (director of public affairs, NYCDEP Bureau of
      Water Supply), and Paul Rush (deputy commissioner, NYCDEP Bureau of Water Supply).

2   Some theorize this is because the water's pH level, at 7.2, is nearly neutral (with purity
      being 7.0). See Rachel Nuwer, "Why Is New York Tap Water So Good?," *Edible Manhattan*,
      March 7, 2013, http://www.ediblemanhattan.com/departments/liquid-assets/theres
      -something-in-the-water/.

3   Tim Sprinkle, "The Secret of New York City's Mythic Bagel-Making Water," *Quartz*,
      October 7, 2014, https://qz.com/263351/the-secret-of-new-york-citys-mythic-bagel
      -baking-water/.

4   Albert Appleton and Daniel Moss, "How New York City Kept Its Drinking Water Pure—
      In Spite of Hurricane Sandy," *Huffington Post*, updated January 23, 2014, http://www
      .huffingtonpost.com/daniel-moss/new-york-drinking-water_b_2064588.html.

5   Appleton and Moss, "How New York City Kept Its Drinking Water Pure." Specifically, the
      authors state that "there was a 75 percent to 80 percent reduction in farm pollution loading."

6   Adam Bosch, personal correspondence with author, June 28, 2017.

7   The program itself is premised on partnership with local organizations. For example,
      the Catskill Watershed Corporation and the Watershed Agricultural Council, along
      with other development corporations, make possible the septic repairs and agricultural
      accommodations discussed in this profile. As Adam Bosch notes, "The partnership model is
      part of what makes our watershed protection program unique, successful, and a model for
      others."

8   Background on the New York City Watershed Protection Program provided by David
      Warne, Adam Bosch, and Paul Rush.

9   Winnie Hu, "A Billion-Dollar Investment in New York's Water," *New York Times*, January
      18, 2018, https://www.nytimes.com/2018/01/18/nyregion/new-york-city-water-filtration
      .html.

10   Adam Bosch, email communication with author, January 19, 2022.

11   The water does undergo limited treatment to ensure quality. For a succinct overview of New
      York's water sourcing and treatment, see Emily S. Rueb, "How New York Gets Its Water,"
      New York Times, March 24, 2016, https://www.nytimes.com/interactive/2016/03/24
      /nyregion/how-nyc-gets-its-water-new-york-101.html?_r=0.

12   Allison Dunne, "Delegation from India Wants To Learn About Catskills Watershed,"
      WAMC Northeast Public Radio, April 16, 2017, http://wamc.org/post/delegation-india

-wants-learn-about-catskills-watershed; Violet Snow, "Catskills watershed lends its expertise across the pond," *Hudson Valley One*, June 20, 2018, https://hudsonvalleyone.com /2018/06/20/catskills-watershed-lends-its-expertise-across-the-pond/.

13   Motoko Rich and John Broder, "A Debate Arises on Job Creation and Environment," *New York Times*, September 4, 2011, http://www.nytimes.com/2011/09/05/business/economy/a -debate-arises-on-job-creation-vs-environmental-regulation.html.

14   Steven Overly, "Donald Trump Tells Detroit Auto CEOs That Environmental Regulations Are 'Out Of Control,'" *Washington Post*, January 24, 2017, https://www.washingtonpost.com /news/innovations/wp/2017/01/24/donald-trump-tells-detroit-auto-ceos-environmental -regulations-are-out-of-control/?utm_term=.cfb0ba3ad90a.

15   Kerri Evelyn Harris (community organizer and politician), interview with author, February 9, 2022.

16   All figures on regulatory compliance and benefits in 2012 taken from Jim Tankersley, "Report: New Regulations Cost $216B and 87 Million Hours of Paperwork. What Do They Reap?" *Washington Post*, January 14, 2013, https://www.washingtonpost.com/news /wonk/wp/2013/01/14/report-new-regulations-cost-216-billion-and-87-million-hours-of -paperwork/?utm_term=.87de12e35564.

17   Lindsey Cook, "Seriously, Go to College," *US News & World Report*, August 17, 2015, https://www.usnews.com/news/blogs/data-mine/2015/08/17/study-benefits-of-a-college -degree-are-historically-high.

18   For this discussion on the Clean Air Act, and all monetary figures, I borrow from Alan H. Lockwood, "How the Clean Air Act Has Saved $22 Trillion in Health-Care Costs," *Atlantic*, September 7, 2012, https://www.theatlantic.com/health/archive/2012/09/how -the-clean-air-act-has-saved-22-trillion-in-health-care-costs/262071/. This article was an excerpt from his book *The Silent Epidemic: Coal and the Hidden Threat to Health* (Cambridge, MA: MIT Press, September 2012).

19   Simon Mui and Amanda Levin, "Clearing the Air: The Benefits of the Clean Air Act," Natural Resources Defense Council, May 2020, https://www.nrdc.org/sites/default/files /benefits-clean-air-act-ib.pdf.

20   Alan H. Lockwood, *The Silent Epidemic: Coal and the Hidden Threat to Health* (Cambridge, MA: MIT Press, 2012), https://mitpress.mit.edu/books/silent-epidemic.

21   "Small Business Owners Favor Regulations to Protect Clean Water," American Sustainable Business Council, July 2014, https://studylib.net/doc/8215811/small-business-owners-favor -regulations-to-protect-clean-.

22   "2021 Climate Check: Business' Views on Environmental Sustainability," Deloitte, https ://www2.deloitte.com/global/en/pages/risk/articles/2021-climate-check-business-views -on-environmental-sustainability.html.

23   Pippa Stevens, "US 'Green Economy' Generates $1.3 Trillion and Employs Millions, New Study Finds," *CNBC*, October 16, 2019, https://www.cnbc.com/2019/10/16/us-green -economy-generates-1point3-trillion-and-employs-millions-new-study-finds.html; L. Georgeson and M. Maslin, "Estimating the Scale of the US Green Economy within the Global Context," *Palgrave Commun* 5, no. 121 (2019), https://doi.org/10.1057/s41599-019 -0329-3.

24   Mohamed Younis and Lydia Saad, "Americans Support ESG Objectives but Unfamiliar with Term," *Gallup Poll Service*, https://news.gallup.com/poll/350258/americans-support -esg-objectives-unfamiliar-term.aspx.

25 H. S. J. Cesar and P. van Beukering, "Economic Valuation of the Coral Reefs of Hawai'i," *Pacific Science* 58, no. 2 (2004), https://muse.jhu.edu/article/54568/pdf; Richard C. Bishop et al., "Total Economic Value for Protecting and Restoring Hawaiian Coral Reef Ecosystems: Final Report," NOAA Office of National Marine Sanctuaries, Office of Response and Restoration, and Coral Reef Conservation Program, NOAA Technical Memorandum CRCP, Executive Summary, https://www.coris.noaa.gov/activities/hawaii_econeval /resources/chapter1.pdf.

26 Cesar and van Beukering, "Economic Valuation of the Coral Reefs."

27 R. Moore, J. S. Gunn, and A. Troy, "Valuing Maine's Nature: Manomet Center for Conservation Sciences," *Natural Capital Initiative Report* 2012-01 (May 2012), https ://www.manomet.org/wp-content/uploads/old-files/Manomet_ValuingMainesNature _May2012.pdf.

28 "The Economic Benefits of Southern New Mexico's Natural Assets," Headwaters Economics and Audubon New Mexico, https://headwaterseconomics.org/wp-content /uploads/NMreport_FINAL.pdf.

29 "New Study Shows Multi-Trillion Dollar Natural Capital Risk Underlining Urgency of Green Economy Transition," United Nations Environment Programme, April 15, 2013, https://www.unep.org/es/node/5990.

30 Linda J. Bilmes, "Putting a Dollar Value on Nature Will Give Governments and Businesses More Reasons to Protect It," *The Conversation US,* May 11, 2021, https://theconversation .com/putting-a-dollar-value-on-nature-will-give-governments-and-businesses-more -reasons-to-protect-it-153968.

31 Capitals Coalition, *Natural Capital at Risk,* Trucost and TEEB for Business Coalition, April 2013, https://www.naturalcapitalcoalition.org/wp-content/uploads/2016/07/Trucost-Nat -Cap-at-Risk-Final-Report-web.pdf.

32 Chari Towne, *A River Again: The Story of the Schuylkill River Project* (Bristol, PA: Delaware Riverkeeper Network, 2012), 11, https://www.delawareriverkeeper.org/sites/default/files/A _RIVER_AGAIN_2012.pdf.

33 Towne, *A River Again,* 12.

34 Towne, *A River Again,* 14.

35 Towne, *A River Again,* 33.

36 Green Amendments For The Generations, "New York Legislator Spotlight: Asm. Englebright," July 13, 2021, YouTube Video, https://www.youtube.com/watch?v =ZYyjVfM4GdY.

37 Unless otherwise stated, all information on the Delaware River in this section is from the Delaware Riverkeeper Network's *River Values: The Value of a Clean and Healthy Delaware River,* April 2010, http://www.delawareriverkeeper.org/sites/default/files/River_Values _Report_0.pdf.

38 Gerald J. Kauffman et al., "Economic Value of the Delaware Estuary Watershed," University of Delaware, October 2011, https://www.wrc.udel.edu/wp-content/publications/DelEstuary ValueSummary.pdf; Gerald J. Kauffman et al., "Socioeconomic Value of the Delaware River Basin in Delaware, New Jersey, New York, and Pennsylvania," October 11, 2011, https://www .state.nj.us/drbc/library/documents/SocioeconomicValueDRB-UDEL-ExecSum.pdf.

39 Kauffman et al., "Socioeconomic Value of the Delaware River Basin."

40 Alexis C. Madrigal, "The Blood Harvest," *Atlantic,* February 26, 2014, https://www.the atlantic.com/technology/archive/2014/02/the-blood-harvest/284078/.

41   Kieron Monks, "Why This Crab's Blood Could Save Your Life," CNN, updated January 5, 2015, http://www.cnn.com/2014/09/04/health/this-crabs-blood-could-save-your-life/.

42   Ted Lee Eubanks Jr., John R. Stoll, PhD, and Paul Kerlinger, PhD, *Wildlife-Associated Recreation on the New Jersey Delaware Bayshore*, New Jersey Division of Fish and Wildlife, February 16, 2000, 49.

43   C. C. Sutton, J. C. O'Herron, and R. T. Zappalorti, *The Scientific Characterization of the Delaware Estuary*, Delaware Estuary Program, 1996; "Delaware River: Our Highway to the Ocean," Adventure Aquarium, September 27, 2021, https://www.adventureaquarium.com/blog/delaware-river/.

44   Kauffman et al., "Economic Value of the Delaware Estuary."

45   D. Munro et al., "Oyster Mortality in Delaware Bay: Impacts and Recovery from Hurricane Irene and Tropical Storm Lee," *Estuarine, Coastal and Shelf Science* 135 (2013), http://hsrl.rutgers.edu/abstracts.articles/Munroe_2013_ECSS.pdf. Significant storms have taken their toll on the oysters, reducing harvests because of the freshwater flow dynamics that had harmful impacts on the Delaware Bay oysters.

46   Green Amendments For The Generations, "Hawaii Legislator Spotlight: Senator Gabbard," July 13, 2021, Facebook Video, https://www.facebook.com/watch/?v=1489004261435665.

Chapter 11: Fighting for a Green Amendment

1   David R. Boyd, *The Environmental Rights Revolution* (Vancouver: University of British Columbia Press, 2012), 5.

2   Chelsey Sanchez, "Kamala Harris Slams GOP, Says Supreme Court Hearings Should Be Held After Election," *Harper's Bazaar*, October 13, 2020, https://www.harpersbazaar.com/culture/politics/a34358908/kamala-harris-supreme-court-hearing-election.

3   Boyd, *The Environmental Rights Revolution.*

4   Zachary Davies Boren, "Major Study Finds the US Is an Oligarchy," *Business Insider*, April 16, 2014, http://www.businessinsider.com/major-study-finds-that-the-us-is-an-oligarchy-2014-4.

5   Nathan Rott, "How the EPA Became a Victim of Its Own Success," *National Public Radio*, February 17, 2017, http://www.npr.org/2017/02/17/515748401/how-the-epa-became-a-victim-of-its-own-success.

6   Joanne Ferrary (New Mexico state representative), communication with author, March 14, 2022.

7   John Dernbach (professor of environmental law and sustainability), interview with author, February 27, 2022.

8   Phara Souffrant Forrest, transcript of house session, February 8, 2021, www2.assembly.state.ny.us/write/upload/transcripts/2021/2-8-21.html.

9   Harold Pope Jr. (New Mexico state senator), comments at Green Amendments training, November 17, 2021.

10   Ted Bohlen (founder of the Hawai'i Reef and Ocean Coalition and Climate Protectors Hawai'i), email correspondence with author, February 2, 2022.

11   Franklin L. Kury, Statement to the House of Delegates of the Pennsylvania Bar Association, 1970. Reprinted in Franklin L. Kury, *Clean Politics, Clean Streams: A Legislative Autobiography and Reflections* (Bethlehem, PA: Lehigh University Press, 2011).

12   Kerri Evelyn Harris (community organizer and politician), interview with author, February 9, 2022.

INDEX

ABOUT THE AUTHOR

Maya K. van Rossum is a veteran environmentalist who joined the Delaware Riverkeeper Network in 1994. As the Delaware Riverkeeper since 1996, Maya both leads the organization and serves as a head advocate, championing the rights of all the communities—both human and nonhuman—that depend upon the river and ensuring that the Delaware River and tributary streams are free-flowing, clean, and healthy with a diversity of life.

In 2013, van Rossum was one of the original petitioners in *Robinson Township, Delaware Riverkeeper Network et al. v. Commonwealth of Pennsylvania*. That landmark case led to a watershed victory that breathed legal life into the state's long ignored Environmental Rights Amendment, protecting people's right to pure water, clean air, and a healthy environment. In the wake of that victory, van Rossum founded the Green Amendment For The Generations movement and organization—coining and defining the term "Green Amendment," determining that forty-eight states were lacking this most powerful provision, and sparking a nationwide campaign to secure Green Amendments in every state across the nation and in the federal constitution. van Rossum's vision and movement are inspiring people, communities, organizations, and legislators nationwide to fight for this most powerful protection.

van Rossum is a licensed attorney in three states: Pennsylvania, New Jersey, and the District of Columbia. In 2002, she founded the River Resources Law Clinic, which operates in partnership with the Temple

University Beasley School of Law and other law schools in the region. There, she accepts legal interns from multiple law schools looking for a hands-on opportunity to learn how they can use their legal skills to protect and defend our environment.

van Rossum grew up in the Delaware River watershed and lives there today with her family.